D1094911

The Scorekeeper

Reflecting on Big Games and Big Stories,

Brooklyn Roots and Jewish-American Culture,

The Craft of Reporting and Art of The Spin

Edward Hershey

Joy Media

Library of Congress
Cataloging-in-Publication Data
The Scorekeeper: a Memoir
Hershey, Edward, author
Chicago: Joy Media LLC

LCCN: 2016953500
ISBN: 978-0-9800954-8-7

Jacket design by Laura Duffy
Book design by Karen Minster

www.joymediaonline.com

Printed in the United States of America

FIRST EDITION

For Naima Simone Hershey,
Tova Madeleine Hershey and
Ellis Baldwin Hershey.

When anyone asked what I was up to these past few years I said, "I'm either writing a memoir or a very long letter to my grandchildren." It turned out to be both (although it may be a few years before your parents want you to read it).

Contents

PROLOGUE

Asleep at the Wheel

xii

PART ONE

The Parkway

PART TWO
The Big Leagues

PART THREE
The Real World

PART FOUR

The Other Side

POSTSCRIPT

Catching You Up

Acknowledgments

Asleep at the Wheel

But for the benevolence of fate at midnight on a highway in Maine you would not be reading this.

Get a good night's rest and leave Brooklyn in the morning. That was the plan. Then the phone rang. An NBC crew would be in Waterville, Maine the next morning to tape a segment for what the network saw as a man-bites-dog piece: Colby College students protesting a faculty decision to bar the Central Intelligence Agency from recruiting on campus.

I smiled. To my mind the story was not the odd juxtaposition some reporters took it to be. Colby's professors retained their Vietnam-era mistrust for government while its students, coming of age fifteen years after the end of the military draft, wanted every option they could glean from a prestigious—and expensive—degree. The oldest of them was no more than ten when Saigon fell and most came from families not directly touched by the Vietnam War, children of fathers who, like me, found ways to avoid the battlefield. Nonetheless, my decades as a communicator told me that news was not what I thought it should be but what the press made it.

"Please wait until the morning," Victoria implored. She was staying behind to find a buyer for our Brooklyn house before completing our unlikely transition to Maine in that summer of 1987. But as a former reporter—we'd met in a newsroom—she understood I had to be there. I finished packing, downed some coffee and drove off with our daughter Rebecca, who was to start fifth grade at her new school that week, and Browser, a shaggy black-haired mutt who had shown up the year before, "just browsing around," as Rebecca put it.

We got off to an inauspicious, even ominous start. My preferred route to New England, taking us over the Brooklyn Bridge onto the FDR Drive to the Willis Avenue Bridge and then the Bruckner Expressway was fast and toll-free, but included Hunts Point, an especially crime-ridden stretch of the South Bronx. Near the expressway ramp a dog darted in front of us. There was a thud and then silence. Even at modest speed no dog was likely to survive a head-on meeting with our Buick Electra and this would be no place to dawdle, even without a canine corpse to ponder. I drove on, but the pain must have shown in my face.

"I understand, Daddy," Rebecca said in her best nine-year-old adult voice. As awful as I felt about the dog, the sense of shame in my concession to the reality of the South Bronx was worse. We had tried to instill pride in Rebecca's black and Latina roots at every turn and here I was afraid to stop—let alone exit the car. Yet even her mother had expressed relief about leaving Brooklyn just as Rebecca was starting to ask about going places on her own in a city so dangerous police dealt with 500 violent felonies each day and many more went unreported. (A month later, as if art was imitating life, Tom Wolfe's *The Bonfire of the Vanities* hit the best-seller lists with a plot that turned on a fender-bender on a ramp of the Bruckner Expressway.)

One interstate highway led to another through Connecticut and Massachusetts, then up the New Hampshire seacoast into Maine. Rebecca was asleep and I was fighting fatigue, but we were almost there. I called Brooklyn from a rest stop to let Victoria know she could go to sleep and drove off again. The next thing I remember is a series of jolts. I had dozed off and the Buick, continuing straight as the road veered left, bumped to a stop in a rutty field. My assumption, reinforced every time I drove that stretch, was that had I lost consciousness seconds earlier or later we might well have plunged over an embankment. Rebecca slept through it, but Browser gave me a quizzical look, seemingly aware he could have become the second dog I'd killed in one night.

After we reached the home we were renting, I put Rebecca to bed and lay awake, unable to shed the chilling realization of what I had almost done. My life was not flashing before my eyes so much as playing out in a newsreel. I even imagined a wire-service account of our demise.

FREEPORT, MAINE, SEPT. 12 (AP)—The new director of public relations at Colby College and his daughter were killed in a one-car accident here last night, police reported. Edward Hershey, 43, and his 9-year-old daughter, Rebecca, died when their auto plunged off of Interstate 95 shortly before midnight. There were no witnesses to the accident, but police said the absence of skid marks suggested that Hershey might have fallen asleep at the wheel.

Hershey was communications director at Long Island University, his alma mater, before he was hired in June for the Colby position. He previously served as New York City's Assistant Commissioner of Correction for Public Affairs and was a reporter for the Long Island newspaper *Newsday*, where he covered such stories as the Attica Prison insurrection and the "Son of Sam" multiple murder case. Hershey also founded the newspaper's union for journalists. He is survived by his wife, Victoria Mares Hershey.

That would do, factual and to the point. But who would run it? I hadn't been at Colby long enough for the Maine papers to pay much attention. *Newsday* might take note, though maybe not. Start a union and you aren't exactly a favored staffer. What about the *New York Times?* Was my body of work noteworthy enough for "the paper of record" to take note of my death?

My profile of Arthur Ashe was in "Best Sports Stories of 1968," and *Pro Football Digest* had reprinted my series on Paul Brown's return to coaching. After leaving sports, my reporting won awards for revealing flaws in charter bus regulation after a fatal accident and for bringing down two of New York's most powerful politicians in a vote-siphoning scheme. And I'd written books with a baseball star and a legendary cop.

But it was a career that touched fame more than achieving it, a life less about making history than footnoting it. I'd interviewed the likes of Mickey Mantle and Joe Namath, Wilt Chamberlain and Billie Jean King. Profiled oddballs like pool shark Wimpy Lassiter and wrestling behemoth Haystacks Calhoun. Pressed retired U. S. Supreme Court Justice Arthur Goldberg on the legality of the Vietnam War and questioned *Li'l Abner* cartoonist Al Capp about his sexual predation. Escorted Tony Randall around Brighton Beach and watched Pete Seeger serenade prison inmates. Chatted with John Lennon's killer and Mick Jagger's ex-wife Bianca. Gave Geraldine Ferraro her first significant ink and Bill Bradley his first political exposure. Even danced (after a fashion) on Dick Clark's *American Bandstand* and saw my name on the Yankee Stadium scoreboard, sending me off to active duty in the Army Reserve.

Mine could be the first biography published as a stack of Trivial Pursuit cards. But was that so bad? Almost every encounter involved a story and often a story behind a story, and I could hardly get through a conversation without referencing one or two. The family joke each time I changed jobs, which I was starting to do with uncomfortable regularity, was that at least it gave me a fresh audience. "You ought to write that down," I heard many times. "Yes," I would invariably respond. "I have to get to it some day."

This book is about coming of age amid the heady if cautious optimism of post-war Jewish life in a borough of underdogs with dreams, coming into my own as a reporter at the height of America's love affair with the suburbs, and coming to terms with the corollary to a lyric John Lennon expropriated: If life really happens to you while you are making other plans, then formulate new ones.

The morning after our near-tragedy I put my daughter on the bus for her first day of school before meeting the NBC crew. As I hoped, we spun the story to portray Colby as a campus where independent-minded students and idealistic teachers could turn a dispute into a learning experience. I would learn, too, in six years there, a dozen at Cornell, and shorter stints at colleges in Oregon and Pennsylvania. Add my time as president of a Shakespearean theater, city alderman, basketball announcer, antiques columnist, labor union strategist and semi-professional storyteller and there is fodder for more tales. But that, as we used to say in Brooklyn, would be a whole 'nother book.

PART ONE

The Parkway

1
Guilt-Edged Coin

JANUARY 1952
Brooklyn

The last thing I expected when I proudly brandished the dime was a morality tale from my mother.

Our bank account may have told a different story, but I never thought of us as poor. We *gave* to the poor. My grandmother defied arthritic legs trudging from neighbor to neighbor to collect clothing and food for displaced Holocaust survivors in Europe and my mother always found a coin or two of *tzedakah* to drop into tin *pushkas* for one cause or another. It was a *mitzvah* to care for the "less fortunate."

And while my upbringing bore little resemblance to the idealized family life on television sitcoms or in the Dick-and-Jane readers New York City schools still used in the 1950s, our Brooklyn neighborhood was idyllic in its own way, a place where children walked home from school for lunch as I was doing the day I spotted that dime as I started across Avenue O.

"Edward," my mother said in a tone that told me something I might not want to hear would follow, "have you thought that if you found that dime it also means someone lost it? Maybe it was Joyce from the corner. She eats lunch in school every day because her mother goes to business. It could have been her milk money."

Finders keepers, losers weepers, I thought, but the words never came out. That was something you said in the playground, not to your mother. Besides, was it really worth 10 cents to make anyone cry, least of all Joyce? Well before anyone used the term, she was a latchkey kid who had to fend for herself until her mother came home from work, a circumstance that housewives on Ocean Parkway associated with profound misfortune. Fathers worked as a matter of course, but mothers went "to business" only if calamities like widowhood or divorce demanded it. They viewed their own days of shopping, cooking, cleaning, and child-rearing as a privilege, and why not? They had unhappy memories of life during the Depression and the war before making their way into the lower echelon of "the middle class."

That was a term my mother invoked with pride one moment to attest to how far she had come and resignation the next to acknowledge the modesty of our circumstances. The living room in our three-room ground-floor apartment—"The landlord's calling it three-and-a-half on the fifth floor now," she would say—had three functions. It was a second bedroom once we opened the rollaway each night and also served as my father's home office. His civil service salary—she called it "a fixed income"—did not go far, and they would often argue over how carefully she stretched her "allowance" for groceries and other necessities between paydays.

Living so frugally required ingenuity and choices. For example, my parents never joined a synagogue. Dues were expensive and did not even entitle members to seats on the High Holy Days each fall, when some *shuls* erected billboards extolling their cantor's credentials as if to suggest soliciting God's forgiveness was contingent on tonal quality. Like many Ashkenazi Jews whose families had emigrated from central Europe, their religious observance was less about spirituality and presence than custom and identity anyway. They honored the *kashruth*, eating only kosher food and using separate sets of dishes for meat and dairy at home, and fasted on the holiest day of the year, Yom Kippur, but even then barely set foot in a synagogue. She mourned the mother she never knew at a *yizkor* memorial service open to all. He would congregate with neighbors on Ocean Parkway and as sundown approached, walk around the corner to the Avenue N Jewish Center to wait outside for the sound of the *shofar*, the ceremonial ram's horn trumpeting an end to the fast.

There were no prayers at supper that night or any other and the question of whether there was a god never came up. But if faith wasn't an issue, respect was. Everyone in the neighborhood understood that a boy who was not confirmed in *shul* at age 13 would subject his parents to shame. Getting "bar mitzvahed" was part of the Jewish trinity, alongside completing college and marrying within the faith. "Just do this," Jewish parents pleaded. "That's all we ask." When the day arrived after years of preparation, it came with a rollicking party and largesse from guests who slid a check or savings bond into the inside pocket of the honoree's new suit jacket. With luck, the take matched his family's outlay for the party.

"Just do this" meant that, in exchange for interminable afternoons in Hebrew school, a boy would hardly ever need to do anything Jewish again for the remainder of adolescence. Thus, chanting from the *Haftorah* on the *bimah* in front of the Torah ark on that *Shabbat* morning became a Hebrew swan song, transforming a ceremony ostensibly welcoming thirteen-year-olds as full participants into a terminal event that gave us what amounted to a get-out-of-shul-free card.

Forgoing synagogue membership was hardly the only economic corner they cut. Scrimping was the norm. My father reminisced about his 1937 Pontiac, but after it gave out he did not own another automobile until he bought a hand-me-down from his brother-in-law when I was eleven. "Eating out," if it happened at all, meant inserting nickels into the slots at a Horn & Hardart Automat or nibbling a nut-cheese sandwich at a Chock Full O' Nuts counter. Restaurant food wasn't kosher, my father would say, and could be risky. "Uncle Nathan worked in those places and you should hear the stories he told." We knew it was not really about such dire tales. We couldn't splurge on restaurants any more than shop for clothing anywhere but at discount stores like Mays in downtown Brooklyn or S. Klein on Union Square in Manhattan and only then when it was on sale.

"The girls"—my mother and her mah-jongg buddies—went a step further, combing charity bazaars for goods priced below wholesale. This bargain hunting became something of a hobby but was undertaken with a degree of discretion. Self-conscious that such outings would seem déclassé to better-heeled neighbors who might overhear them, they referred to the bazaars as "bees" so often that I assumed it was just another name for them.

One place my parents were determined to avoid compromising quality for price was in health care. That called for creativity, and two of my early medical issues—a wandering right eye that required surgical reattachment and very bucked teeth—were cases in point.

A finessed application qualified me for clinical treatment for the indigent at Columbia Presbyterian Hospital's famed Harkness Pavilion where my eye surgery was performed. We would take the subway to Washington Heights in upper Manhattan on an appointment day and spend hours in one waiting area and then another before reaching an examination room where medical students took notes as a prestigious specialist examined me. I didn't mind being the center of such attention, but once when the doctor asked a question I deemed personal, I responded with a line I'd heard during televised Congressional hearings. "I decline to answer on the ground that it might incriminate me." Clearly taken aback—this was the McCarthy Era and invoking the Fifth Amendment was seen by many as an act of disloyalty—he observed, "You've probably been watching a little too much television, young man." My mother made her own discomfort clear in the talking-to I got on the long subway ride back to Brooklyn.

My teeth were deemed too important for any clinic so we made the rounds of orthodontists. They all said that while ordinarily they would wait several years to treat a six-year-old, my overbite was pronounced enough to warrant immediate treatment. It came down to two, and the more highly regarded of the pair was considerably more expensive. But the look on my mother's face when his office manager quoted the cost led her to suggest an alternative. Orthodontic appointments qualified as excusable absences in city schools so if we only went on weekday mornings when patient load was light she could lower the price to $2,000 (the equivalent of nearly $20,000 today) and it could be paid in installments. During the six years I wore braces and even thereafter my mother would point to my mouth and, sounding half-proud and half-rueful, declare, "That's my mink coat."

2

Too Good for America?

A pair of bronze plaques out front labeled our six-story apartment house "Parkway Terrace," although no one ever called it that. We lived at 1440 Ocean Parkway or simply "1440"—distinguishing it from 1420 at Avenue N and 1500 at Avenue O.

Up and down "the Parkway," which spanned the six miles between Prospect Park and Brighton Beach, nearly everyone was Jewish, reflecting a demographic reality of midcentury New York. The city may have been diverse as a whole, but it was less a melting pot than a collection of ethnic neighborhoods. And few were more homogenous than those housing the two million Jews who comprised a quarter of its populace in 1950 (before many started migrating to Long Island, Westchester and New Jersey to form suburban Jewish enclaves).

This Jewish-American circumspection about how—and where—to live reflected a perceived need to stick together for support and even protection. The "American dream," as historian James Truslow Adams defined it, was "a land in which life should be better and richer and fuller for everyone, with opportunity for each according to ability or achievement regardless of social class or circumstances of birth." But after living through the Great Depression without losing focus, watching relatives succumb to the Holocaust without losing faith and facing endemic anti-Semitism without losing heart, my parents' generation had come to view the American reality with a grain of kosher salt.

Banding together was one way to counter—or at least circumvent—the limitations and indignities of bias in employment, housing, education, and social access. "They would not let us in, so we bought the place" became a laugh line in the Catskill Mountains "Borscht Belt" and on the Miami Beach "Gold Coast" where Jewish resorts emerged in areas previously "restricted" to gentiles. But such humor belied a widespread effort to hide in plain sight. Avoid making waves. Better not to be noticed. Don't invite trouble. If such wariness rankled my coming generation of war babies and post-war boomers it was intended to shield from anti-Semitism, it also meshed with the superstitious reluctance to tempt fate that Jews shared with others—those who knocked on wood or carried amulets: Never *ever* discuss how well things are going for fear of attracting the evil eye.

"Don't give it a *kinehora*," someone was almost sure to interject, wagging a finger at anyone foolish enough to express satisfaction (especially in anticipation of good fortune). That was the Yiddish term for a taboo so ubiquitous it predated birth and lingered beyond the grave. Pregnant women refused to anticipate motherhood by assembling layettes, and it was (and for the most part still is) customary not to name a child for a living individual for fear that the angel of death might one day confuse the two and mistake the namesake for an older relative whose time has come.

Economics, too, played a part in neighborhood homogeneity. Most Jewish families arrived on Ellis Island as my grandparents had with few resources, looking to predecessors for the support nineteenth-century Jewish-American poet and communal leader Emma Lazarus envisioned in words adorning the Statue of Liberty:

> *"Keep, ancient lands, your storied pomp!" cries she*
> *With silent lips. "Give me your tired, your poor,*
> *Your huddled masses yearning to breathe free,*
> *The wretched refuse of your teeming shore.*
> *Send these, the homeless, tempest-tost to me,*
> *I lift my lamp beside the golden door!"*

Some immigrants joined sponsors in other parts of the country but many remained in New York, taking refuge in tenements on Manhattan's Lower East Side or other areas with relatively affordable housing, including the Brooklyn neighborhoods of Borough Park and East New York where my parents were raised. After marrying in November 1941, they moved into 1440 Ocean Parkway, my home when I came along thirty months later. How Jewish was our neighborhood? "Like Ivory Soap," people would say, "99 and 44 one-hundredths percent pure."

One December after Mrs. Weinberg, the teacher in charge of our weekly school assembly, led a rendition of "Deck the Halls," she asked if anyone knew what holly was. Hands shot up all over the auditorium. "It's bread!" one child volunteered. "No," Mrs. Weinberg said. "That's *challah*. Now can anyone tell us what holly is?" Not a hand in the room remained up.

The famed creators of Central Park, Frederick Law Olmsted and Calvert Vaux, who designed Ocean Parkway as an expansive European-style boulevard connecting their Prospect Park to the Atlantic Ocean, thought that stately manors would eventually line the parkway. But as Brooklyn's population grew nearly tenfold between 1860 and 1930 (when it counted more than 2.5 million residents, slightly fewer than it has today), apartment buildings rose to house tenants who had earned their way out of inner-city tenements. With "the smell of cookin' in the hallways," as Neil Diamond put it in "Brooklyn Roads," they became tight-knit communities of interdependent neighbors.

"1440" had a blond brick façade and some art deco touches when it was built in 1939, but few residents took note of the décor. They were more concerned with substance than style, especially when it came to rules governing the city's rent control law, calculating how much a paint job or permission to affix a TV antenna to the roof would allow the landlord to add to the rent. And on Election Day they voted their pocketbooks. The building had 60 units and so far as anyone knew Democrats occupied 59 of them. When he wasn't vacationing in Florida, the landlord resided in the 60th. "Mr. Shikora is a *Republican*," my mother would say, setting the word off with the sort of sinister emphasis you might apply to a known despot. He even *looked* the part, a latter day Ebenezer Scrooge who had curly white hair and wore three-piece suits.

At least the landlord's political affiliation seemed logical to her, since everyone knew Republicans were the fat-cat party while Democrats looked out for the little guy. She was upset when people in our economic bracket failed to appreciate this distinction. At dinner the evening after Election Day in 1952, she recounted an incident that morning at the Glick Brothers kosher butcher shop on Avenue P with a woman from 1500, one apartment house over. "Someone said, 'Did everyone vote right?' And she said, 'I voted right! I liked Ike.'" my mother said. "I almost died. I didn't say a word, but can you imagine? You should have seen the *shmata* she had on! How could a woman wearing a coat like that vote for a Republican? How can people be so stupid?" My father merely shook his head and said, "She's *nuts*!" It was a word that served him twice over as an epithet and an expletive—his favorite depiction of behavior he deemed irrational and a euphemistic substitute for common vulgarities he would never utter out loud (and I find repulsive to this day).

My parents considered the man Ike had trounced, Illinois Governor Adlai Stevenson, a worthy heir to Franklin D. Roosevelt—intellectual, erudite, and charming. War hero or not, Eisenhower was hardly trustworthy given that he had run with villainous Dick Nixon, who had red-baited his way into the Senate by defiling liberal Congresswoman Helen Gahagan Douglas. Worst of all, Ike was a Republican. If they knew the Democrats had turned to Stevenson only after failing to recruit Eisenhower, they never mentioned it. For that matter, FDR's failure to focus more on saving Jewish lives during the war or lift immigration barriers to refugees fleeing Hitler never came up. Like most American Jews, they revered FDR. As for Stevenson (who would lose to Eisenhower again in 1956), they reconciled themselves to the idea that he was just "too good for the American people."

3
The Cheap Seats

We celebrated my ninth birthday thrice over with a family dinner on the actual date, Sunday, May 3, a party in school the next day, and the best imaginable birthday present that Saturday, a Dodgers game with my father at Ebbets Field.

The batch of cream puffs my mother baked for the school party had become confections of legend at P.S. 238 and even evoked a smile from my third-grade nemesis, Mrs. Smith. I was growing used to teachers faulting my classroom deportment—I talked too much—but Mrs. Smith seemed to relish demeaning me with a snide, dismissive sneer in the British accent that made her sound like comic actress Hermoine Gingold absent the daftness. When she minced no words in castigating me to my parents on Open School Night, this antagonism advanced from a mere annoyance to the stuff of anxiety dreams. ("Class, this is a day you will remember for the rest of your lives," Mrs. Smith declared when television networks capitalized on faster planes and film processors to provide same-day video of the coronation of Queen Elizabeth II. "It is something you will tell your grandchildren about." Whenever British royalty suffered a setback over the years I took satisfaction from how far off she proved to be.)

Third-grade travails were far from my mind when I awakened that Saturday to prepare for the ballgame. I took one of my father's yellow notepads and, with more precision than I ever applied to penmanship drills, offset the thin blue rules with perpendicular lines to create my own version of the scorecard sold at the ballpark so I could track every play wth letters, numbers and symbols in traditional scorekeeper shorthand.

A boy's first trip to Ebbets Field was a rite of passage in Brooklyn, where devotion to the Dodgers was about more than baseball. It reflected the collective dreams and disappointments of the denizens of a borough whose very mention on radio or TV was a punch line. I never figured out what was supposed to be so funny but clearly understood they were laughing *at* and not *with* us, especially when actors like William Bendix caricatured our patois with dese, dem and dose in heavily accented "Brooklynese."

Until 1896 Brooklyn had been its own city, and while merging with the other New York City boroughs made economic sense, it left future generations with a diminished sense of identity. Manhattan *was* New York, an attitude reinforced by subway signs in Brooklyn pointing riders "To City" as if we were apart from it. And as if to reinforce this image, the Dodgers, too, had been a punch line in the decades before World War II—laughingstocks of the National League who lost with a zany futility typified by the day that three runners wound up on third base. But Branch Rickey, an astute executive who sportswriters nicknamed "the Mahatma," changed that. Integrating the game with black stars like Jackie Robinson, Roy Campanella and Don Newcombe was just one example of his foresight and eye for talent. Rickey assembled so many good players that from 1947 through 1956 the team won 61.4 percent of its games, a record unmatched by any team in any decade before or since. Yet even these Dodgers, who were celebrated in Roger Kahn's book, *The Boys of Summer*, cultivated an underdog's image by often letting the big one slip away.

We were gathered around our first television when they lost the National League pennant to the Phillies in the final game of the 1950 season after Cal Abrams was tagged out at home plate with what would have been the winning run. "Only one Jewish player on the team," my mother lamented. "Why did it have to be him?" A year later our time-honored motto—"Wait 'til Next Year"—became an even more painful rejoinder after the Dodgers saw a 13–game lead evaporate and lost a playoff series to the Giants on Bobby Thomson's "shot heard 'round the world." They did win the National League pennant in each of the next two years, but lost the World Series to the New York Yankees. The Dodgers faced the Yankees in six World Series from 1947–1956 and lost five of them—disappointments that came each fall at about the same time as the Jewish High Holy Days, leading me to secretly wonder if they were not paying for my sins.

"Next year" always began in late winter with exhibition games broadcast from Florida by Walter (Red) Barber, whose down-home style and knack for understatement survived well into the twenty-first century in the voice of his protégé, Vince Scully. When the season began I would scoot home from school to catch the end of a day game on television or finish my homework in time to watch a night game with my father until bedtime intervened.

On the day of my Ebbets Field debut we rode the Brighton Beach El to the Prospect Park station and walked to the ballpark in a swarm of fans, passing the landmark Bond Bread factory with its clock tower as well as taverns, hot dog carts, and street vendors hawking souvenirs. Then there it was. As accurate as they are, accounts of how decrepit and outdated Ebbets Field had become by the 1950s are hard to reconcile with my memory of the hallowed edifice that came into view at that moment as the crowd surged forward like pilgrims en route to Mecca.

Yet, the tug between promise and disillusionment I associate with the Dodgers became part of that day, too. When we reached the rotunda behind home plate some fans entered the ballpark and others peeled off at gates alongside the first base line. But we kept going, circumnavigating half the structure until we reached the bleacher entrance. He favored the bleachers, my father proclaimed, because he liked "sitting in fair territory." But I knew his preference was about price and not location. The cheapest seats closer to the action cost $1.25, while tickets to the bleachers were 60 cents (up, my father noted, from 50 cents when he had last been there). Looking down at a big-league baseball field once we had climbed to the top deck, I was struck by the colors below from greener-than-green manicured grass and bright Dodger blue grandstands to the uniforms of the players taking batting practice and the advertising signs on the right and left-field walls. Black-and-white television failed to capture such vibrancy.

But it soon became apparent that our view from a backless bench nearly 400 feet from home plate would not do even an exciting game justice. I'd waited so long for this day and now, with the action so distant and the sun baking down on us (ergo the term "bleachers"), it was as if we were on the outside looking in, like being in steerage except that we were the ones high up. That feeling was only reinforced when I went down to the men's room and noticed a forbidding iron fence separated us from everyone else at the game. It upset me and also made me ashamed for allowing myself to feel so frustrated and deprived.

We anticipated the game would be a low-scoring duel between two of the league's best pitchers, Brooklyn's Preacher Roe and Robin Roberts of the Philadelphia Phillies, but neither was in top form. The Phillies scored twice in the eighth inning to surge ahead, 5–4, and when Roberts retired the first two batters in the ninth, the game seemed all but over. Then Robinson drew a walk, bringing Campanella to the plate. Campy swung and drilled one to center field where Richie Ashburn retreated until both he and the ball disappeared beneath an overhang that obscured the last 20 feet of the outfield from those of us in the bleachers. Had Ashburn caught the ball for the final out? For a few confused moments there was no way to know. Then the crowd roared and Robinson leapt for joy, rounding second base. Campy's blast had won the game, clearing the wall to send us home exulting over a feat we had not really seen.

Better seats would have turned my first Ebbets Field outing into a fabulous day, but that was not my father's way. Phil Hershey was hardly miserly—except when it came to money. He was generous when anyone needed help with tax returns or a job application. After retiring, he volunteered to tutor schoolchildren and manage the estates of elderly widows. But growing up poor, scraping for room and board in college only to graduate into a jobless economy, and starting a family on a civil servant's salary had taken a toll. Even years later when he could well afford to stop cutting corners he never did.

After a bout of heatstroke led to his hospitalization and pushed the dementia that had plagued him for nearly a decade past the point of no return, my sister Nancy and I rushed to Florida. The days we spent monitoring his care also gave us a chance to inventory his financial worth. It was no small task. His investing had become a late-life hobby spread among dozens of holdings, 50 shares of this and 100 of that. We kept a running count of each valuation and were taken aback when the aggregate topped $1 million. When we related that to him in the hospital, hoping he would grasp the significance, there was a glimmer of recognition. "I guess," he responded with a smile, "you could say I'm a millionaire."

4

Coney or the Catskills?

AUGUST 1953
Mountaindale, New York

When winter melted into spring the Hersheys of Ocean Parkway mulled two options: summer at the seashore or in the mountains, Coney Island or the Catskills?

Had the decision been his alone, my father would have always chosen the shore. Since childhood he had escaped Brooklyn's summer heat for the ocean a short ride away and by the 1950s his destination was Washington Baths, a refuge for middle-class Jews in Coney Island that provided lockers, showers, a saltwater swimming pool, and his favorite, a Russian-style steam room, for a modest seasonal fee. There were also concrete tennis and handball courts and a ubiquitous speaker system piping baseball broadcasts or pop music. To this day I cannot think of those times at the beach without hearing Doris Day singing "Que Sera Sera, Whatever Will Be Will Be," which topped the charts in my last full summer there in 1956.

By then we owned a car, but in the earlier years heading for the beach entailed riding the Culver Local seven stops to the end of the line and walking along Surf Avenue, a major commercial thorough-fare parallel to the ocean. We'd pass Nathan's Famous hotdog empo-rium and anonymous food stands smelling of burgers and onions by 10 a.m. and Steeplechase Park with its signature electric horse ride and 250-foot-high parachute jump, transplanted to Coney Island from the 1939 New York World's Fair. Just past Raven Hall, an Italian-American counterpart to Washington Baths, we'd head for the board-walk entrance where my father invariably checked that the gatekeeper punched the correct date on his season pass.

Invariably was the word, too. Sidney Farber, the rock-hard gym teacher at P.S. 238, did not look or sound like my father but when he opened the first day of class with a drill sergeant's refrain—"There's a right way, a wrong way, and my way. You'll do things my way."—that's who came to mind. Phil Hershey applied the purity, beauty, symmetry and constancy he saw in mathematics and physics to all aspects of life. He sought order, structure, moderation, and balance in how our apart-ment was decorated; how the dials were set on every appliance (with the radio centered between treble and bass and the toaster midway between light and dark); and even how he tore and folded each length of toilet paper he used. Once he decided on the way something ought to be done, there was no varying from it.

His days at the beach, and thus ours, were preordained. Barring a sudden rainstorm we always knew where to find him—in the pool, taking steam, reading in the bleachers above the handball courts after lunch, swimming again and so forth—down to the minute. What choice was there but to accept and adapt to his schedule?

My mother, who had long since ceased resisting such regimenta-tion, spent a good part of those days playing mah-jongg in the women's solarium which, like its men's counterpart, was also a haven for nude sunbathing (back when beachgoers associated it with Vitamin D, not skin cancer). But had it been left to her, we'd have spent every summer at a bungalow colony in "the mountains" where she could breathe country air and feel evening breezes, I could play on grass instead of concrete or asphalt, and we could go berry picking together—outings that evoked memories for her of a childhood I knew nothing about.

For decades Faye Hershey's personal story started with her mother's death shortly after her birth in 1915 in Brooklyn. That turned out to be half-true, a revised narrative reflecting how self-conscious she felt about being an immigrant. She was actually born in the city of Vitebsk (also the birthplace of the Jewish artist Marc Chagall) in what is now Belarus, the third child of Nachum Goronin and Nechama Onikul Goronin, who died when she was an infant. Nachum immigrated to the United States, leaving her in the care of an aunt and uncle and boarding her older sister and brother with other *shtetl* families. He resettled in New York, found tailoring work, remarried and fathered a son and, after prodding from family members, sent for ten-year-old Faygel and her twelve-year-old brother and fifteen-year-old sister (who passed for eighteen so they could make their way to Rotterdam and sail for New York without adult escort). I was well into adulthood before my mother shared any of this. Only then did I hear about berry picking in the Russian countryside—attached to a poignant tale of losing a shoe in the woods—and understand why my Hebrew middle name, anglicized to Norman, honored a beloved uncle who raised her there.

Geologically speaking, the Catskills are not mountains at all but an aging plateau. But they were mountains enough for generations of New Yorkers attracted by lush greenery and cooler temperatures 100 miles north of the city. The region was a hotbed of Bund and Ku Klux Klan activity in the first half of the twentieth century when resorts often advertised themselves as "restricted" to gentiles before Jewish-owned resorts proliferated in such numbers the area became known as "the Borscht Belt," a development that came about almost by chance. Building on their successful rooming house in the sleepy town of

Ferndale, in 1919 a Jewish couple named Grossinger opened a hotel on a hillside in Liberty catering to prosperous vacationers attracted by the quality of three kosher meals a day as well as the quantity. Guests there (and later at the Concord in Kiamesha Lake, the Nevele in Ellenville, Kutshers in Monticello, the Laurels in Sackett Lake, Brown's in Loch Sheldrake, and the Pines in South Fallsburg) ordered as many dishes as they cared to sample.

With this abundance came a second Borscht Belt staple: humor. Headliners like Milton Berle, Red Buttons, Sid Caesar, Eddie Cantor, Buddy Hackett, Danny Kaye, Alan King, Jerry Lewis, Phil Silvers, Jonathan Winters and Henny Youngman started in the Catskills, honing routines on stage and off. Until they *were* headliners, comics went from table to table in the dining room and chaise to chaise at the pool *tummling*, kibitzing with guests. The closest we got to these high-end retreats was when we drove by them. Lesser hotels like the one depicted in the movie *Dirty Dancing* and affectionately labeled "schlock joints" (the way patrons call favored diners "greasy spoons") were also out of our price range.

Our summer sanctuary was a tiny cottage in a bungalow colony with access to a lake, fields, a casino where residents could play cards or watch television, and something upscale resorts lacked: a sense of community. From late June until Labor Day housewives relished a respite from the city watching their children in relatively idyllic surroundings, but their husbands paid a price for this escape. After fending for themselves all week back home, they faced a long drive Friday evening— one notorious stretch over the Wurtsboro Hills could bring traffic to a crawl—and went back late Sunday or before dawn Monday for the next workweek. It was hardly a ride in the country, so to speak. What never occurred to me (at least consciously) at the time was that if conjugal activity was one reward for such weekly treks then my parents must have been very quiet about it given that I slept on a cot a few feet away.

His four weeks of annual vacation (a tradeoff for the low salary of a civil servant) meant that my father endured fewer of these taxing turnarounds than most of the men, which may be why he agreed to spend four summers from 1948 through 1953 in the Catskills. The one I recall vividly was the last of them, starting with my introduction to something unheard of on Ocean Parkway: an interracial marriage. He was Jewish and a hotel chef, she Hawaiian and a singer who played the resorts. Everyone fawned over their infant son and treated them as full-fledged members of our little summer community and she reciprocated by inviting all of us to see her perform. "I would like to sing you something in my native tongue," she said before the final number. It was in Hebrew. Even at nine, I detected an air of self-congratulation to this exercise in tolerance and understood how unwelcome the same family would probably be in our own apartment house in Brooklyn.

Yiddish, not Hebrew, was the foreign tongue I associated with Jewish culture. It was my parents' first language, and it was still spoken by their generation, but one I was not destined to learn. Except for an occasional phrase—*Nishtdugadacht* ("It shouldn't happen!") my mother would say after a death or some other tragedy—they used it only to communicate something I was not supposed to hear. It led to an exasperating experience that summer. One evening with a trip to see an off-color Yiddish comedian in the offing when no babysitter could be found my parents took me along. After all, they reasoned, I would not understand a word. I sat stone-faced amid a room full of people laughing uproariously for a solid hour.

Sometimes my father and I would hitch a ride to the Olympic Hotel a couple of miles away and pass for paying guests. We'd saunter onto the grounds as if returning from a little hike and spend the day at the hotel pool, allowing time for our bathing suits to dry before hitching back. Some days he even played for the hotel softball team against visitors from nearby resorts. A similar game when my parents were on vacation before I was born became a family heirloom story. After his side won, a player on the other team handed him a $5 bill. It was a money game for fairly significant stakes ($80 now, accounting for inflation). "We did not have a dime with us," my mother liked to recall. "I don't know what we'd have done if Daddy's team had lost." Games at the Olympic were just for fun, but one cost him plenty. Ranging back for a pop fly he crumpled to the grass. He had torn ligaments below his left knee and was hobbled for the balance of the summer, softball forever in his past.

The other children my age that summer, three boys and a girl, were always game for daily adventures. However unable I was to account for them, vague stirrings drove me to think of Deena as more than another playmate. She was not as pretty as pert, bouncy Susan Greenberg and tall, lithe Roberta Cohen, *femmes fatale* at P.S. 238 whose allure was acknowledged in little slam books clandestinely crafted in class by other girls and described in hushed tones by boys in corners of the schoolyard. But, theoretically at least, she was accessible.

And for two months I was among equals. That was not how it went back in Brooklyn where I was perennially selected last—and sometimes not at all—when we chose sides for street games. If we were an odd number I was usually the odd man out, designated "official catcher" for both teams. It was a slight I came to view with relief because it spared me the risk of striking out or flubbing a catch. For such a devoted sports fan, I was an awful player, lacking speed, strength, hand-eye coordination, or any other attribute of athletic prowess. Occasionally, I also provided running commentary, trying to sound like Red Barber. When an adult asked, "What do you want to be when you grow up?" I said "an engineer" because when I heard my mother tell someone her brother was one she seemed so proud. Besides, I understood how impractical it sounded to say I planned on a career in sportscasting.

I did want to please my parents, even if I chafed at her tight apron strings and his tight-fistedness. And they did find little ways to reward me as if to signal recognition of my frustrations. Once that summer when "the Toy Man" came to our bungalow colony, my mother saw me eyeing a horseracing game and stunned me by shelling out a dollar for it. And one Friday my father came up from the city with two new packs of baseball cards, a gift tinged with the irony of an O'Henry tale. I had sold my modest cache of cards to a playmate during the week. My mother took me aside and suggested that I try to cancel the transaction. I did and my father never knew.

She could prove handy in such an awkward moment, but near summer's end there was nothing I could do to spare her a hurt that I found confusing and galling. As Labor Day approached, life seemed close to perfect. Even my father's damaged leg was almost healed. Then came the farewell party. My excitement mounted when cartons of hot dogs and cold cuts arrived from Kaplan's, the kosher deli in Monticello. What a tasty exclamation point on a lovely ten weeks! Then anticipation turned to disappointment and outrage when I learned that this was to be an adults-only event.

I could hardly believe it. Weren't kids people, too? My summer friends agreed it was a pretty bum deal, but did not share my passion for pastrami and sour pickles enough to think it was a big deal. This was my battle to fight. There was always one cool guy in every collection of adults who seemed capable of seeing things from a kid's perspective. I approached ours. He was sympathetic but explained that the partygoers wanted to let their hair down, share jokes that children ought not hear, and generally comport themselves in adult ways. The presence of children would inhibit that, he explained patiently, adding, "Sometimes you just have to learn to accept things in life, even if you think they aren't fair." It was not advice I wanted to hear. My indignation continued to rise and time was growing short. This was not right. I had to say something.

Morty, a tart-tongued character with a curled mustache who was our version of a Borscht Belt *tummler*, was overseeing arrangements like a field general preparing for battle, supervising people setting up tables, assembling decorations, and running extension cords for lights and a turntable. I marched right up to him. "Don't we kids deserve to come to the party?" I asked. "Haven't we been here all summer, too?" He seemed a little flustered and I took that as a signal to press on. "I understand you want to be able to tell jokes and say things children aren't supposed to hear," I said in the deepest voice I could muster, fighting off an urge to cry. "What if we just came for the first hour? Then we can go back to our bungalows." After another back-and-forth or two, Morty yielded. The kids could stay for the first half-hour.

That sounded fine. I could scarf down a lot of cold cuts in half an hour. What's more, I had engaged a man six times my age on equal terms, made my case, and reached a win-win solution. How responsible and triumphant was that? Bursting with pride and vindication, I walked off anticipating the spoils of victory. How could I have gauged it so badly? As Morty and I negotiated people nearby had stopped to listen, something I understood when I heard a female voice with a Bronx twang observe with a cluck and a chuckle, "A regular little Walter Reuther, he is!"

Back in our room, my mother laced into me as she never had before. "You've made me so embarrassed and ashamed," she screamed (and I do mean screamed). "And in front of everyone! How could you do this to me? You were the only one. After all I do for you, that's my reward? How can I go out there and face these people?" In its way the upbraiding was as useful a lesson as any she imparted, one that I would have to re-learn from time to time, about unintended consequences and alternate perspectives—and underscored something I tried to remind myself when I had a child of my own. A person of authority, even a parent, can be wrong.

5

Waiting for George

It was a steamy Thursday morning. I can be positive of the day because my father's weekly *Civil Service Leader* arrived in the mail every Wednesday. When it didn't come the absence elicited an "Aw, nuts!" followed by his plea to my mother (more an instruction, really) to intercept George the mailman the following morning. "Oh, Phil," she would say, "it's probably just a day late." But after token resistance she always acquiesced. (Hearing his real name told me she was annoyed. They almost always used pet names. He was Tootsie and she was Budgee. Faye or Phil betrayed annoyance or worse.)

As we sat in the vestibule the next morning waiting for George to deliver the mail and discussed what the rest of the day would bring, both the subject and my mother's tone abruptly changed. "Life goes by very quickly, Edward," she said with a far-away stare. "Make the most of it." Of all the advice she ever proffered—from an array of aphorisms to fit almost any occasion to more specific counsel—that non sequitur on a summer morning stands out.

Attractive and well liked at 38 (points of pride my mother worked at), Faye Goronin Hershey was grateful for what she had, starting with life itself. As a teenager she had nearly succumbed to lobar pneumonia in the third-floor tenement apartment she shared with her father, stepmother, and half-brother. There was very little money and she went to work as soon as it was legal, finishing high school at night. At a party when she was 21 a young college graduate showed an immediate interest and wound up driving her home. "I was worried about her," my father liked to recount. "She came with some really rough-looking boys and I was concerned. I wanted to make sure she got home okay."

Faygel and Fishel (the Yiddish names they answered to with family) were married three years later and she moved into his parents' apartment in a sturdy brick two-family home in Borough Park where his mother tutored her on cooking what he liked. Theirs was the Eastern European Jewish version of a mixed marriage. The Hershkowitz family was from northern Poland near Galicia, hearty rough-hewn people with a cuisine to match. The Goronins were of Latvian stock, and took a more delicate approach to gastronomy and life. Each group looked upon the other with comic disdain. I once heard a comedian define *meshuga* (Yiddish for "crazy") as a "*Litvak mit* [with] a herring." And whenever Phil said or did something she took to be boorish or self-indulgent, Faye would roll her eyes and declare, "Phil, don't be such a *Galitziana!*"

When the two-family house came up for sale Phil and his parents considered making an offer, but caution trumped aspiration. My grandfather was struggling and his son was a lowly civil servant facing the uncertainty of what the country's coming involvement in World War II meant for every man his age. The house was sold to someone else, a missed opportunity Faye always rued. After Phil received his draft notice, he said his farewells, and took the subway to the induction center on Whitehall Street in lower Manhattan. But he was home before nightfall. A congenital condition he considered of little consequence rendered him 4F.

The deferment came at a cost both during and after the war. Between the draft and the domestic war effort, the unemployment insurance claims Phil evaluated at work disappeared and the state reassigned him to a office on the eastern tip of Long Island. For more than a year he arose well before dawn on Monday mornings to catch the "milk train," staying over some days but returning to Brooklyn on others, a commute that nearly matched the length of his workday.

Back in the city after the war his path up the civil service ladder was slowed because veterans could add extra points on tests to compensate for their years away. That seemed equitable given the loss of time their service entailed—not to mention the risk—but it meant he would ace an exam and then find himself behind candidates who scored over 100 with "veterans preference" points.

That was one issue hampering Phil's rise. Another was how civil service officials gamed the system. Exams were administered statewide and any of the top three scorers could be promoted to fill an opening. It was assumed New York City residents would be reluctant to relocate to the far reaches of the state so upstate positions were often offered to them until enough declined for someone local to become one of the top three. It was probably just as well that my father decided not to move us to Buffalo, Rochester, or Syracuse, but I secretly wished he would. It would be a gutsy and unexpected thing to do and I knew that was the last thing to expect from him.

The younger of two surviving children (two died in infancy), my father was an avid and adept student with a single-mindedness that elicited equal measures of admiration and exasperation. The oft-told exemplification of this came on an October afternoon in 1928 when the huge German *Graf Zeppelin* made land over Brooklyn, completing its first transatlantic voyage. Residents poured outside to glimpse a modern wonder of the world. Not young Philip. He refused to leave the kitchen table, "Let me finish my homework first!" he demanded as his mother and sister beseeched him to come and then dragged him out.

Then something unexpected changed his life. About to graduate from high school, he expected to enter the first class at Brooklyn College, just elevated from its prior status as a branch of the City College of New York. CCNY was called "the poor man's Columbia," a sobriquet with a double connotation. Even in a city of two million Jews, Columbia held to a longstanding Ivy League practice of limiting the number of Jewish students it would admit. So enrollment soared at its Upper-Manhattan neighbor, tuition-free City College, creating pressure to expand into what would become a multi-campus public university.

Philip had taken a statewide exam the prior fall to compete for a stipend he could use for textbooks and supplies. Before handing in the test booklet he checked a box that made him eligible for a full scholarship at Cornell, an Ivy League university more than 200 miles northwest of the city. Just two students from each of the state's 150 legislative assembly districts were chosen and in an area filled with ambitious achievers the odds were long. But as he headed for Coney Island one morning in June a friend shouted "Congratulations!" The *New York Daily Graphic* had listed his name among the Cornell scholarship winners.

Days after turning seventeen, Philip Hershkowitz boarded a bus for Ithaca, the farthest he had ever been from Borough Park. He cherished the academic opportunity Cornell offered and took full advantage of it. Socially and economically, he struggled. Cornell's founders believed a college should educate students, not babysit them, so freshmen had to find their own accommodations. Those wealthy enough pledged fraternities. Others moved into one of the boarding houses that were a cottage industry in Ithaca, a choice limited for Jews to houses not "restricted."

If you knew him for more than a few minutes you probably knew where my father had gone to college. He was a proud Cornell alumnus. You could not enter our apartment without seeing his large framed diploma. Yet, except for fleeting references—I knew he washed dishes to offset the cost of room and board and that he once cadged a long ride home for Thanksgiving in an open-air "rumble seat" in the freezing cold—he never discussed the dark side of his college years. He also never returned to Ithaca or connected with New York City's large contingent of Cornell alumni, and although he enjoyed sports I had to campaign before he agreed to take me to see Cornell's football team play at Columbia. We returned home happy when the Big Red rallied to win, but it was the only Cornell game we ever attended together.

The depth—and sublimation—of his disaffection was apparent sixty years after his graduation when I called to remind him that I was interviewing for a job at his alma mater. Profoundly afflicted with dementia, he would fade in and out of conversations, but the word "Cornell" seemed to ground him. "Yes," he said slowly. "I've been thinking about that, Edward. You know I went to Cornell. But I don't think you should tell them that. I'll tell you why. I went to school with some pretty rich boys and over the years a lot of them have given money to Cornell, something I never did. These are things they can look up. If you tell them I went there, they might hold it against you."

After I accepted Cornell's offer I visited my parents in Florida and told my father that I was about to go to work there. "Now, Edward," he said, again suddenly focused, "I have something to tell you. Listen closely, this is very important. When you get there you'll want to go to Cornell United Religious Works. C-U-R-W. They'll show you where you can live in Ithaca and help you out with other things." It stopped me cold. Why had he been able to summon the name of an obscure campus agency after sixty years? Added to his prior admonition to keep his Cornell degree a secret, it was compelling evidence of how intimidating and alienating his college years were. "They'll tell you where you can live in Ithaca," he said, meaning where Jews were allowed. With his razor-sharp mind bereft of almost all else, *that* he remembered.

He had planned to teach but graduated in 1934 into a historically brutal job market. Down slightly from its peak as a result of FDR's early reforms, national unemployment was still nearly 22% and most jobs paid very little. In New York City, where 110 deaths that year were attributed to starvation, substitute teachers earned $5 a day. The private sector was not much of an option either. Positions available to someone named Hershkowitz were restricted to "Jewish firms" and the path to most of those involved bloodlines of their own. The sons of bankers, lawyers, and successful businessmen—the frat boys at Cornell—had first call. Federal and state government with their merit-based systems for hiring and promotion seemed to present the only reasonable option. That was what eventually led him to the state labor department in 1937.

He still kept taking tests, and after World War II scored third highest in the nation on one of them—for a position in the FBI. It led nowhere. Anti-Semitism was not as overt in the public sector, but still the rule in a number of federal agencies. The State Department, notorious for turning a cold shoulder to desperate Holocaust refugees before, during and after the war, was one. And J. Edgar Hoover's FBI was another. My father never even got an interview. That led him to cease resisting repeated advice from a number of sources, including his older sister whose married name, Simmons, was ethnically neutral. "Phil," she said, "you have to Americanize your name."

Everyone understood that was a euphemism for making it less Jewish, something that galled him because it seemed to capitulate to intolerance. Hersh was a common derivative of Hershkowitz, but my father thought it was too plain. So we all went to court one day in 1948 and became just about as American sounding a family as you might imagine—the Hersheys. The name took on a touch of irony when medical tests attributed attacks of respiratory asthma striking me with alarming frequency to food allergies. I was especially allergic to chocolate.

6

Keeping Score

SEPTEMBER 1955
Brooklyn

The artistic sensibility and physical prowess that came easily to some kids was nearly impossible for me.

Art? I could not color inside the lines or draw anything resembling something. Music? "Edward," the choral music teacher whispered to me in third grade, "when the other children sing just move your lips." I could not find a beat, carry a tune, or detect pitch. And to this day

I cannot whistle. Dexterity? Others made their Duncan yo-yos "go to sleep" or "take a walk," but I could not even coax mine back up once I let out the string. I came to terms with all but one of these shortcomings: my lack of athleticism.

I adored sports so my athletic inability was doubly discouraging. Whether it was punch ball on the sidewalk in front of our apartment house, touch football on the side street around the corner, or three-man basketball at the playground two blocks away, the words "Let's choose sides" were a signal to brace for deflation. I was always the last to be chosen and assigned the position of least possible damage. It wasn't that I didn't try, just that attributes you needed to play well—fleetness afoot, arm strength, fast reflexes, agility and hand/eye coordination—were not part of my game. I was a klutz, a noun defined in one dictionary as "a clumsy, awkward person," derived (naturally enough) from the Yiddish word *klots*, a wooden block.

My klutziness was never more evident than in a street game called *stickball,* which involved hitting a "spaldeen"—Brooklyn parlance for a pink rubber ball manufactured by the A. G. Spaulding Company—with a sawed off broomstick. A sewer cover in the middle of the street served as home plate with the next cover representing second base and fenders of parked cars designated as first base and third base (which once drove off with Mitchell Nodell's jacket). Good hitters sent the highly resilient ball soaring over a fielder standing two sewer covers away, but when it was my turn to hit I might as well have tried to swat a fly with a pencil. I remember connecting just one time, perhaps validating an adage about broken clocks, and even then the ball sailed well foul. Of course, I struck out on the following pitch.

Games like stickball, punch ball, touch football, and three-man basketball were strictly for boys. Girls played jacks or "A My Name is Alice." Jacks involved bouncing a ball and picking first one, then two and ultimately ten small six-pronged metal pieces (the jacks), catching the ball before a second bounce each time.

In "A My Name..." the girl bounced a ball, lifted her leg over it on its upward flight and caught it after reciting a phrase like so: "A [bounce, lift, catch] my name is Alice [bounce, lift, catch] and I come from Alabama [bounce, lift, catch] and I eat apples [bounce, lift, catch] and my dog's name is Asta. B [bounce, lift, catch] my name is Betty [bounce, lift, catch] and I come from Boston..." and so on through the alphabet. Boys never played these games, a gender separation for which I was secretly grateful. I wouldn't have been any good at them either.

I *was* adept at one aspect of sports—tracking and analyzing results, a trait I probably inherited from my father, even if I applied it to games and not math or science. My mother enjoyed the double takes from subway riders who saw my head buried in the *New York Times*. I was reading box scores. When my Uncle Abe gave me a book of baseball records I memorized it cover to cover. And I pored over another book of sports lore so many times that to this day I know how the "Miracle Braves" rallied from last place to win the 1914 pennant and Philadelphia Athletics owner-manager Connie Mack shocked the baseball world by starting old sore-armed Howard Ehmke in the 1929 World Series opener. (He won, striking out 13 Cubs, a record that stood until Carl Erskine—"Oisk" to Dodger fans—struck out 14 Yankees in 1953.)

My idols were not players but sportscasters, especially Marty Glickman, a ubiquitous voice on New York radio announcing basketball, hockey, and football and hosting shows before and after Dodger broadcasts. A heralded sprinter from Brooklyn's Madison High and Syracuse University, Glickman became a footnote to bigotry at the 1936 Olympics in Berlin when the notoriously anti-Semitic U.S. Olympic chairman Avery Brundage ordered coaches to pull him and another runner from a relay team to spare Adolf Hitler the indignity of watching two Jews win gold medals. He had developed into a smooth and knowledgable announcer who could detail game action in a stream of perfectly enunciated words. Lying in the dark well past bedtime with my Philco radio turned low, I hung on every one. "Tricky Dick dribbles into front court...guarded by Cousy at head of the key...behind-the-back to Braun right of the circle...now to Gallatin in the lane harassed by Brannum... finds Clifton alone in the corner for a two-hand set shot... *gooooood* like Nedicks."

When there were no games to see or hear I made up my own. My favorite was Ethan Allen's All-Star Baseball played with a spinner and number-coded discs. I compiled copious statistics and if no one was in earshot, I also announced: Walter Mitty meeting Red Barber. Then, in the winter of 1955, life overtook make-believe. Little League Baseball arrived in Brooklyn. There were meetings to recruit parents as managers, coaches, and umpires; permission slips and medical forms to be signed and tryouts at sprawling Marine Park where men with clipboards took notes. Boys over nine who would not turn thirteen before summer were eligible. Despite my athletic ineptitude, not trying out didn't seem like an option. I owned a first baseman's mitt with extra webbing to ensnare throws from infielders, a kind of leather Venus flytrap, so I tried out for first base.

The West Highway Little League (named for Kings Highway, a stretch of trendy shops everyone called "the Highway") had four teams with flannel uniforms advertising sponsors. Metal spikes were not allowed but players could buy shoes with hard rubber cleats protruding from the soles and batters wore protective helmets. That was a good idea given one obvious imbalance once we started practicing on a baseball diamond two-thirds the dimension of a major league field. Most batters were overmatched against strapping twelve-year-olds firing a hardball from 46 feet away.

Early practices amounted to a second round of tryouts, and just before the start of the season I was cut from the roster and reassigned to a "minor league." It was a merit-based decision, but that did not reduce the hurt. At home that night I ranted through tears that if only my parents had allowed me to try out as a catcher (a position they deemed dangerous) I might have made the team—but knowing (as they did) that I was grasping at straws. I would not have been a good catcher either. To his credit my father let me vent.

I don't remember how I heard that the league needed scorekeepers, but I know nobody envisioned what I proposed. I volunteered to keep score for the whole season. "Every game?" the elderly man who served as commissioner asked. "That's quite a commitment, young man. Are you sure?" It may have been an offer he could not refuse. I suspect nobody else had stepped forward. He gave me a new scorebook that I treated with care and reverence worthy of a sacred trust. I never missed a game. I went when I was sick. I went straight to the field after a day at the beach. I even showed up when it rained on the off chance the game might be played.

On Saturday mornings I donned a "minor-league" uniform—baseball pants and a generic T-shirt—to play on a dusty field adjacent to an amusement complex on Lower New York Bay in the far reaches of Bensonhurst where the competition was such that I could hit and make plays in the field. But I harbored no illusions that I belonged in the games I tracked in my scorebook on weekday evenings. Watching prepubescent prodigies like Ken Gershon (a future college classmate who became a successful high school basketball coach), the Quagliarello twins (sometimes suspected of impersonating each other so the better pitcher could exceed a limitation on innings), and Larry Yellen (who went on to sign a $55,000 bonus contract with the Houston Colt 45s) told me I was where I belonged.

And while the designation "official catcher" for an odd man out in street ball was hardly meaningful, the title of official scorer carried weight. Deciding if a hard grounder that skipped past the third baseman was a double or a two-base error impacted the hitter's batting percentage and the pitcher's earned run average, and could determine whether a no-hitter was still on the line. I updated season statistics after every game and a couple of weeks into the season supplied each manager with a detailed compilation of his team's records. It was nothing I hadn't already done for imaginary games but with a difference. This mattered. One manager altered his lineup in response to a trend my analysis revealed. Players looked at me with newfound respect and, just as important, I saw myself that way, too.

At the end of the season, local leagues across the country selected all-star teams to compete in single-elimination tournaments on the first leg of a long road to Williamsport, Pennsylvania for the Little League World Series. I went along to keep score when our West Highway All Stars faced off against the North Highway All Stars at Marine Park. Alas, our road to Williamsport was short. We lost our first and only game.

In September with sixth grade starting and the Dodgers running away with the pennant en route to what would be their only World Series victory, my summer of keeping score was just a memory. When we were invited to the West Highway Little League awards dinner at a restaurant on Kings Highway, I was surprised my father wanted to go. He rarely spent money unnecessarily and, besides, I was only a minor leaguer. I enjoyed being there but felt out of place as the champions, the all-stars, and finally the most valuable player received medals and trophies.

Well, not quite finally. "We have one more award for a young man who had an extraordinary season," the toastmaster said. "In fact, he participated in every game. This is for our official scorer, Edward Hershey." Beckoning me to the dais, he handed me a trophy as large as the one he had just given the MVP. I understood now why we were there. In May, on the evening I was cut from the team, I managed to fight back tears until I reached home. This time, as the room burst into applause, I started to cry.

7

The Bully in 1 F

Fearful of missing the end of the seventh and deciding game of the 1955 World Series if I walked home from school, I stopped at an auto repair garage that had a radio. Just as I arrived, Dodgers leftfielder Sandy Amoros made a spectacular catch of a drive by Yogi Berra of the Yankees and threw the ball to shortstop Peewee Reese who fired to Gil Hodges at first base to double up Gil McDougald and preserve Brooklyn's 2–0 lead. Three innings later, Elston Howard grounded to Reese who threw to Hodges to secure the Brooklyn Dodgers' first (and, as it turned out, only) championship. Listening to the mechanics shout at the final out was a highly personal experience that I might not have traded for a box seat along the first base line. I can still smell the motor oil.

A few days later my mother and I took our last morning subway ride to the orthodontist's office where before-and-after plaster impressions of my teeth dramatized the success of my six years of treatment. It was a sweet morning that abruptly turned sour when we returned to an empty sixth-grade classroom at P.S. 238. My classmates were elsewhere in the building taking one of a battery of citywide exams to determine eligibility for a Special Progress program that allowed students to complete grades 7–9 in two years. My mother was near panic. "Make the S.P." had been her mantra since failing in her efforts to enroll me in kindergarten in September 1949 when I missed the deadline by three days. Children who reached their fifth birthday after April 30 waited another year to start school. That sounded arbitrary to my mother who reasoned that I was big for my age and smart, and I'd missed the cutoff by only *three days*. Nada. Rules were rules. No exceptions. "We are going to get that year back," she declared resolutely over and over and over, year after year after year. And now I had missed one of the tests required to make it happen. She refused to leave the building without assurance that I would take a makeup exam.

By then, her child-rearing responsibilities had doubled. At 41, she had given birth to a girl. Though I never knew it, she had suffered two miscarriages in her thirties and so my parents had waited a while to tell me she was pregnant. By then I'd overheard enough indiscreet inquiries and whispered conversations to figure it out. I was excited but also disconcerted. *Women can die in childbirth,* I thought, without even knowing she had dismissed medical advice to abort the fetus for her own safety given her age and medical history. Far less calamitous, how could a family of four function in our cramped apartment?

The rounder my mother got and the more real the prospect of a new baby became, the calmer I felt, and I was more excited than afraid when my father awakened me on a July morning before dawn with "It's time to go to the hospital." Except for a milkman on his rounds the streets were desolate on the way there. My mother disappeared into an elevator and we camped out in the waiting room. I'd read every issue of *Reader's Digest* by mid-morning when her obstetrician appeared to say she was not quite ready to deliver, but he wanted her to stay. We drove home and my father headed for Coney Island. Why waste a good beach day? "I was so embarrassed," my mother reported later. "Nobody could believe that I was about to give birth and my husband was at the beach."

There was still no word by bedtime. When the phone rang at 3 a.m. my father shot out of bed, slamming his forehead into a dresser drawer. "It's a girl," he said when he returned. "Go back to sleep." After twelve years, I had a sister. Would she also be a liberator? With a baby commanding her attention would my mother have less time or inclination to baby me?

Her apron strings did not come completely undone but were loosened. For example, when I announced that I wanted to go to Ebbets Field to see the Dodgers try to clinch the pennant on the last day of the season that September she asked, "By *yourself?*" When I nodded, she suggested I go with a friend but acquiesced after none could be found. Duke Snider's two home runs helped Don Newcombe beat Pittsburgh and I exulted in the idea that I was part of a historic triumph.

In truth, I would rather have shared the celebration with someone, but I was accustomed to spending time alone. I never had what you could call a best friend. I thought that might change when I developed an unlikely rapport with popular and handsome Dickie Greenberg (a useful nickname since there was another Richard Greenberg in our fifth-grade class). Dickie lived in a single-family brick house three blocks down Ocean Parkway where we spent afternoons playing board games and trading thoughts that reached such a level of intimacy I was able to confess the crush I had on a girl in our class.

"Have a great summer," I said on the last day of school before he headed off to sleep-away camp and he replied, "See you in September." Those were the last words we ever exchanged. When he failed to appear on the first day of sixth grade, I called. His father answered. No, he said, his son was not there. Then, after a long pause, he added, "Dickie doesn't live here anymore." The Greenbergs were moving to Long Island and Dickie had not even called to say good-bye. *I guess we were not that close after all,* I thought.

By then it was not surprising to hear that anyone on Ocean Parkway had moved to the suburbs. Starting in the early Fifties one family after another left for a dream home with a lawn and a backyard in a stellar school district a short drive from a gleaming shopping center. The first departure with a direct bearing on us was when Elsie and Irving Fein and their two daughters moved to Long Island. The Feins came closer to resembling the model American household portrayed in shows like *Father Knows Best* and *Ozzie & Harriet* than any family I knew. They owned the first television I ever saw and even ate *trayf* at home, sometimes filling the hallway with unfamiliar scents like shrimp and bacon. My first visit to an airport came the night we accompanied Elsie and the girls to LaGuardia when Irving returned from a business trip to Pittsburgh. Planes were not very well equipped for air pressure changes back then, and on our ride home somebody asked how his ears felt. Irving, a jovial man who sported a mustache and smoked a pipe, said chewing gum had been a big help. "Doesn't the gum get sticky in your ears?" one of the girls asked and everyone laughed.

About a year after they moved, the Feins invited us and another 1440 family out for a visit. It was my first look at a suburb and their new quarters were a big step up from Apartment 1G. When Irving ignited the backyard grill the smell was intoxicating, but as the afternoon wore on my sense of wonder began to wear off, probably starting when lunch was served to the children and adults in separate rooms. Was everything a little too perfect? Whatever was bothering me, I fell asleep that night feeling less envious of Dickie Greenberg, Ginny and Wendy Fein, and all those kids who left us behind. I would spend fourteen years as a young adult on Long Island no more than five miles from that house in Westbury. By then my vague uneasiness had developed into a full-blown aversion to suburban life.

The Nodells, the family accompanying us on our visit to the Feins, were hardly jetsetters but were more assimilated than we were. They belonged to a large Reform Jewish temple and ate at Chinese or Italian restaurants on Sundays. "We're going to the chink's," Carrie Nodell would say, using a word so common on Ocean Parkway that I thought "chinx" was innocent shorthand for Chinese food rather than a racial slur. Marty Nodell gained a measure of fame late in life when comic book collectors discovered he had created the Green Lantern, first drawn under the pseudonym of Mart Dellon to preserve his reputation because comics were considered such low art.

Marty was a commercial artist at Cunningham & Walsh, an ad agency like those portrayed a half-century later on *Mad Men*. It was work that seemed exciting compared to my father's job, sizing up unemployment insurance applicants. But the downside became clear in 1956 when the Italian Liner *S. S. Andrea Doria* sank after a collision with a Swedish cruise ship in the Atlantic that killed 52 people. The Italian Line, a major client, ceased all advertising and Marty was laid off. He caught on at an agency in Chicago where he helped create "Poppin' Fresh," the Pillsbury doughboy. But when I visited the Nodells in Wilmette outside Chicago when I was there for a college newspaper convention in 1964, it was clear Marty's heart was still in New York. "Chicago seems like an exciting place," I said, aglow from my first plane ride. "Two Newarks on a lake," he scoffed.

The suburban migration did exact one undeniable toll, a diminished pool of playmates. As families left, young couples or older empty nesters rented the apartments they vacated and soon nobody who remained was much of a match for me. Freddy Sake in 3C, son of one of my mother's mah-jongg partners, was whip smart but socially and physically immature. Michael Garson in 2A, the son of a liquor salesman whose family ran with the building's faster set, was sweet but immersed in the piano playing that would lead to a career as keyboardist for David Bowie and The Smashing Pumpkins. Mitchell Nodell in 6 G, two grades ahead of me, wasn't exactly a bully but usually got the better of me in anything we did together.

Now Victor Dubitsky in 1F, *there* was a bully! He lived with his parents and a brother and cousin, each several years his senior. The older boys were tall, slender and well mannered. Half a foot shorter and squat, Victor was a talented singer with professional ambition, but his stature rendered that a long shot and his demeanor did not help. He had an evil smile and a cutting word at the ready for any occasion and was less than an average student, a rarity in the building.

All this imbued him with resentment and anger, and I was a handy target for his constant goading, usually accompanied by some guffaws and an unspoken invitation to bystanders to chime in.

While none of it ever became physical beyond an occasional "noogie" applied to my arm, two incidents suggested nothing was beyond him. "Wanna see something?" a kid asked one day, beckoning several of us down an alley we used as a lurking spot for Ringalevio, a street game that combined hide-and-seek and tag. We were soon looking at a kitten in the bottom of a trashcan. Victor found a broom, walked over to the can and crushed the kitten to death while the rest of us stood there. It was by far the most brutal and sadistic act that I had ever seen close up and it alerted me that he was not just a bully but a danger-ous one, a point he drove home one evening when Victor reached into his pocket, withdrew a firecracker, stuck it in my mouth and waved a match back and forth. Suddenly the fuse lit.

For a moment we each froze, with only the crisp crackle of the burning fuse breaking the silence. Then Victor slapped the firecracker from my mouth and stamped it out on the ground. Unlike the kitten in the trashcan, I'd managed to use one of my nine lives. "I never meant to light it," he said, shaking his head as I looked down at the smolder-ing fuse and then up at his face still just inches away. The smile was gone, replaced by a look of fear. "I'll give you credit, Hershey," he said. "You've got guts!"

I don't know if a witness to either of these incidents ever spoke of them, but I never said a word to anyone. And while his taunts contin-ued, after that Victor seemed less intimidating.

8

Camp Harmony

AUGUST 1957
Hopewell, New Jersey

Every spring my mother would suggest sleep-away camp and I would decline in part out of fear of missing out on something at home and in part just out of fear. Except for a week in the hospital for eye surgery when I was six, I had never been away from home. Notwithstanding how hard I tugged at her apron strings, had my mother groomed a mama's boy? Was it Alexander Portnoy meets Stockholm syndrome?

But this time my mother held three aces and played them all, arguing 1) my baby sister needed too much time and attention to allow for other family activity, 2) my cousin Sandy would be a counselor at the camp and right there if I needed anything, and 3) our neighbor Rose Dubitsky had bemoaned a lost job opportunity for her son Victor, meaning the bully in apartment 1F would be around all summer. Case closed.

On the last Saturday in June my father drove me to Camp Harmony in Hopewell, New Jersey, a hamlet up the road from Princeton. Hopewell had once been at the center of pure pandemonium, scene of the 1932 kidnap-murder of Charles and Anne Morrow Lindbergh's infant son and the subsequent trial, leading to the execution of Bruno Richard Hauptmann. A quarter-century later its bucolic somnolence was a perfect setting for a sleepy little sleep-away camp, and Harmony was as sleepy as they came.

The 1950s were a golden age for summer camps, which had become almost essential for a well-rounded childhood in the eyes of Jewish parents who could afford them, but that success had raised expectations in the marketplace. Competitors with fancy facilities and sophisticated programs were crowding out mom-and-pop operations like Harmony that depended on word-of-mouth referrals. Just sixty campers lined up to salute the flag to a bugler's scratchy recording of "Retreat" that first evening—a far cry, longtime campers said, from its bustling heyday not many years before.

Harmony's pop was David Purmell, a sixty-seven-year-old Latvian-born arboriculturist who bought a 230-acre fruit farm in 1931 and nine years later converted it to a camp he named to honor his wife Anna, a concert pianist before arthritis crippled her. A half-century had not thinned Purmell's accent, and his announcements above the crackle of a primitive loudspeaker were a source of bemusement. Music was a principal draw. John Chagy, the composer son of a famed Latvian-American Jewish cantor, gave piano lessons and staged a Broadway musical on family visiting day. His son Alan had grown from a babe in arms to a senior camper and daughter Lynda Mae had matured into a teenager counselor as flirtatious as her brother was shy. Most coun-selors were well off enough to spare them sweltering summers on con-struction crews or resort staffs for college tuition. For them, the eight weeks at camp was about fun—and romance. Some arrived in pairs and most of the rest quickly coupled off.

One cabin of "senior boys" aged twelve to fourteen was composed of returnees wise to the ways of camp. Ours had the misfits. Bernie, a quintessential nerd, was setting up his low-frequency radio station when I arrived. Paul, raw-boned and innocent, lived far enough out in the exurbs of New Jersey to speak with a country twang. David, slight and quiet, was not as nerdy as Bernie but hardly cool. Wayne, from a blue-collar Queens neighborhood, was even-tempered and unpreten-tious with a perpetually goofy expression masking a quick wit. Azi was an outcast among outcasts, pudgy and socially challenged, so driven to please he blurted his way into conversations with non-sequiturs that only invited more mockery. Once we were wise enough to the ways of camp to try the time-honored practical joke of "Frenching" a bed by folding the top sheet so an unsuspecting target could not climb all the way in, Azi was the natural victim. I wish I could say I was imbued with enough empathy to defend him, but I was content not to *be* him. It was not exactly an all-star crew, and as we traded stories for well over an hour the first night after lights out, I was certain of this much: No matter the game, for eight weeks I would not be the last player chosen.

The social side of camp life had been on my mind because I'd finally begun to approach girls. For a year I'd timed my route home from school to chat with Susan Goldstein until we reached her house, never letting on that our convergence was more than coincidental. Then in May, with my bar mitzvah behind me and afternoons my own at last, I fell in with an after-school clique a few blocks from our house—a safe distance from anyone who knew me mostly for my awkwardness. It was there that a pony-tailed eleven-year-old caught my eye. Sandy, whose parents owned a neighborhood bakery, lived quite far away and one afternoon I volunteered to walk her home. To my delight and dis-belief, in a matter of blocks we were holding hands. That was as far as it got. Big move, eh? Yet it told me I might finally be ready to actualize my romantic yearnings.

So in addition to sewing name tags into my clothes and buying me new sneakers and a tennis racquet, my mother acquiesced to a couple of extra purchases—a jar of Max Factor hair slicker and (oh how I cringe just to think about this) a pair of Pat Boone's trademark white buck shoes. I wore both to the rec hall for the opening night talent show where an array of piano solos and tap dances ensued until my world spun to a halt in a heartbeat. I fell head over white buck heels in love with one of two girls in white leatherette jackets and matching caps who sang a hit record by the young Hollywood star Sal Mineo.

"Can't figure out what it's all about,
you're always on my mind
You never miss with your sweet kiss
but you leave my heart behind.
I wanna you to start movin'—
come on hold me tight
Start movin' in my direction—
and let's start our lovin' tonight!"

Corinne was everything I wasn't—slender, demure and one of two gentile campers in the whole place. For a time, we danced at Saturday night socials to "It's All in the Game" by Tommy Edwards, "Tonite, Tonite" by the Mello Kings and "The Great Pretender" by the Platters until it turned out that I was the one pretending. She took me aside one night and said, "Ed, I'm not sure how to tell you this. I like you but I don't want to dance every dance with you." Devastated seems too mild to describe how hard this uncoupling hit me. I can still hear every word six decades later. When several boys sneaked off on a "raid" of the girls' side on the final night of camp to cuddle with summer girl-friends (after carefully encasing their pre-adolescent genitalia in jock straps to avoid the embarrassment of a possible erection), I had no one to visit.

That said, I enjoyed the summer. As I suspected that first night, the limited talent pool elevated my own game. I was picked early when we chose sides and sometimes did the choosing. I played Colonel Pickering in "My Fair Lady," the visiting day show. Following in the footsteps of the third-grade chorale director who said "just move your lips" and the rabbi who told me to speak rather than chant the *haftorah* at my bar mitzvah, John Chagy converted the part of Henry Higgins' sidekick to a non-singing role. With rehearsal foundering on the eve of the show, Chagy stormed off and a longtime counselor appeared as if on cue to deliver a show-must-go-on pep talk. The next day we brought down the house, although it was not exactly a tough audience. My key line could have been our mantra: "I doubted you'd do it, I surely thought you'd rue it, but succeed you did!"

Two days later I was introduced to another camp tradition. As older hands smirked, two counselors started arguing during dinner and one shouted, "This is war!" A chorus resounded, "Color war!" The ostensible disputants were captains of the red and white teams through four days of sports culminating in a competitive sing. It was no accident that this was a late-summer staple at most camps just as malaise began to set in with one day of swimming, softball, and arts & crafts blending into the next. But everything about sleep-away camp was new to me, and I barely slept that night in anticipation, especially after seeing the first day's schedule.

We senior boys were more than just competitors. We were the evening entertainment. A ping-pong table was transported from the rec hall porch to the stage, where Alan Chagy and I faced off in front of the entire camp. We'd played often and while we were fairly well matched, Alan always won. Maybe that's why I felt loose when he took an early lead in the opening game of a best-of-three match. Then I made an improbable shot and then another and another to draw even. Several serves after we tied at 21, I won consecutive points to take the first game. Alan did not panic but I played out of my head, pulling improbable returns from my hip pocket and sending unreturnable shots careening off the edge of the table. The second game was not nearly as close. When I exited the stage in triumph, teammates clustered around as if I'd homered to win the World Series.

During rest hour after lunch the next day Alan appeared at our bunk and motioned for me to follow him. "I have to see something," he said when we reached the ping-pong table back in its usual place on the rec hall porch. "Your serve." I tried as hard as I could, but he beat me two straight games.

9

A Game for the Ages

DECEMBER 1958
The Bronx

In Brooklyn, where there had always been a "next year," we hoped until the very last that Dodgers owner Walter O'Malley was bluffing. The Borscht Belt comedian Phil Foster even recorded a song called "Keep the Dodgers in Brooklyn." But it was not to be. The move to Los Angeles was announced shortly after the 1957 season, making Brooklyn fans the ultimate underdogs. We had no team at all.

I confronted another, more personal loss that fall. My grandfather had been diagnosed with terminal cancer in the spring and it kept creeping into my mind at summer camp when the rest of the real world seemed far away. I'd experienced only fleeting connections to death. An elderly neighbor who talked baseball with me died of a heart attack and one of my father's uncles jumped off the roof of a building (an aspect of his passing discussed only in guarded whispers). But this would be my most direct brush with mortality. It was less about grieving for him—we did not have much of a relationship—than wondering how I was supposed to respond. I hadn't been back from camp a day when my mother caught me by surprise asking, "Why don't you go see Grandpa?"

Nathan Goronin, an austere, remote man, rail thin with slender hands that had once sewn clothing to provide for his family but now kept shaking, appeared older than his seventy years. What few words he spoke in a soft, raspy voice were almost all in Yiddish. If someone asked, "How's the soup, Papa?" and he responded, "*Es s nisht schlekt* [It's not bad.]," it was practically cause for celebration. My lasting memory of him stemmed from a Passover Seder four years before and still jarred me.

We would spend one Seder with my father's family and the other with my mother's in apartments crammed with cousins and aunts and uncles at a makeshift table in the living room. But the similarity ended there. As informal and accessible as the first one, that's how stilted and imposing the second night felt. The service was long and barely decipherable for me and my mother's stepmother was not much of a cook. When dinner arrived, the tasteless *knaidlach* floating in watery soup and overcooked chicken hardly seemed worth the wait.

When I started attending afternoon Hebrew classes, I inherited the role of asking the ceremonial "four questions" that serve as a prelude to the telling of the story of the exodus from Egypt in the *Haggadah*. My debut went well enough the first night, coached along by supportive smiles, but soon after I began on the next night I sensed a commotion. This grandfather was used to a dirge-like rendition he probably once recited himself. The sprightly tune I had learned seemed akin to sacrilege. "In my whole life I never heard such a thing," he rasped as others tried to mollify him. "Papa," someone whispered, "this is what they taught him." I pretended not to notice but I was mortified, a pit in my stomach betraying the embarrassment everyone else at the table tried to spare me.

I did identify with one aspect of my grandfather's life. He was an avid Brooklyn Dodgers fan. So, as I embarked on my journey to visit him in the days before his passing, my mother advised, "Talk to grandpa about baseball." Gazing into the dark tunnel as the A train trundled toward Van Siclen Avenue after making the requisite subway connections, I felt a burgeoning sense of maturity—and doubt. What would I say to a dying man about the Dodgers, who were only weeks away from deserting us?

He never acknowledged his impending demise or their coming departure but did complain about the poor play of what would be the last Dodger team in Brooklyn, which was mired in third place. "Shit, that Hotches [Hodges] doesn't hit," he said in his accented English. "They throw him a curveball and he can't hit." After two hours I was en route home, feeling that this, and not my bar mitzvah the previous May, was my coming of age, the day my grandfather felt comfortable enough to toss off an expletive as I said goodbye to him, to the Dodgers, and much more. He died on Thanksgiving weekend a month after the Dodgers and New York Giants packed up and went west.

The Dodgers' exodus provided sobering insight into the ephemeral nature of associations and allegiances. I had so little interest in baseball that even hating the Yankees lost most of its appeal. I started rooting for the other New York Giants, the city's pro football team. The Giants had some establishment trappings, including a pair of stars with Hollywood looks in Frank Gifford and Kyle Rote and even played home games at Yankee Stadium, but also boasted a host of "lunch-pail" players with ethnic names to match—Karilivacz, Modzelewski, Robustelli, Stroud, Svare, Svoboda, Wietecha and Huff. And like the Dodgers, they also signed black players like Emlen Tunnell, Roosevelt Brown and Roosevelt Grier.

I longed to see the Giants play at the stadium where my junior high school ID card would reduce the price of a ticket to $2, but my mother would not hear of it. Hadn't I gone to Ebbets Field by myself, changed subway lines twice to visit a dying grandfather, and ridden my bicycle clear to Coney Island? No dice. "Edward, you are not going all the way to the Bronx by yourself and sit in the freezing cold all day," she said, "and that's that."

So I hatched a plan. Well, not much of a plan. I would simply sneak out of the apartment before anyone else was up. It would be the most direct act of disobedience in my young life. I awoke early, quietly closed my sofa bed, donned several layers of clothing I stashed the night before, packed a sandwich, and left a note. All that remained was to extricate my winter coat from a closet in the bedroom where my parents and baby sister slept. Either I was not quiet enough or my mother opened an eye at the wrong moment but just as I exited the room, coat in hand, I heard "Edward?" She was out of bed and in my face about as fast as Frank Gifford could skirt right end. "What are you doing?" she shouted. "Do you want to give me a heart attack?" Part of me was relieved because even as I activated my plan its likely repercussions began to dawn on me. Sitting in the stadium contemplating the wrath awaiting my return would surely have tempered my enjoyment of the game.

As it turned out, the sheer audacity of my aborted escape led to a positive outcome. She relented and I got to see Gifford lead the Giants to victory over the Chicago Cardinals the very next Sunday. The following season, in 1958, I went to most games, including one that I would treasure always. On the final day of the regular season the Giants needed to beat the Cleveland Browns to tie for first place and force a playoff. The temperature was in the 20s with intermittent snow, making anyone who went outside feel "chilled to the bone through and through," as my mother put it, combining metaphors for emphasis in a futile appeal for me to stay home. Or, as she said more succinctly that morning, "Edward, you'll get pneumonia!"

After two hours waiting on line and two more in my seat before the kickoff, even three pair of socks, two pair of gloves, and a set of long underwear under several layers of wool did not seem like enough. The score was 10–10 in the waning minutes and when Pat Summerall's 33-yard field goal attempt sailed wide, all seemed lost. A tie would keep the Browns in first, sending them into the championship game against the Baltimore Colts. Some fans had departed when a poor Cleveland punt gave the Giants one last chance.

After three incomplete passes, Summerall trotted in for a 49-yard field goal. What were the coaches thinking? Hobbled by a knee injury, he had missed half his 22 attempts that season and never even tried one that long. Even a desperation pass seemed a better bet. But in one of those unlikely turns that make games worth watching to the end, his kick was long and true.

I returned the next week in even nastier weather to watch the Giants win again but did not see the Colts beat them in overtime at Yankee Stadium a week later in what many called "the greatest game ever played." The cheapest ticket was $10 (about $85 today) and the telecast was blacked out in New York. Besides for my money—all $2 worth—nothing could top that miracle kick in the snow.

10

Does It Have a Beat?

APRIL 1959
Philadelphia

Does anyone have a good first day of high school? Doubts enveloped me on a rickety green school bus during the two-mile ride to the far reaches of a desolate neighborhood called Bath Beach. Was I taking the right courses? How could I get to room 412A from here? Would I catch the bus home where it dropped me off?

You fended for yourself from day one at Lafayette High. Built at the close of the Great Depression, the school was on the other side of the tracks in more ways than one, a half-block from the West End El with such a lack of amenities it was fodder for upperclassmen selling

swimming pool passes to unsuspecting newbies. There *was* no pool—
or much else in terms of recreational facilities beyond a gymnasium
with lockers and showers that looked like no place I cared to spend
more time than absolutely necessary. What we did have even before
baby boomers came of high school age was an excess of students,
requiring a de facto double shift with ten class periods extending from
early morning to late afternoon. This surplus also made the education
enterprise a no-frills affair. Aside from perfunctory annual sessions, I
met with my "guidance counselor" only when I needed him to authorize a class change.

My cousin Sandy, who edited the *Marquis,* the school literary magazine (pronounced Mar-KWISS in true Brooklyn fashion), introduced
me to her counterpart at the *Lafayette News,* the school newspaper.
When I told him I wanted to be a sportswriter, he called over the
sports editor who said, "You can cover cross-country. The first meet is
up at Van Cortlandt Park a week from Saturday. Go find Coach Yudell
that Monday and he'll fill you in on the results."

Two things came to mind. First: *cross-country?* My idea of sports
involved balls and bats, baskets and backboards, pucks and nets, and
yard lines and goalposts. Aside from a vague notion that it involved
running up and down hills, I knew nothing about cross-country. The
other: *Go find the coach and he'll fill you in?* That was no way to cover
any story, let alone my very first. The park was several blocks past the
last stop on the Broadway Local, a longer ride than I had calculated.
I had to run a race of my own to reach the starting line where several
hundred runners were shedding sweat suits. I nearly panicked before
spotting the maroon-clad Lafayette team, just about startling coach
Simon Yudell. He had never seen a *Lafayette News* reporter at a track
meet, let alone at a single race in the far reaches of the Bronx.

Not that I saw much of the race. Nobody did. At the sound of
the starter's pistol the runners took off across a quarter-mile field
before funneling onto a two-mile trail through the hills. About fifteen
minutes later the best of them emerged at the head of a quarter-mile
straightaway to the finish line led by twins from Brooklyn Automotive

High who broke the tape hand in hand in a photo that made the Sunday papers.

Stopwatch in hand, Yudell stood in a line of coaches and called out each Lafayette finisher's time for his student manager, Marty Goldman, to record on a clipboard. The first, Harold Tepper, was well back in the pack.

Yudell had been an intensely successful soccer coach at New Utrecht High way back when my father attended and later at Lafayette before a heart condition forced him to give it up. He had mellowed into a gentle, bespectacled man who never raised his voice. "You really don't have to come all the way up here for these races," he told me, "but if you want to do it, I'd be happy to pick you up next week."

The track team's exploits commanded only a few inches of copy in the school paper each month, but I discerned a way to use the assignment to my advantage. By the indoor season I was also the team statistician, logging times with my own stopwatch at daylong meets sponsored by Catholic high schools at a cavernous armory in Washington Heights.

We sat in stands above a 220-yard oval track marked out on the drill floor, which was restricted to runners, coaches, officials and real sportswriters. Their press table was my destiny. First, I would have to overcome an imposing obstacle—large men in black with white collars stationed at the doors, the first priests I had ever seen up close. I would wander downstairs during the long day and lurk in a warm-up area, conjuring how to make my way past these forbidding figures.

By the third meet I had a plan. Clipboard and stopwatch in hand, I waited for an optimal moment to fall in with several others, nodded to the guardian of the door and headed for the press area. "You're Ralph Blumenfeld," I said to a writer I recognized from the photo atop his column on high school sports in the *New York Post*. "Right you are," he said with a smile, "and you are ... ?"

"I'm Ed Hershey from the *Lafayette News*," I announced, wondering if a squadron of priests was about to descend on me. After some small talk he asked, "How would you like to be my Lafayette correspondent?" My head was practically spinning just from meeting a real newspaperman. The idea that I could contribute to his column was beyond mind-boggling. I copied down Blumenfeld's direct line at the *Post*. "Call me any Friday evening you have something I can use," he said before I excused myself and headed back upstairs flushed with excitement. After that I spent as much time as I could each week trying to glean at least one tidbit that would give me an excuse to make that Friday call, hands just about shaking, to announce (once I'd gotten through after a series of busy signals), "Ralph, this is Ed Hershey from Lafayette High School."

Lafayette's runners asked the same question over and over that winter. Would they go to the Penn Relays? For Brooklyn kids who rarely left New York City, it represented more than the chance to run in a world-class meet at historic Franklin Field. It was a voyage to a distant and exotic locale. So the excitement was palpable on the final Friday of April as 13 of us—10 competitors, the coach, the manager and a wide-eyed reporter-statistician—boarded a chartered bus for the 90-mile trip to Philadelphia.

Our adventure began with the ride, which nowadays might be called a multicultural experience. We shared the bus with teams from two other schools, Wingate and Lane, composed entirely of blacks. When the city closed Lafayette in 2006 few white students remained, but in 1959 that was all we had. Lafayette's diversity was ethnic and not racial, a split between Jews and Italian-American Catholics, and reflected a different form of bias. Most Jews—even academic laggards like me—took college-prep classes. Many Italians were channeled into less challenging programs—general studies for boys on a path to blue-collar work, commercial diplomas for girls en route to clerical or sales jobs before marriage. And, of course, there were only boys on the bus. Girls did not compete in track and field or any sport until the federal government enacted Title IX in 1972.

We checked into Philadelphia's venerable if austere Arch Street YMCA and headed to a nearby Horn & Hardart Automat. Catholics on the team grumbled that since it was Friday they had to order shrimp

instead of meat. I smiled to myself. Shellfish was *trayf*—non-kosher. I
was not supposed to eat shrimp on any day. After lunch it was off to the
races. The high school relays were on Saturday so we spent Friday afternoon watching an array of stars expected to compete in the 1960 Rome
Olympics. As the afternoon wore on and the novelty wore off, someone
said, "Wanna see if we can get on *American Bandstand*?"

ABC had turned *Bandstand* from a local dance show into an American phenomenon. At 29 going on 17, host Dick Clark had the clean-
cut face to pitch acne cream and a demeanor that connected well in
living rooms where homework played second fiddle to rock and roll.
Kids everywhere knew the names of the regulars from West Philly and
Clark's perennial question to three teens rating a new record—"Does it
have a beat?"—was a national punch line.

It seemed unlikely anyone could just show up and get in. But we
hopped an El and in half an hour were on line outside WFIL-TV
watching the regulars walk by, nod to a guard, and enter a stage door.
There were familiar couples, Justine and Bob and Kenny and Arlene,
and right behind them Pat Molittieri, a pert brunette with an easy
smile and flowing skirt. To me, she was Natalie Wood and Ann-Mar-
garet rolled in one. Then, almost before I realized what was happening, the guard approached our line and started counting. He was still
counting when he passed me. Moments later he beckoned us through
that door.

Forget that I could hardly dance a step or that the day's live performers were the hopelessly dippy Teddy Bears lip-synching their lame
hit, "To Know Him Is to Love Him." (Did it have a beat? Hell, it
barely had a pulse!) We were on Bandstand. I was 10 feet away from
Pat Molittieri on American *effing* Bandstand! That was as close as I
would get. She was single, but far out of my league. I sat in the bleachers on the side of the set, scanning the crowd for a likely partner and
waiting for the first strains of a slow record. Once, like a kid at a fourth-
grade social too timid to cross the gym, I started and then went back
when the song turned out to be too fast. When I did take the plunge
and secured an appropriately unglamorous partner, I concentrated on

getting through it, thinking to myself, "Forget where you are. Pretend this is the rec hall at Camp Harmony."

Social ineptitude aside, I had never been timid about engaging authority. During a commercial break I strode to the base of the podium where Dick Clark was perched above a large lectern. "A bunch of us are from the Lafayette High School track team in Brooklyn," I called up to him. "We're in Philly for the Penn Relays." He smiled that Dick Clark smile and said, "That's great. Is there a team captain I can talk to?" I nearly knocked over a couple of people racing across the set to find Steve Aiello. In minutes he and Clark were chatting on the air. I smiled at dinner that night when Steve recounted the experience to the others, proud that I'd made it happen.

As expected our two relay teams lost on Saturday. That night we dined at Tad's Steakhouse (not exactly prime, but $1.19 with garlic bread and a baked potato) and set out in search of a different sort of exposure. "My cousin told me we need to check out the Troc Theater," one of the runners said. "Troc" was short for Trocadero. Locals smirked that it stood for Theodore Roosevelt Opera Company, and it really was a former opera house that was now a relic of a different sort, a burlesque palace. Banished from New York City in 1937 as a source of "moral corruption," burlesque was alive if not well in Philadelphia.

I wasn't sure if you had to be eighteen or twenty-one to enter. I was a week short of my fifteenth birthday. "One, please," I told a woman in the ticket booth in the deepest voice I could muster. Not to worry. Burlesque was fading for reasons that had nothing to do with morality. It was passé, too tame and seedy for the budding sexual revolution. So management was not turning away any paying customer and police had more important duties on Saturday night than to check IDs in the balcony at the Troc.

For better or worse, it was vintage burlesque. Baggy pants comedians doubled up on double entendres. (The first syllable of the word "scrutinize" was a running gag in one skit.) An off-color (and off-key) baritone warbled suggestive lyrics like "Oh, to See My Old Gal Flo Again." A candy barker hawked worthless trinkets between the acts.

And strippers past whatever prime they once had gyrated to the beat of a small band.

Then the emcee announced, "Now straight from her national tour, the star of our show, Cupcake Cassidy!" The woman who walked on stage was a cut above her predecessors, younger and more enthusiastic when she punctuated a pause in the music by tossing off another article of clothing. Down to nearly bare essentials (pasties covering her nipples and a G-string down below), she attached a pair of tassels to ample breasts and rotated them one way, then the other. She was what the trade called a tassel twirler. I had watched once and future Olympians at Franklin Field that afternoon but when she started those tassels going in concentric circles I thought to myself that it was the most marvelous feat of athleticism I'd seen all day.

Inexperienced even for my age, I was having some trouble accounting for the excitement welling up inside. But after we got back to the Y, the hormones took over in the dark. Suffice it to say that when we boarded the bus for home the next morning, I left my pre-pubescence behind in Philadelphia.

11

Hershey from the J-A

DECEMBER 1960
Manhattan

When Harold Tepper anchored Lafayette High's distance medley relay team to victory in a novice race (restricted to runners who had never won a gold medal), another coach walked up to Simon Yudell, slapped him on the back, and said, "Sy, you old son of a gun, you've still got it!" Yudell beamed but Tepper knew better. Yudell was a kindly coach who knew little about track.

In the 1940s and '50s Lafayette coaches defied poor training facilities to mold winning football, baseball, and (in Yudell's heyday) soccer teams, but by 1960 football and soccer had faded. While Lafayette was on the rise in basketball and still competitive in baseball, that success stemmed more from youth programs in basketball at the Jewish Community House of Bensonhurst and baseball in Prospect Park. It was there that a keen-eyed manager suggested to a Lafayette first baseman named Sandy Koufax that he might want to try pitching.

"These guys think by jogging three or four miles that they're training," Tepper scoffed one day as we watched several teammates set off on a long, loping practice regimen through Bath Beach. "They won't get any better working out like that." He understood that maximizing his own potential meant looking elsewhere for effective coaching. I could identify. Malcolm Largmann, the earnest *Lafayette News* faculty advisor who would go on to a distinguished career as a high school principal, did not have much useful advice for an aspiring journalist.

Tepper found a mentor in Ted Foy, who had run for New York University and the New York Pioneer Club, a populist alternative to the imperious (not to mention racist and anti-Semitic) New York Athletic Club. Foy trained a small group of runners from across the city and had no use for anyone unwilling to work hard. That was fine with Tepper, who built leg strength and stamina by taking the stairs two steps at a time to deliver bags of laundry to upper-floor apartments for his father's dry cleaning business. "Teddy's just what I need," he told me after a few weeks of Foy's tutelage at Van Cortlandt Park and the 369th Regiment Armory in Harlem, the Pioneer Club's home base. "I can't believe how much stronger I feel."

When I accompanied him to a training session there, Van Cortlandt Park was almost eerily quiet in contrast to the tumultuous scene I'd come upon at the start of a cross-country race the prior fall. Aside from Foy's little troupe the lone figure on the track was Pete McArdle,

an Irish immigrant who was a bus mechanic for the city transit authority and on his way to fulfilling two dreams—gaining American citi-
zenship and a place on the U. S. Olympic marathon team. "Pete's got a
clock in his head," Foy marveled as McArdle ticked off lap after lap in
precisely the same time.

The armory presented another sort of vivid contrast. Every passenger on the Lenox Avenue line on our way to Harlem, every person we
passed on the walk from the 145th Street station, and everyone else in
the old drillshed was black. I thought of the bus to the Penn Relays we
had shared with two all-black teams in the spring and further back to
the day a friend of my mother's who taught in an overwhelmingly black
elementary school invited us to a class outing in Prospect Park. The
students were my age and I fit right in but felt as if I had been transported to another country.

There were no children of color in my years at P.S. 238, just one at
Seth Low Junior High and none among 1,241 graduates pictured in my
high school yearbook. The impact of such profound segregation would
eventually reverberate politically and socially but was not readily discussed on Ocean Parkway. About the closest I ever heard anyone come
to acknowledging that racism might be a problem was the day a parent
upbraided a clueless child for reciting the version of a street rhyme that
started, "Eeny, meeny, miney mo, catch a nigger by the toe…"

Later, when Southerners told me that Northern racism, less brutal
if not less endemic than the antics of Bull Connor and the Ku Klux
Klan, would be harder to reverse no matter how many liberals joined
the NAACP or marched in protest, I took it for self-serving deflection.
But I reflected on their words again and again in an ensuing decade
of upheaval in New York—marked by riots after the assassination of
Martin Luther King Jr. and acts of police brutality; rampages during
power blackouts; and white resistance to control of schools in minority
communities and low-income housing in middle-class neighborhoods.

The potential for resentful blacks to lash out should have been obvious. Negro women left their homes to clean apartments in our part
of Brooklyn every day, a migration I spotted one morning when the

Brighton Beach El pulled into the Prospect Park station. The "Schvar-tzes" (Yiddish for "blacks" and often a derogatory term) stood shoul-der-to-shoulder three deep across the platform awaiting a southbound train, having transferred from the Franklin Avenue Shuttle.

More subtle examples could be just as telling. We had white build-ing superintendents at 1440, but for years the super up the street at No. 1420 was a black man named Willie. One day as my mother and I passed by, another black man—not Willie—was leaning against the building. "I wonder what *he*'s doing there?" she said in a hushed, almost ominous voice. The fact that I remember her aside so vividly tells me I was probably jarred by it. I guess it did not compute. How could my mother adore Jackie, Campy, Newk and the other Dodgers, yet feel put off, even threatened, by the sight of a Negro on our street? It would be a while before I could put this uneasiness into focus, but venturing into Harlem for the first time amounted to a more tangible experience with an unfamiliar world.

Like Harold Tepper, I was already looking past Lafayette. While my associations with sports would not yield the college scholarship his running could (and did), I sensed they could pay off in other ways. So I expanded my purview. I kept score for the Lafayette baseball team, charted plays for a new football coach and, in a move that spared me the obligation to take gym class, volunteered to work for the athletic director. In exchange for answering the phone and handling paper-work each day I received credits for physical education without having to undress and shower in a dank and drafty basement, lug smelly gym clothes around, or expose my lack of athletic prowess.

More of my tips to Ralph Blumenfeld found their way into the *New York Post*, including one touting Ted Foy's protégés as contenders in the first high school cross-country run of the 1959 season—an item that made Ralph seem like a Svengali when Tepper and one of the others ran 1–2. It led to a feature story in the *Post* about his unusual training method delivering dry cleaning for his dad. That cemented my bond with Blumenfeld who told me, "I really appreciate your help. I can't pay you but I think I know someone who can. Give Morrey Rokeach a call at the *Journal-American*. I think he has a budget for high school stringers."

I did, and one evening the following week the phone rang. It was "Morrey Rokeach of the J-A." Could I come to his home near Brighton Beach to help compile football statistics? If this call seemed strange to me, can you imagine how it sounded to my parents? But my bylines in the school paper and contact with sportswriters had started to impress them. When my father dropped me off, Rokeach opened the door and called out, "I know it's a school night. I won't keep him too long and I'll drive him back."

Whatever romanticized impressions I had about newspapering vanished as soon as I got a good look at the disheveled man inside, T-shirt outside his trousers and cigarette dangling from his lips. Morris ("Morrey") Rokeach was 35 going on 60. He had a chain smoker's rasp, drank coffee all day long, and was given to a tantrum if anything interfered with how he tried to organize his world. Organize was the word, too. He filed copious accounts of every aspect of his work in loose-leaf binders. In one way, this established a handy reference source. In another—and this was pointed out to him by every supervisor and colleague he ever knew as well as his long-suffering wife—it took much more time and effort than it could possibly save.

But Rokeach took such criticism as a badge of honor. That night he proudly described losing his first full-time job as a wire service reporter in Lorain, Ohio after graduating from Ohio State. The service used a bell system to prioritize the news it sent to newspaper and broadcast wire rooms across Ohio. Newsworthy dispatches from population centers like Cleveland and Cincinnati moved on the wire with one or two bells while bulletins could carry three, four, or even five bells to alert editors to a calamitous event like an earthquake or an assassination. That meant reporters at remote outposts like Lorain often had to wait to transmit stories, and one night as story after story bumped his, Rokeach decided he'd had enough. He moved a report on a city council meeting as a three-bell bulletin and went home—only to awaken the next morning to another bulletin. He was fired. So he picked up and moved back to New York where he caught on in the sports section of Hearst's *Journal-American,* one of the city's seven daily papers.

My efforts that first evening prompted an invitation to join him at the *Journal-American* office on South Street in lower Manhattan the following Saturday to take phone reports on football games. There was no budget for my office work so Rokeach handed me $10 after sending my last story to the sports desk. "I'm sorry it can't be more," he said. I'd have done it for nothing. It was like being dropped into a newspaper movie. With the first copy deadline at 3:30 Saturday afternoon to produce a "bulldog edition" for readers who liked to bring a Sunday paper home Saturday night, the sports department was bustling. A half-dozen copy editors sat "on the rim" of a U-shaped desk opposite a "slot man" who was flipping stories at them like a dealer in a casino. Copy boys rushed edited stories downstairs to Linotype operators who set them in molten type for compositors working from the slot man's "page dummy" to place in metal frames called "chases" once they cooled.

In December Rokeach asked me to cover a track meet at the armory where a year before I sat in the balcony, wondering how I could talk my way onto the floor. Carrying a new Olivetti Lettera 22 portable typewriter I'd purchased with some of my bar mitzvah money, I brushed past a priest at the door without breaking stride announcing, "Ed Hershey of the *Journal-American.*" And then there I was at age sixteen on press row. Because of the early deadline, I had to file my first story after only two events were over and with a quaint means of conveyance. Western Union placed typewriter keyboards at Yankee Stadium and Madison Square Garden, but it didn't pay to install such equipment at the armory where it would be used a few times a year. So the first newspaper dispatch of my young career was transmitted one letter and space at a time in Morse code by one of the three remaining telegraphers in New York who could handle the key deftly enough to send it with the speed my deadline copy required.

I led with the 60-yard high hurdles, won by Tyrone Pannell, a tall, muscular runner from Bishop Loughlin. Pannell would go on to run for Manhattan College and then the U. S. Marine Corps before shipping out to Vietnam. On November 30, 1965, a booby-trapped artillery round struck the platoon he commanded, wounding several of his men and killing him instantly five weeks after his 24th birthday. One of more than 58,000 Americans to die in combat in Southeast Asia, he is buried in Long Island National Cemetery a few miles from where he grew up in Amityville, Long Island. Pannell left a wife and an infant daughter. The prior August he wrote this letter to his daughter, subsequently published in the book, *Dear America—Letters Home From Vietnam.*

> Dear Tracy: The things I want to say to you can never be fully expressed in words. I want so very much to say the things that will make you understand how very much I love you. Before you were born I, like most men, wanted a son. But when I saw you for the first time just a few minutes old, I knew I could never love a son the way I loved you. For a son grows and becomes a man while a daughter is always a child to be loved and cared for. More than anything I want you to know me and love me. The next time I see you, you will be a little lady, walking and talking. Learn how to say, "Daddy, I love you with all my heart."
> Love,
> Daddy

An Internet memorial page has a photo of Tracy and her daughter, Pannell's granddaughter, tracing his name on panel 3E row 18 of the Vietnam Veterans Memorial in Washington, D.C.

12

My Double Life

Some students drop out. I dropped in. By my junior year at Lafayette High I had rigged my schedule to end each school day by 11:30 a.m. I studied just enough to flirt with a B average. If a class entailed more commitment than that I dropped it, but one subject I could not drop was French. Three years of foreign language was required for an academic diploma.

So I muddled through and that led to a scene on Open School Night eerily similar to the day my third-grade teacher predicted that I would never amount to anything. "Edward is capable of far more than the tripe he produces for my class," Madame Gerard told my mother, adding that she would fail me unless I got 75% in the upcoming State Regents exam, a score that would mandate a passing grade. Talk about incentive! I bought all the study guides and dove into them, but a few weeks of cramming could not quite overcome three years of indifference. I came up just short with a 72 and had to repeat French.

I had one exciting class in my junior year, an elective called English TTF, which stood for theater, television, and film. We saw Broadway shows like *Once Upon a Mattress* with a young Carol Burnett and *A Raisin in the Sun* with Sidney Poitier, Ruby Dee, Claudia McNeil, Glynn Turman, and an electrifying teenager named Diana Sands who chatted with us outside the stage door. There was also provocative, even daring, off-Broadway fare with plays by Samuel Beckett and Berthold Brecht as well as Jack Gelber's *The Connection,* an unsparing depiction of drug addiction staged at Julian Beck and Judith Malina's Living Theater.

That was an exception in three unremarkable years. After a time even sports did not excite me. In my sophomore year, the football team fought epic battles against Brooklyn Tech and New Utrecht under Sam Rutigliano, who later coached the Cleveland Browns. But he was gone after that, succeeded by a physical education teacher who had not even played college ball, and the team lost every game. The year after I graduated, Gary Goldberg, who would later create the television sitcom *Family Ties,* led the basketball team on a wild ride to the city championship game, but in my time the team lost more than it won. The track team, too, faded after Steve Aiello and Harold Tepper graduated. So by my senior year all I wanted to do was move on.

Besides, no matter the season, there was work for me at the *Journal-American.* When football gave way to basketball I spent Tuesday and Friday nights in the office taking basketball scores. "It's too much, Edward," my mother protested without much conviction. She probably realized I would always find something to do instead of homework, and this at least seemed constructive. Her concern for my safety was another matter. Unless I got a ride, my way home started with a six-block walk on dark, desolate streets to the East Broadway subway station often followed by a long wait on a lonely platform. I banked on the idea that I did not present a lucrative target and while I was never accosted, there was hardly a moment when I was not alert to the potential danger. I saw it as a risk worth taking and feigned indifference to my parents' concerns.

The highlight of the scholastic sports calendar was the annual public high school basketball tournament at Madison Square Garden with weekday tripleheaders starting in late morning. I had the best seat in the house, volunteering to spot for public address announcer John Condon, whose rich baritone was a familiar part of every game at the Garden for decades. When the first game ended I'd race to the pressroom to call a story into the *Journal-American* for the evening edition. Finally, after the arena emptied following the final game, I'd stay behind and mingle with sportswriters who could get me in to see pro or college games that night, find an empty seat behind the press table and try to appear as inconspicuous as possible. It reminded me of a day not many years before when Mitchell Nodell and I wandered down to the box seats in the late innings of a game at Yankee Stadium, a pair of ragamuffins in T-shirts among the bankers and brokers. When an usher glanced our way Mitchell whispered, "Look like you belong!"

Working at the *Journal-American* at sixteen meant that I also had to "belong" when I related to coaches after games and at meetings where they voted on "all-city" teams. At one of those, Jefferson High football coach Moe Finkelstein chided his Tilden counterpart, Bernie Mars, by insisting that he had better runners than Tilden's Ronnie Bliey whose spectacular play was the talk of the city. The coaches chose Bliey, but Finkelstein wanted the last word. In three days the teams would meet on Thanksgiving. "We'll kick to Bliey every time," he said. Bliey took the opening kickoff 88 yards for a touchdown, then ran for a two-point conversion and, after Jefferson scored, took the ensuing kickoff 92 yards for another score. Finkelstein ordered an onside kickoff rather than test him a third time.

Jefferson wore Tilden down but even as the score mounted there were no more deep kickoffs. "Why did you stop kicking to Bliey?" I asked after the game. "You said you would kick to him every time." Finkelstein looked at me incredulously before responding in Brooklyn fashion: "Ya think I'm crazy?"

This double life—high school student by day and sportswriter on nights and weekends—could create awkward moments. After a track meet on Randalls Island in the East River, Boys High coach Marty Lewis offered to drop me at a subway stop across the Triborough Bridge in Queens to spare me a long bus ride. I was grateful, but taken aback when he suggested, "Have time to stop for a beer, kid?" I assumed he did not appreciate how much of a kid I really was. I was about to turn 17. It was not my first beer but was close enough and tasted very sour. "How," I wondered to myself, "can anyone like this stuff?"

Then there was the afternoon Lafayette's football team scrimmaged against Tilden. I was there in my student capacity but greeted Bernie Mars and his assistant, Ace Adler, by their first names with the Lafayette coach in earshot. "These men are Coach Mars and Coach Adler to you," he said, unmasking me. I sheepishly assured them all that I meant no disrespect, but took silent satisfaction from every Lafayette loss after that. My two worlds conflicted again when a track meet in New Jersey came on the Saturday I was to take the Scholastic Aptitude Test. Probably concerned that I would choose the meet over the SATs, my father picked me up at school after the test and drove me to Washington Heights to catch a bus over the George Washington Bridge.

When a class I scheduled in my final semester failed to draw enough students and was cancelled, I nearly panicked. No likely substitute jumped off the schedule, threatening my 11:30-and-out schedule. It precipitated a rare conference with my grade advisor:

MR. K: Here's a class in merchandising. It's the second half of a
         unit, but I don't see why you can't take it as an elective.
ED H: Sign me up.

It was a window into a side of the school that I had not experienced, a class comprised almost entirely of girls studying for a commercial diploma. "This semester," the teacher said when I introduced myself, "we are studying textiles." To this day I can distinguish between thread counts in muslin and percale. My term project was on men's clothing at S. Klein on Union Square, the discount store where we bought all our finery. The manager struck me as a bit of a peacock for someone running an off-price department. He seemed flattered to be interviewed. "Someone in my position learns how to maximize a sale," he explained, in an office affording him a view of his domain. "If I spot a good prospect from the quality of a man's wristwatch or his wife's jewelry, I move out onto the floor and take over the sale." I smiled to myself. Nothing any member of our family wore on our shopping excursions to S. Klein's would ever prod him to even think about leaving his office.

13

Graduation Day

Whenever Morrey Rokeach sent me for coffee I tried to ingratiate myself with the weathered old hands on the *Journal-American* sports desk by volunteering to fetch some for them, too. A collection of rumpled, acerbic has-beens relegated to marking up copy in the final years of careers that had once put them in major league press boxes or at ringside for big fights, they were the human equivalent of the linotype machines downstairs—vestiges of bygone days soon to be rendered obsolete. But even if they did not know what to make of me, they were generally pleasant and one even added a touch of ribaldry. "I go for coffee so often I think I know every crack between here and the lunchroom," I said, handing him a cup after stirring in milk to create the shade of "Florida tan" he always wanted. "I know every crack in the building," he snapped back, "and there's a secretary on the second floor who is something else!" I was flustered enough to blush but managed to nod, smile, and say, "I'll bet."

Most of the paper's sportswriters were also aging veterans with two notable exceptions, each a thirty-year-old future Pulitzer Prize winner. Dave Anderson, a hockey and tennis writer who had worked at the *Brooklyn Eagle* before it closed in 1955, would become a columnist at the *New York Times*. Jimmy Breslin, a stylist who could go five or six paragraphs into a game story before noting the score or even who won, befuddled the desk men who were fairly certain he was not long for the newspaper business. He would find more appreciative editors at the *Herald-Tribune*, emerging as a seminal figure of the New American Journalism and later a highly honored columnist and author of such books as *The Gang That Couldn't Shoot Straight*.

The sports editor, Max Kase, a jowly man with a gruff voice and crusty manner, had founded the B'nai B'rith Sports Lodge at a time when the New York Athletic Club barred Jewish members, but he knew how to play the other guy's game. As toastmaster at banquets the paper sponsored to honor its all-city players, Kase sat alongside the widows of Babe Ruth and Lou Gehrig and introduced an array of celebrities. One night Otto Graham, the old Cleveland Browns quarterback then coaching at the Coast Guard Academy, concluded a story with this punch line: "The band played 'There's a Goldmine in the Sky' and the next day 20,000 Jews joined the Air Force." Such anti-Semitic humor in a ballroom full of students, parents, and coaches shocked me and so did the roar of laughter it evoked—with Kase guffawing as much as anyone.

For better or (more probably) worse, those times were different in many ways. Take the telephone. Now when a reporter interviews a subject by telephone rather than face to face it is divulged in the story but back then the phone was viewed as a modern breakthrough. The *Journal-American* even inserted a facsimile of an old cradle phone over the legend "J-A Phone Exclusive" into stories. This gave rise to a legendary (and probably apocryphal) yarn about the reporter who rewrote a piece of wire copy profiling a Catholic priest in New Jersey who ran a program for wayward youth. His inspiring story, based on a phone interview, made the front page. When the reporter arrived at work the next day he was summoned by an editor who said, "We got a call about your story. It turns out that priest is a deaf mute. What do you have to say for yourself?" The reporter purportedly snapped back, "That's not what he told me!"

Stories created from whole cloth—"pipe jobs" in city room parlance—were rare, but inventive augmentation was not. One Friday morning in December 1960 two airliners collided over New York Bay: one crashing in Park Slope, Brooklyn, the other on Staten Island, killing 128 on board the planes and 6 on the ground. Miraculously, a badly burned eleven-year-old boy survived his fall from the sky. Doctors and nurses worked feverishly in a Brooklyn hospital in a quest to save him that would end at ten o'clock the next morning. That night two of the paper's top reporters, John Horan and Dom Frasca, were hammering out Saturday's front-page story in a corner of the *Journal-American* city room where I compiled basketball scores when a colleague, John Mitchell, arrived from the hospital. "How's this for a lead, John?" Frasca asked, "The clock on the wall said 1 a. m. Down the corridor at Methodist Hospital little Stevie Baltz was fighting for his life." Mitchell responded, "That sounds good, except for one thing. There is no clock on the wall." They looked at each other for several seconds of silence before Horan settled the issue. "I guess there is now," he said.

I wonder, I thought to myself, *if they teach you that in journalism school?* By then my eyes were on the middle leg of the requisite trinity Jewish parents expected of their male progeny, the one between "get bar mitzvahed" and "marry a nice Jewish girl"— "get a college degree." Nowadays many families start college searches by middle school. Not in 1960. At the start of my senior year I dutifully applied to the tuition-free public city university system, secretly fearing that Brooklyn College would admit me despite my mediocre grades. I'd won a State Regents scholarship just as my father had thirty years before and scored well on the SATs, but I wanted to go to Long Island University in downtown Brooklyn because of its journalism program. I also figured it would be easier academically. But L.I.U. was a private school and charged tuition, so I suspected I would have to enroll at Brooklyn College if I was accepted there.

I gave no thought to the third expectation, marriage, since I was about as much of an underachiever socially as academically. I'd heard of spin-the-bottle games at parties in junior high, but was never invited to one or to high school "frat parties" with supposedly more advanced goings-on. Even when the hormones started to kick in, I was too shy to act until I actually went on a date just after my fourth and final summer at Camp Harmony. As in prior years, my efforts at summer romance ranged from fleeting to unrequited. It was time to demonstrate, at least to myself, that I could do this. I approached the least threatening female I knew, a pleasant but plain girl who lived in

a two-family home adjacent to our apartment house. She was literally the girl-next-door. For all I knew, it might have been her first
date, too. We went to Coney Island, held hands, and kissed when we
reached the top of the Wonder Wheel, a first kiss on a first date that
felt more obligatory than romantic. There was no second date.

I did finally have someone close to a best friend, Jerry Glazer, who
shared a love of sports that I put to the test early in our friendship.
With the Dodgers gone I listened to Orioles broadcasts on a clear
channel station from Baltimore. One night when Rocky Colavito of
the Indians hit his fourth home run in a game against the Orioles, my
reporter's instinct took over. I had to be the only person in all of New
York privy to a feat accomplished five times in the history of the major
leagues, surely news worth sharing. So in one of those misjudgments
one appreciates an instant past the moment it can be undone, I phoned
Jerry. His mother's half-sleepy, half-alarmed voice validated my worst
second thoughts. All anyone answering the phone in the Glazer household would expect to hear at that hour was news of a severe injury or
death. To make matters worse, Jerry's father was a butcher who arose
before dawn, something Jerry noted in the morning and Mrs. Glazer
reinforced the next time we met. I was just grateful she allowed me
back in the apartment.

We had the same sophomore biology teacher, but I was in an "honors" section and Jerry was not, and it taught us an early lesson in how
expectation can influence perception. One morning the same homework assignment was due in both classes and (surprise) I had not done
mine so I copied his almost word for word—and received a better
grade. Sick of hearing about my underachievement, part of me envied
Jerry but another part nurtured perverse pride in gaining as much as I
could from as little effort as possible. The most absurd example came
later—in fact, at the very end.

Lafayette's graduation exercises were at Loews Kings on Flatbush
Avenue, one of the few theaters in Brooklyn large enough to accom-
modate a class of 1,200. When we arrived I was pulled from the line
of gown-clad marchers and ushered onto the stage alongside merit

scholars and other super achievers of the Class of '61. Why? To the amazement of Jerry and other classmates who often teased me about my gym evasion, I received the New York City Association of Health and Physical Education Certificate of Honor "in recognition of exceptional qualities of character and outstanding service in the conduct of the Health Education program of Lafayette High School."

By then my silent entreaties had been answered. Brooklyn College rejected me. Queens College, another branch of the city university that was also free and prestigious, did give me a scare by accepting me. But whether it was the two-hour commute each way attending Queens would entail or how uncharacteristically enthusiastic I seemed about studying journalism or even reluctant recognition that academic rigor was not a good match for me, my parents agreed to pay $35 a credit for me to go to L.I.U.

Jerry, who was the one going away to college to study optometry in Boston and using some of his own money to do it, put in as many hours as he could at the Smilen Brothers greengrocery on Avenue J that summer. Cash was less a concern for me so I jumped at a chance to earn $125 for eight weeks as a junior counselor at a summer camp in Pennsylvania's Pocono Mountains. It was an offer from the Lafayette athletic director who saved me from taking gym class and handed me my graduation prize. Thus, the end of high school reinforced what I had learned on the first day when my cousin Sandy escorted me into the *Lafayette News* office: Connections count.

PART TWO

The Big Leagues

14

Coming Up for Air

College started anomalously—on a threadbare velvet seat in the cavernous Brooklyn Paramount Theater, listening to Long Island University Athletic Director Buck Lai conduct freshman orientation from a stage where vaudevillian Rudy Vallee crooned in the 1930s and disc jockey Allen Freed introduced stars like Chuck Berry and Bill Haley & the Comets at rock 'n' roll shows in the 1950s.

Allen Freed's rise and fall—he was ruined for accepting "payola" from record promoters—might have been an object lesson for Lai's timeworn warning: "Look to your left. Now look to your right. One of the two people you just saw won't be here at this time a year from now." Two classmates traded nervous glances with me. "Not us," one said bravely, but by the time the university had transformed the old movie palace into a gymnasium and lecture halls in my sophomore year, Lai's prophecy proved an understatement. Both were gone.

The theater and an adjoining twelve-story building—purchased a few years before largely through a donation from real estate tycoon William Zeckendorf—was the first real home for an institution that had operated in rented space since its founding in the 1920s. Sometimes called "Second-Chance U" for the students who transferred in after starting elsewhere, L.I.U. was known mostly for a scandal of its own a decade earlier when gamblers induced some of its basketball stars to fix games. And even its prime benefactor and longtime board chair, Zeckendorf, was about to go bust. Academically, socially and economically, we were a good match—classic Brooklyn upstarts and underdogs. I felt at home from day one.

I didn't major in journalism so much as in *Seawanhaka,* the weekly
student newspaper named for a seagoing Indian tribe that first inhab-
ited Long Island. And, contrary to the notion I had when I walked
into the paper's office my first day on campus, I had a lot to learn. Perhaps better put, I had a lot to *un*learn. The sports lingo that peppered
my copy in the *Lafayette News* and even the *New York Journal-American*
was off-limits. A small, fleet soccer forward was not a "will o' the wisp"
nor was a left-handed fastball pitcher "a flame-throwing southpaw." At
first, this exercise in excising clichés didn't take. An editor critiquing
one of my stories was exasperated to note that I didn't even know what
the word cliché *meant.* "Roy Rubin's practice whistle ushered in a new
exciting era" my first basketball story gushed, going on to describe a
"dribbling whiz" who was part of "a slick playmaking duo with speed
to burn."

Hackneyed phrases slowly started disappearing from my copy and
I even branched out to cover news stories. A prior foray into news in
my senior year of high school had not exactly made journalism history. Assigned to do a piece on a citywide controversy over high school
press freedom I sought an interview with Lafayette Principal Joseph
Bellafiore. Weeks later, when I entered the athletic director's office
he demanded, "Where were you? The principal wants to see you!" I
walked to Bellafiore's office in a panic, wondering who had spotted me
cadging a smoke and what the consequences might be, thoughts that
only darkened in ten minutes sitting in an anteroom. Once escorted
inside, I realized I was not in trouble but had been summoned in
response to my nearly forgotten request for an interview. He had to
hand me a pad and a pen.

My first college news story was more successful. It led the paper.
The university had canceled student invitations to controversial outside
speakers like Malcolm X as well as retired Army General Edwin A.
Walker, an avowed segregationist, and Robert Welch, founder of the
radically conservative John Birch Society. The ban was lifted after students protested and Malcolm X spoke to 500 students with 200 more
turned away for lack of space. Those of us expecting a firebrand instead

heard a calm if intense man decrying the historic subjugation of black people. "Blacks are the world of tomorrow and whites are the world of yesterday," he told the largely white audience, castigating blacks for not rising up. "The black man in the United States is a beggar because he is not willing to die for what he believes." He never used the word "Negro," nonetheless *Seawanhaka* headlined the story, "Malcolm X Calls Negro A Beggar." If Malcolm associated "Negro" with subjugation the editors of an all-white college newspaper did not.

While *Seawanhaka* editorialized against the exclusivity of fraternities, in reality we were a de facto fraternity. Part classroom, part laboratory and all hangout, our office was a city room in miniature where lively debates crackled over clacking typewriters. Copy was due Monday so it could be edited and sent to a print shop in Manhattan in time for galley proofs to await us when we arrived Tuesday afternoon to finalize each week's edition, which was delivered Wednesday morning. The International Printing Company was a grimy storefront in a bleak part of town called Alphabet City. Nearby, the East Village was becoming trendy, but Alphabet City (so named because avenues east of First Avenue below 14th Street were designated with letters) was to be traversed quickly and in groups.

At dinnertime we headed three blocks down to Katz's deli, a frequent stop for politicians who posed under a vintage sign urging customers to "Send a Salami to Your Boy in the Army" and later the site of Meg Ryan's faked orgasm in the movie *When Harry Met Sally* (1989), setting up Estelle Reiner's signature line, "I'll have what she's having." Katz's anchored a collection of Jewish-American *nosherai* emporia on Houston (pronounced HOW-sten) Street, relics of the old Jewish Lower East Side. There was Yonah Schimmel's for knishes, Russ & Daughters for dried fruit and smoked fish, and Henry's, a smaller deli with a sign declaring, "This Is the Only Kosher Restaurant in this Vicinity"—a dig at its neighbor, which sold meat lacking rabbinic certification. That did not eat into much of the patronage Katz's attracted day and night. Kosher or not, customers lined up three and four deep, less in queues than a swarm, shouting orders to countermen the way floor traders bought and sold stock. Franks were near the front, sand-wiches farther along, and French fries and Dr. Brown's soda toward the back so it took several trips to assemble a complete (if not exactly balanced) meal.

Back at the print shop after dinner we worked well into the night revising inked proofs the way newspaper people had for decades, a pro-cess that would eventually give way to cleaner methods, then automa-tion, and finally computerization rendering traditional printing crafts obsolete. By the time a twelve- or sixteen-page edition arrived on cam-pus the following morning, we were starting on the next issue.

This weekly ritual plus some freelancing for the city dailies kept me busy even without scholarly endeavors, had I been inclined to pursue them. But like my grandfather, who would order "onion soup without the onions," I sought a college degree with as little college as possible. He wanted only the broth and I wanted just the froth. Studies were a qualifier, a price for the right to be a collegian and leave with the req-uisite diploma.

I watched hour-long class periods evaporate a minute at a time in rooms overlooking a digital display atop the Dime Savings Bank alternately flashing the bank's interest rate, the temperature, and the time of day. Yet by my senior year I ranked 222nd in a class of 719 because I had good journalism grades and avoided difficult courses. Literature? Realizing a class on Chaucer was taught in Middle English, I dropped it for an easier alternative. Language? I started with Russian but one D and one F later backtracked and slogged through two years of French. Science? With no physics or chemis-try in high school, I banked on making it through biology, but the textbook might as well have been written in hieroglyphics—and I couldn't tell one organ from another in a dissected fetal pig! Earth science—known on some campuses as "rocks for jocks"—was added to the curriculum in my junior year, allowing me to fulfill the science requirement.

Even journalism was less than alluring with its resident faculty of one, a sad-faced man with no field experience whose soporific lectures covered the same ground in one course after another, regardless of its title. The saving grace was a coterie of professional journalists who served as adjunct instructors, exposing us to real-life perspectives. A *New York Times* sports editor tested our ingenuity in one class, distributing a list of local events and assigning us to cover one with this proviso: We could not say we were students and had to purport to represent a real news organization.

Steve Seplow and I zeroed in on a tax conference at Pace College because lunch was involved. A good reporter, we reasoned, never passes up a free meal. He registered on behalf of a weekly he freelanced for and I invented a plausible-sounding paper. With lunch about to begin we were alone at the press table—it was not exactly an event of wide interest—when a classmate entered the room, started speaking with the organizer, and then pointed in our direction. She was violating the spirit of our assignment and giving us up in the process. "Quick!" Steve whispered. "Eat your fruit salad!"

What I had going for me that the fellows alongside me that first morning at orientation may have lacked was a survivor's instinct and will. Cramming for finals could not completely compensate for a semester's indifference, but I learned that it would get me through. I would camp out in the living room with a pot of coffee and a pack of Herbert Tareyton cigarettes, playing "Kind of Blue" by Miles Davis and "Ahmad Jamal at the Pershing" low enough on the hi-fi to avoid disturbing my parents and sister in the bedroom.

At the end of my freshman year one of these semi-annual efforts nearly ended in disaster. On the D train heading for what I thought was an afternoon history final, I glanced at my schedule and realized I'd mixed up the days and times. The final had started at 9 a.m. The history department chairman, an imposing man who wore dark glasses for an eye condition that made him seem like the heavy in a horror film, cackled after I presented myself in search of redress. A make-up exam, he warned, would be "twice as hard" as the test I'd missed, but he granted me one and I passed the course with the same C that I had the semester before.

En route to campus on a finals morning the following year, another revelation probably added years to my life. Two blocks from the El and barely on time, I heard a train in the distance. I ran the rest of the way, took the two flights to the platform two steps at a time and just caught it. Once inside what I could barely catch in the crush of rush-hour passengers was my breath. I'd been contending with a chest cold and had switched to a milder cigarette brand, but as more commuters squeezed in at ensuing stops it felt as if my next gasp for air might be my last. When the train reached my stop, DeKalb Avenue, I tossed the last pack of cigarettes I would ever own into a trash receptacle.

An initial foray into the timeworn collegiate pastime of drinking was also, shall we say, sobering. I'd summoned the courage to ask our freshman class president on a date to see the L.I.U. senior show. She was tall and smart and attractive, but not the sort of alluring girl I considered out of reach. She accepted, but then I came into a pair of tickets to the city high school basketball championship game at Madison Square Garden where Lafayette High was playing for the title that same night. I backed out, fibbing about a family obligation.

That evening in the dorm I was in a group that included a short buxom girl I'd noticed at L.I.U. basketball games who was outgoing, flirtatious, and provocatively attired. As the group dispersed I kept talking to her. "I have tickets to the high school basketball championship at Madison Square Garden on Saturday night," I said finally, "Would you like to go?" She did not hesitate. "Yes," she said, "I'd love to." I showed up at the dorm and waited for her. And waited. Finally, I phoned upstairs. A roommate answered that my date had taken ill, but I had little doubt that she had forgotten or gotten a better offer.

Dumb, dumb, dumb, I thought to myself. That's what you get for trying to play out of your league, let alone opt for cheap over classy. The ballgame had lost its allure. I decided to catch the senior show after all. As it let out, someone invited me to the cast party where I ran into the class president I'd ditched. It was like a scene from the movie *Marty,* except without a happy ending. She stared such daggers at me that I didn't bother to compound my caddishness with an explanation.

Instead, I hit the bar. Hard. In what seemed like almost no time the room was spinning. The following morning's headache was my first experience with a hangover.

15

Reporter-in-Training

JUNE 1963
Kings Point, New York

"I'm covering a high school tournament in Farrell, Pennsylvania over Christmas break," *New York World-Telegram & Sun* sportswriter Paul Zimmerman told me at a high school basketball game. "Want to come along? I'd love the company." Sitting in his Volkswagen Beetle as we drove through the Holland Tunnel early one morning a week later I unfolded a Pennsylvania map to locate Farrell. "Turn it over," he advised. "It's on the other side." No wonder he wanted company. Our destination was a few miles from the Ohio border. I smiled, remembering why I had agreed to come along. Our roundtrip amounted to 800 miles of opportunity.

A hulk of a man with a crew cut and an owlish expression behind thick eyeglasses, Zimmerman, who would become "Dr. Z," *Sports Illustrated's* uncanny prognosticator and author of *A Thinking Man's Guide to Pro Football,* brought a fresh perspective to his craft. Unlike peers who took the time-honored path from the grandstand to the press box, he was an athlete who still played club rugby at 29 and saw games from the inside. A chance to learn from him was reason enough to accept his invitation, but I had another motive. The *World-Telegram* paid a college student $25 a week to assist its scholastic sportswriter. This was work I had done off the books at the *Journal-American,* and the position would open up in a year or two.

As the miles passed, Zimmerman waxed on about everything from his sexual conquests to his passion for food. He said he aspired to write a book about all-you-can-eat restaurants in New York but learned the hard way that his own appetite had its limits. "Some guys in our Army unit in Germany entered me in an eating contest," he said. "I never had a chance. I was in against professional eaters who would travel from town to town. They'd wolf down everything put in front of us and then make side bets eating extra food between courses." He also regaled me with outlandish tales of rugby buddies like a devil-may-care sidekick named Al Ginepra. "We're at a basketball game at Stanford," he said, "and the Cal players come out for warm-ups, all 6-foot-3 blond guys, chiseled features, not an ounce of fat on them. Al turns to me and says, 'How can anyone who ever had a pimple on his face root for a team like that'!"

I tried to hold up my end of the conversation, but my inexperience showed—and eventually got me in trouble. When we finally left the Pennsylvania Turnpike not far from Pittsburgh, Zimmerman pulled over for directions and I cranked down my side window. "Go three red lights and hang a left," the fellow I asked started. "Does that include the green one up there?" I interrupted. He gave me a strange look and, glancing down at our New York license plate, said, "We call 'em all red lights out here." Zimmerman shook his head. "What's the matter with you?" he snapped as we drove off. "Are you trying to get us killed? People out here don't like New Yorkers as it is." I apologized and protested that it had been an innocent question and he softened, adding, "It's amazing. More than half the people in this country still live in places like this."

The team we drove all that way to see, Adelphi Academy, a small private school from Brooklyn with a big-time college prospect in 6-foot-8 Judd Rothman, was trounced twice. But the trip did give me a leg up on my own future. After he was promoted to cover track and field meets at Madison Square Garden, Zimmerman started providing commentary for television—and hired me to arrange live interviews. I darted between tuxedo-clad officials to collar race winners like mile champion Tom O'Hara (who confessed he hated to run at the Garden "because the smell of the popcorn machines where we warm up downstairs makes me nauseous") before escorting them to a press area (where I once watched legendary columnist Jimmy Cannon bark vulgarities into a broadcaster's microphone to render the tape unplayable so he could not turn the answers to Cannon's questions into sound bites).

Then came the real prize. Zimmerman recommended me for the position I coveted as assistant to his successor on the *World-Telegram* high school sports beat, a gentle giant of an ex-Marine named Dick Joyce who told better stories than he wrote, but was exceedingly kind in a milieu where kindness could be in short supply. The biggest story we ever covered together was the announcement of where Power Memorial Academy star center Ferdinand Lewis (Lew) Alcindor—who would one day become Kareem Abdul-Jabbar—had decided to play college basketball. The school reported that Alcindor had boiled his choices down to five, and the late-morning timing meant we could just make that day's final edition if we moved fast, so Joyce and I devised a plan. He would exit the Power Gym on West 61st Street to signal me, standing at 61st and Amsterdam Avenue, so I could race a block down to the nearest pay phone to call in the news. I even taped an out-of-order sign to the phone to assure it would be free. It went perfectly. Joyce made a big U with his arms to indicate Alcindor was headed for UCLA and I raced to the phone—only to discover it really *was* out of order! I had to run an additional three blocks and barely made the edition.

Since the *World-Telegram* did not publish on Sundays, I also worked Saturdays at the *Herald-Tribune* and that led to some freelance opportunities. My first story, on an L.I.U. soccer star from Lithuania named Rimantis (Ray) Klivecka, ran under the headline: "L.I.U. on Beam with Ray" and earned me another assignment, a clinic that Allie

Sherman of the Giants was conducting for high school coaches at the U.S. Merchant Marine Academy in Kings Point on Long Island. I planned to take the Long Island Rail Road and then a bus or a cab to get there until my mother provided an unanticipated alternative. I'd passed my driving test, but had not driven alone yet. After what I presume was a delicate negotiation with my father, she handed me the keys to the family car. *I guess,* I thought to myself, *my parents are starting to see career possibilities in this obsession with sports.*

Transcendent moments are identifiable in retrospect, but how many strike us as they happen? This was one. Driving to cover a story on the head coach of the Giants felt like I was in an episode of "The Twilight Zone," transported to a new dimension with a sense of possibility and empowerment that approximated adulthood. I filled a steno pad during Sherman's presentation and then approached him for a brief interview before getting reaction quotes from the high school coaches at lunch. I composed the story a dozen times in my head on the drive back to Brooklyn before settling on a fairly straightforward lead on Sherman's advice about pass protection. It might seem counterintuitive, he told the coaches, but linemen should "fire out," moving forward when the ball was snapped on pass plays before forming a pocket shielding the quarterback. That allowed them to remain aggressive and also confuse the defense, neither giving ground at the outset nor giving away that the play was a pass.

I phoned the *Herald-Tribune* dictation machine and my story ran the following morning. Under the headline—*Some Giant Advice: 'Be Practical'*—were the words "Special to the Herald Tribune" since freelancers ("stringers" in newspaper parlance) did not get bylines. It could not have been more special to me.

16

Artful Dodger

Avoiding the draft—we did not say evading, which smacked of disloyalty if not criminality—was desirable for every young man I knew even before the war in Vietnam made it essential. At best, military service amounted to a waste of two precious years. It was like a real-life board game. Steer clear of the draft until your 26th birthday and you were home free. That was the goal, and there were plenty of approaches, starting with an automatic deferment for full-time students in good standing. Thus, after dreaming of escaping the classroom practically from the day I entered kindergarten, I began to contemplate an unlikely option: graduate school.

My first choice was the bastion of academe that (to my relief) had rejected me four years before. Brooklyn College had a new master's program in television with a modern studio—"state of the art" was the phrase of the day—serving as laboratory. Students paid no tuition, received a stipend for living expenses, gained experience by producing programs for the city, and developed contacts interning in the capital of the television world before leaving in two years with a prestigious credential. Applications flooded in from far and wide, which should have made me a long shot given my uneven academic record, but as a locally tax-supported institution Brooklyn College needed to enroll some city residents. That was one factor in my favor. I had two others: a strong journalism background and compelling recommendation from Dr. William Birenbaum, provost of the L.I.U. Brooklyn campus.

Birenbaum arrived at the outset of my senior year. He was an innovative, accessible reformer, the polar opposite of his predecessor John Baiardi, a gruff, imperious biologist who looked and sounded like

Green Bay Packers football coach Vince Lombardi. I knew that first-hand from a run-in the prior spring. After cigarette machines were removed from the campus I wrote a tongue-in-cheek news brief attributing the decision to "Chancellor John H. G. Pell (not as in Pall Mall)." Baiardi summoned me to say he considered the reference an egregious insult. An affable if aloof New England patrician, Pell was an interim caretaker during a search for a true academic leader in the aftermath of the death of his predecessor in a plane crash. The last thing that administrators priming Pell for a donation wanted was to embarrass him. I conceded nothing as Baiardi lectured me from behind a large desk and resisted the temptation to debate him about freedom of the press. That may have helped me escape with a stern warning.

After Baiardi took another assignment, Birenbaum arrived from the New School for Social Research, and set about changing a range of policies that seemed antithetical to his concept of higher education. One was a dress code barring "coeds" (as female students were known then) from wearing slacks to class unless the temperature fell below twenty-five degrees. But when he liberalized a rule on compulsory class attendance only for Dean's list students, I felt it fell short and sought an interview. The tone was far different from my humbling in the same office months before. "Bill Birenbaum," he said as I entered, walking from behind that same desk to extend a hand. We chatted at a conference table where he contended that total elimination of attendance requirements would not fly with a faculty he needed on his side. I left unsatisfied but pleased. I had been treated as a reporter, not just a student.

"The two of you have a good rappaport," my friend Steve Ende joked. Even as he tried to coax me into cultivating more intellectual curiosity, Birenbaum seemed to use our further exchanges to understand students quite different than those he knew at the New School. I was flattered, which in itself presented a dilemma. Would our kinship limit my ability to cover him with impartiality? And was it really friendship or more a reflection of mutual need? Such questions were not as vexing in college, where sources in positions of authority were also teachers and the paper served as a laboratory, as they would be in the professional world. Birenbaum was as surprised as anyone that I would consider graduate school, and he smiled widely when I walked into his office brandishing my acceptance letter.

So my last months at L.I.U. would not be my last days as a student but I still relished them, especially after Ende and I landed a free dorm room. As student chair of an annual urban affairs conference he recruited me to publicize the event and after a time we were practically sleeping in the conference office in the residence hall. That begged the question: Why *not* sleep there? The dean in charge, Dorcas Fick (with a name straight from a Victorian novel and a reputation to match) approved the idea with one proviso: no female visitors. We readily agreed and each day transformed the office into a bedroom and back, exposing me to part of campus life commuting students never experience—sharing late-night revelations with a roommate that can seem so profound and original when you are that age. "You know what I love about the zoo?" I said one night after we'd turned the lights out. "It isn't a picture or a movie. You're looking at a giraffe, a real live fucking giraffe!" And on a day dominated by news of Middle East strife Steve observed, "Have you ever noticed that Israelis are always called commandos and Arabs are always called terrorists?"

Some promises are hard to keep. One Saturday night when Steve was away Dean Fick's no-female edict was not the only barrier I broke. I'd come close a couple of times in backseat trysts worthy of a comic novel, but a sweet, ebullient red-haired freshman finally brought out the best in me, so to speak. It came off so smoothly that it felt like an out-of-body experience, as if I was watching someone way more adept, thinking as we consummated the act, "Is this really happening?" At the risk of mixing a metaphor, it seemed almost anticlimactic.

The urban affairs conference itself made news when the University of Mississippi sent a delegation two years after lethal rioting accompanied James Meredith's enrollment and nine months after the Goodman-Schwerner-Chaney Freedom Summer murders. The Ole Miss students exuded Southern charm and we responded in kind, treating them to a ride on the subway (where one of them expressed amazement over the need for a sign reminding riders not to spit) and a bagels-and-lox brunch (when another tempered adventurous eating with caution, asking for "just one lock, please."). Some accused us of pandering to racists, a charge I sought to refute by noting that with L.I.U. dorm students hosting visitors, by chance one of the Ole Miss women was paired with a black coed from L.I.U. She was distressed when my comment made the papers, fearing that if word got back she might be ostracized.

We had our own racial issues. Harlem had erupted in rioting the prior summer and just across Flatbush Avenue in Brooklyn that winter, members of the Congress on Racial Equality shattered a plate glass window at Junior's during a protest against the popular deli's policy of hiring only white waiters. But even historian James Silver's book, *Mississippi: The Closed Society,* an unsparing depiction of the stultifying atmosphere at Ole Miss, failed to prepare me for the idea that a white student there might be shunned for sharing a room with a Negro. In the end, we got to see for ourselves. At the invitation of our unlikely visitors, ten of us spent our spring break at Ole Miss attending classes and touring such landmarks as Parchman Prison and the sprawling Delta Pine & Land Plantation. Males stayed in graduate housing and females in sororities where they got insight into Southern social pressure on Saturday night. A woman down the hall kept the lights off in her room so no passersby would look up and realize she had no date. To us, it was as ludicrous as warning riders not to spit on the subway.

Then, too soon, my undergraduate days were over. Our commencement speaker, U.S. Interior Secretary Stewart Udall, was not inspiring but the day held a special reward for me. I was named George Polk Outstanding Graduate in Journalism. A CBS war correspondent killed in Greece in 1948, Polk is memorialized by L.I.U. each year with awards recognizing the nation's top investigative journalism. I wondered if I would ever earn one. But that part of my future was on hold. I indulged myself in a final idyll at the children's camp in the Pocono Mountains where I'd worked three of the prior four summers, then returned to start graduate school.

It proved a short stay. My mindset moved rapidly from "This really doesn't interest me" to "I'm not sure I'm suited for this" to "What am I doing here?" The program director's deadly lectures reminded me of the soporific one-man journalism faculty at L.I.U. The studio was as modern as advertised, a plus for students from places like California, Texas, and Utah with experience in television, which is to say everyone in the program but me. And while sympathetic colleagues assured me that I would get the knack of it, what was apparent to me was that I wielded a camera and manipulated a tech board about as well as I fielded a grounder and dissected a fetal pig. If crews for our shows had been selected like teams for punch ball, I'd have been the last one chosen every time.

One evening after driving to the campus for a class, I was unable to find a place to park. I circled back to try again and when the second pass failed to yield a space, I kept on driving. By the end of the week I had arranged for a part-time public relations position at L.I.U., where I enrolled in graduate education courses. That would maintain my 2–S student draft status and could lead to another deferment since schoolteachers were also draft-exempt. Teaching was not my idea of a promising career, but I only had to do it until I turned twenty-six. I never notified Brooklyn College, and for years concluded the story of my brief time there by adding, "They must still be waiting for me to come clean out my desk."

17

The Wrong Abe Cohen

"I must tell you," *New York World-Telegram & Sun* managing editor Herb Kamm said moments after giving me my first full-time job, "that this might not last very long."

Few people were better positioned to know that the paper's days were numbered. Kamm was in secret merger talks with executives of the *Journal-American* and *Herald-Tribune* and would later serve as executive editor of their short-lived amalgam, "the Widget"—the *New York World-Journal-Tribune.* "I'm grateful for the opportunity," I told him. "If worse comes to worst, it will look good on my resumé."

I was succeeding a local legend, octogenarian Brooklyn sports editor Jimmy Murphy who believed there were three important aspects of any story—names, names, and names. "Names sell newspapers," he told me when I paid a courtesy visit to him in Far Rockaway. The idea in Murphy's era was to load notes columns with them—a high school shortstop's errorless streak, a Brooklyn kid playing college soccer, the results of a handball tournament in Brighton Beach—and even when you covered a game, the more names you squeezed into your copy the better. He gave me a headstart, a two-inch thick folder of items he hadn't gotten to. There was no point in arguing, so I nodded and managed to mine some features from these leads—and the steady stream arriving daily from correspondents who knew if they mailed something to Jimmy Murphy he'd print it.

When Herb Kamm's prediction came true, on Saturday, April 23, 1966, I went to the composing room to retrieve the metal blocks that were used to print stock headlines I developed for columns of my own, mementos that would become paperweights. The New York

Newspaper Guild instructed us to report outside the *World-Telegram* on Barclay Street (where the World Trade Center twin towers would later rise and fall) to picket against what the union deemed a lockout. But my first shift on a cold, drizzly day was also my last. Someone handed me a flyer headed "Why We Are Picketing." The third bulleted item decried management intentions to retain some recent hires and lay off others with more seniority. As it began to rain harder and I grasped that I was demonstrating against my own interests, I discreetly leaned my sign against a wall on the far side of the building and left, wondering if my newspaper career was at an end nearly as soon as its start.

Returning to journalism was secondary to a more pressing priority: the military draft. The graduate education courses I was taking at L.I.U. could lead to an obvious option. The city was so short of teachers it waived some requirements for applicants, qualifying me for an interview, which was conducted by Harry Levine, principal of Nathaniel Macon Junior High School in Brooklyn. A small, bespectacled, balding man, he looked up from a sheaf of prepared questions and asked, "How would you like to work for me? You're a big guy with a strong voice. We could use a fellow like you."

After waiting out seventeen years to avoid sitting in a classroom, I would be standing in front of one in September. But without any income in the interim, I moved back in with my parents and discovered something unusual afoot in the old neighborhood: a lively political campaign in an area where organization Democrats normally faced nominal or no opposition. Mel Dubin, a young engineer who had turned his design for a new-fangled home-heating radiator into a successful business, was running in a primary against nineteen-term Congressman and Democratic district leader Abe Multer.

I'd interviewed Multer for a term paper once. With "reform Democrats" like Ed Koch bucking "Tammany Hall bosses" in Manhattan he portrayed his role in a different light. Multer walked me through the history of the party as a de facto public welfare agency before FDR's New Deal made social services a government function, helping with job applications, landlord troubles and, yes, even parking tickets. "Do you know how many tickets we have fixed in all the years I have been here?" he asked rhetorically. "None. That's how many. Not a one. People come in here with a ticket and a story and one of my people says, 'Don't worry, we'll take care of it.' And we do. We pay it. It's a good investment for us. It buys loyalty."

The Dubin campaign was about something loftier than fixed tickets: ending the Vietnam War. On the surface it seemed like a quixotic endeavor, yet most voters in the district were liberal and many had sons and grandsons facing the draft. With time on my hands I decided to volunteer. When I reached the top of the stairs at Dubin's walkup headquarters, Steve Solarz just about leapt from behind his desk to greet me. At twenty-five, he had abandoned doctoral studies at Columbia to comanage the campaign. I knew the turf, a valuable asset because many volunteers were anti-war activists from outside the district, so Solarz assigned me to drive Dubin to events and cruise around the neighborhood in a sound-car alternately delivering a spiel and playing a song recorded by a local folk group. This attracted quizzical looks, and that was almost the point. We needed to alert voters prone to overlooking primaries that there was an election in June.

By May, Dubin was gaining traction, buoyed by national attention when syndicated columnist Drew Pearson accused Multer of shady off-shore banking deals and bolstered by groups like Women's Strike for Peace and celebrities like the actor Tony Randall, who worked the Brighton Beach boardwalk one hot afternoon. *Schvitzing* from ten blocks of greeting elderly Jewish residents passing the day on benches, Randall suggested we return to his waiting limo. "Sure," I said, "but why don't we go back on the other side of the boardwalk so we can meet different people?" Randall arched his head. "Young man," he said in an exaggerated stage voice, "we can be here for the next twenty years and we will be meeting the *same people!*"

To counter Multer's organizational advantage, the campaign assembled a slate of insurgents for lesser offices to run with him, creating an instant organization much as mayoral candidate John Lindsay had the year before in his upset victory. This was sound reasoning, but it would backfire because of two blunders, one a miscalculation and the other a snafu that could only happen in Brooklyn. Old hands advised campaign leaders to avoid challenging Irwin (Bobby) Brownstein, a popular state senator and district leader from Bensonhurst who aspired to the Congressional seat himself and would not regret a Multer defeat. But that seemed inconsistent to campaign leaders.

"If you feel we have to run someone in Bensonhurst," Mike Scott, who was running for the State Assembly in another part of the district, advised Dubin and Solarz, "we could do worse than a friend of mine, a community activist named Abe Cohen." They found a challenger for Brownstein's party leadership post, but days before nominating petitions were due they still had no state senate candidate. Then, as if by fate it seemed, a man mounted the stairs on Quentin Road. "I'm Abe Cohen," he said. "From Bensonhurst."

Dubin rushed over in response to Solarz's call. At first Abe Cohen seemed surprised that anyone would want him to run for office but soon agreed to fill the State Senate slot. Two weeks later at the formal campaign kickoff at the Casa del Ray catering hall on Coney Island Avenue, Mike Scott walked over to Solarz and asked, "Who's that schmuck over there that's been bending my ear half the night?"

"What do you mean?" Solarz responded. "That's Abe Cohen, the guy you recommended. He's running for the State Senate against Brownstein."

"That's not *my* Abe Cohen," Scott said. The Abe Cohen on the ballot was an affable postal carrier with little intellectual rigor or political presence. Dubin would win the rest of the district but lose so badly in Bensonhurst that Multer survived for one last term in Congress.

Dubin tried and lost again to his machine-backed successor, Bertram Podell. He returned to his business and lived a long and honorable life but never again dabbled in electoral politics. Solarz was later elected to the State Assembly and then Congress after Podell pleaded guilty to influence peddling—only to follow Podell to prison as well for his role in a scandal connected to the Congressional Post Office. Before that, whenever our paths crossed I could make him blush by recalling the time he blew an election by running "the wrong Abe Cohen."

18

Hard Lessons

AUGUST 1966
Roscoe, New York

Why would anyone name a street anywhere in Brooklyn, let alone the heart of the borough's signature black neighborhood, for a North Carolina Congressman who opposed adoption of the U. S. Constitution and fought for slavery and states' rights? Yet there it was—Macon Street—and when the city named a junior high school after the street on which it stood in Bedford-Stuyvesant, it had the ring of an inadvertent inside joke.

When I arrived in 1966 Nathaniel Macon Junior High was a joke in the worst sense of the world, a cruel microcosm of everything wrong with urban education starting with Principal Harry Levine and the English teacher he personally recruited, Mr. Edward Hershey. I planned to teach until I turned twenty-six and no longer needed a draft deferment, but a summer working with teenagers made me think I might enjoy teaching after all and even do it well.

An ad in the *New York Times* led me to Lincoln Farm, a summer camp for teens 120 miles north of the city that combined progressive educational principles with an authoritarian streak worthy of military school. The camp attracted affluent parents seeking a more meaningful experience for their children than the eight weeks of indulgence available elsewhere. A few campers were on scholarship, including a smattering of non-whites at a time when integrated camps were unheard of, except for those sponsored by charities or left-wing groups. I had not seen one black camper or counselor in eight summers at two traditional Jewish-American camps. Non-white staff was restricted to kitchen and grounds work, something I learned to my chagrin—and shame—the summer before at Pocono Highland Camps.

I convinced the owner to allow me to recruit a basketball team of high school stars to serve as junior counselors and play against teams from other camps under the lights on our outdoor court. Three black players from George Westinghouse Vocational High in Brooklyn were in the group I assembled. That's when the camp owner told me that unlike the whites, they could only have kitchen jobs. "Ed, I know your heart's in the right place, but we just can't put them in with the kids," he said. "If word got out, we would lose families. It's out of the question." The honorable response was to withdraw the offers. Instead, in a summer when civil rights activists my age were dying in Mississippi, the black players washed dishes while the whites organized softball games. This is high on any list of my least-proud moments.

Lincoln Farm was very different in other ways, too. Campers took morning classes in farming, forestry, and carpentry and by August the vegetables they grew were served in the dining hall and the camp had a new bunkhouse they helped construct. Afternoons were occupied by such traditional activities as swimming and land sports with evenings devoted to programs like the journalism seminar I led. Another attraction, for parents at least, was an inviolate ban on alcohol, drugs, and cigarettes mandating expulsion without a refund for transgressors. A week into the summer a taxicab pulled up to transport a camper caught smoking to the bus station as others watched. It was so chilling a sight that I wondered if it had been staged just as one I would recall two summers later at an army base in Georgia as I watched a soldier arrested after going AWOL marched past our basic training unit in handcuffs.

Every other weekend, groups of campers rode flatbed trucks to concerts, museums or summer-stock theater and camped out for two nights. Two counselors accompanied each group, one designated the trip leader and charged with finding extra activities and spending an allotment of cash for meals. The first trip I led was to the St. John Terrell Music Circus in Lambertville, New Jersey, for a remarkable double-bill featuring two African-American legends, comedian Dick Gregory and jazz trumpeter Dizzy Gillespie. I added two stops that proved popular, the quaint Delaware River town of New Hope, Pennsylvania and the Stangl Pottery factory in Flemington, New Jersey, but nothing could top Gillespie's high notes and Gregory's irreverence. Typical: a riff on his dumb brother-in-law taking a television in for repair amid the Harlem riots and looting. "The cops arrested him," Gregory reported, "but they let him go. He told them, 'Who would *steal* a Motorola?'"

My next weekend destination was the Long Wharf Theater in New Haven where our group took in a Chekhov play and met director Jon Jory, son of Hollywood actor Victor Jory. The Yale campus was one obvious addition to our itinerary, and at the last second I added the New York Giants summer training facility at Fairfield University, which became the talk of camp. Maybe that was why I felt so positive about my third outing to the Baseball Hall of Fame and the Farmers Museum in Cooperstown, N.Y. Instead, it became my undoing, producing one of those hard lessons that show up when you least expect them.

The problem began when a camper took ill. While the group watched a stock car race we bundled her up in the truck cab. The next day she was treated for flu symptoms at an emergency room near the state park where we spent the night. "I'll be OK," she said when we offered to head back early, so we stopped at a supermarket to buy food for that evening's campfire. Chuck steak was on sale for 39 cents a pound. "That's cheaper than franks and burgers," I told my assistant trip leader. "Let's do it. It'll make the kids feel special." To the campers it might as well have been prime sirloin. I was still feeling an afterglow for snatching excitment from the jaws of disappointment on Monday afternoon when the camp owner summoned me to his office.

"Did you feed them *steak?*" he asked. I started to explain, but he would have none of it. Campers were bragging about it and word would surely reach parents who did not expect their $1,000 tuition to pay for fancy meals. "Let me be frank," he said. "I consider this a serious breach of judgment. If I do send you out on another trip, it will not be as the leader." The upbraiding made me feel like the kid who'd been sent home in the taxicab—and for what I considered a rank injustice. But this was *his* camp. My best option was to learn from it: An unintended consequence is no less real than any other.

Still, I returned to the city buoyed by how well I had done with the kids, only to learn very quickly that summer camp in the Catskills was not a junior high in Brooklyn. With no training in classroom management, educational theory or adolescent psychology, I was ill prepared. The best of my students entered seventh grade reading at a fifth-grade reading level. And the principal who recruited me, Harry Levine, was hardly helpful. A Depression-era graduate of Cornell like my father, he seemed to see his position less as a capstone to his career than an escape from it. He rarely entered a classroom and made certain he would not even have to see or hear students by prohibiting them from using the corridor outside his first-floor office. To walk from one side of the first floor to the other they climbed stairs to the second floor, crossed over and came back down again.

Small wonder demand was mounting in minority areas for a say in how schools were run—and who ran them. It was a matter of intense debate after the new Lindsay Administration authorized a "community control" experiment in three districts—the South Bronx, the Two Bridges section of Manhattan, and Ocean Hill-Brownsville, an area of Brooklyn so impoverished it made Bedford-Stuyvesant seem prosperous. But what portended progress for black and Latino leaders was perceived as a dire threat to teachers' job security, a point hammered home by Albert Shanker, their union president, who was so forceful a

presence that Woody Allen made his name a punch line in his movie
Sleeper (1973). ("According to history," actor John McLiam explains
the war that destroyed America, "a man named Albert Shanker got
hold of a nuclear warhead.") He was an unlikely opponent of minority
rights, having marched with Martin Luther King, Jr. and their mutual
friend Bayard Rustin, but the dispute made Shanker's thick glasses
and perpetually mussed hair the face of what newspapers called "white
backlash."

The flashpoint came when new community school boards sought
to replace some teachers with "better role models" for students, evok-
ing charges of anti-Semitism because many of those they wanted to
transfer out were Jewish. They almost had to be. So many Jews taught
in the city that each autumn the entire system shut down when holy
days fell on school days. And not just for the *High* Holy Days but for
Sukkot and *Simchat Torah,* which few of us observed. "Mr. Hershey," a
sweet, chubby seventh-grader named Alberta piped up in class a few
weeks after the last of these breaks, "You got any more o' them Jewish
holidays comin' up?"

These crosscurrents would boil over into a bitter thirty-six-day
teacher strike at the start of the 1968–69 school year, but I had more
immediate problems. I was in way over my head and nobody knew it
more than the seventh graders I was trying to teach. As one disastrous
day led to the next, I had to focus less on reading levels than decibel
levels in a losing battle to maintain order in the face of mayhem. I
would pass classrooms where teachers had control and children were
learning, but I was at a loss about how to make that happen. Clearly, it
took more than "a big guy with a strong voice."

19

Second Shift

One phone call changed it all. My old L.I.U. classmate Steve Ende, back in New York after a grad school debacle of his own at Georgia Tech, had landed in the sports department of a new daily paper on Long Island called the *Suffolk Sun*. There was one more opening for a sportswriter and he'd told his editors that I was their man. "But I'm teaching," I said, "or at least trying to."

"So?" Steve said. "Do both. We're a morning paper so you won't have to start working until school is out. It'll be great. We can even find a place to room together again." I drove to the paper's office in an industrial park forty-five miles east of Brooklyn to meet Larry Conroy, the sports editor. We were more opposite than alike—for starters, he was a hard-drinking Irish-American—but we shared a bond. A veteran of the *Herald-Tribune* sports desk, he too had been laid off when it merged with the *Journal-American* and *World-Telegram & Sun*.

"Are you sure you can do this?" he asked, almost incredulous at the idea that anyone could simultaneously teach in Brooklyn and cover sports on Long Island. "I'd sure like to try," I said. "I'm a newspaperman, not a schoolteacher." He sent me to see the managing editor and it was immediately clear that my offhand remark about my resumé the day Herb Kamm hired me in New York had been prescient. The *Sun* loved the idea of attracting refugees from papers in the city. It hardly seemed to matter that I'd only been on staff there for three months. I was hired.

Steve Ende and I rented a house in Hempstead halfway between the school and the *Sun* office, allowing me to drive to Brooklyn weekday mornings and then out to Long Island or to a ball game at Madison Square Garden or Shea or Yankee Stadium. Because the *Sun* had a thin sports staff, at age 23 I would be covering the major leagues far sooner than I could have if the *World-Telegram* had survived.

Suffolk Sun publisher Gardner (Pat) Cowles III was scion of one of two branches of a family publishing empire. One, based in Minneapolis, had a track record in newspapers. Pat was from the other side of the family, son of *Look Magazine* publisher Gardner (Mike) Cowles, Jr. Daddy staked him to a pair of small dailies in Florida where he did well enough to earn the chance to start the *Sun,* which was like no newspaper any of us had seen. Housed in a new single-story building next to a Germaine Monteil cosmetics plant, it had pastel colored desks coded by department. "Looks like an insurance office," Conroy complained the day we met. The modern décor belied a decrepit mechanical operation with hand-me-down presses purchased from the *Newark Star-Ledger.* That was one challenge. Another was *Newsday,* the only source of local news and advertising for two million Long Islanders east of Queens County.

Newsday was as much the model as the competition, an unlikely success story launched in the 1940s by Alicia Patterson, socialite member of another publishing family, owners of the *Chicago Tribune* and *New York Daily News.* One of her first editorial crusades, a successful campaign for zoning changes to provide affordable housing for World War II veterans and their families, led to massive suburban residential developments like Levittown, propelling *Newsday's* growth. Nassau County's population doubled between 1950 and 1960, and the paper's circulation followed suit. Expansive Suffolk County to its east was growing apace but still largely undeveloped, with half of Nassau's population in more than five times its size.

Demographers expected Long Island's population center to drift eastward to Yaphank, site of a new county office complex sixty miles east of Times Square, and the *Sun* aspired to be part of that future. But *Newsday* was not about to see its market saturation diluted and used every advantage it had to keep the new kid on the block from gaining a foothold. The *Sun's* approach to this David-and-Goliath match was to shoot for the ankles not the forehead, seeking to be anything *Newsday* was not. *Newsday* was delivered in the afternoon with the bulk of its subscribers in Nassau County, so the *Sun* would be a morning paper focused exclusively on Suffolk. *Newsday* was a tabloid so the *Sun* would be full-sized. Like almost every daily newspaper, *Newsday* was black and white so the *Sun* would experiment (very primitively) with color. All this assumed that there was a niche for a new paper and the *Sun* had the funding and expertise to fill it. But those would turn out to be faulty assumptions.

Conroy, the sports editor, and columnist Pat Putnam, an award-winning sportswriter in Miami who had come north with the Cowles Florida contingent, taught me a lot about covering sports but had less success acquainting me with their after-hours world. I felt very adult one night at the Sky Lounge, a favored hangout adjacent to a small airport a mile from the *Sun's* office, hearing myself bark, "Jack Daniels on the rocks with a twist"—until Conroy bellowed from the other end of the bar, "Hershey, that stuff's too sweet. Order a man's drink!" Conroy and Putnam were so prone to drinking mishaps they could have served as object lessons for the temperance union. One night after downing a few at the Sky they decided to drop by a new bar where Conroy yelled, "Any Guinea worth his weight will fight!" Several takers sent him to the hospital. And heading home after another drinking bout, Putnam tried to drive straight through the Smithtown traffic circle, totaling his car and nearly himself.

Given my schedule, there was little time to carouse anyway. I was up at dawn each day for the twenty-mile rush-hour drive to Brooklyn and home past midnight after covering a game in the city or driving forty miles to the *Sun's* office in Deer Park and then twenty miles back to Hempstead. My beats included the Knicks and the Jets. Steve was a rabid hockey fan so he took the Rangers. We each covered lots of high school games and split the lone Suffolk-based pro sports franchise, the Long Island Ducks of the Eastern Hockey League. The Ducks were pros in the sense that they earned modest salaries in a league full of toothless veterans nearing the close of minor-league careers and under-educated Canadian youngsters who could not skate well enough to go much higher—hard truths that hardly mattered to several thousand vocal fans at a dingy rink in Commack.

Because our slow and unreliable presses started early to ensure a full run of the next morning's edition, I would call in a brief story as soon as a Ducks game ended, visit the locker room for quotes, and drive to the office ten minutes away to complete a detailed account in time for the scheduled nightly stoppage to re-plate the presses with later news. After one game I raced back with a dazzling lead in my head, unscathed by a spinout on the icy Sagtikos State Parkway, only to learn there would be no re-plate. The presses had been so balky those in charge did not want to chance stopping them for fear they would fail to restart. Another time I arrived to see a headline that read "JETS NIP DUCKS" over my early story. "Nice head," I told Joe Deacon, who had edited it. "Only problem is they were playing the Blades, Joe, not the Jets." A moon-eyed shmoo of a man whose goofiness was usually unintentional, Deacon recovered with as quick a retort as I have ever heard. "Blades," he said, "wouldn't fit."

By spring I'd worn out my welcome at Macon Junior High. The strain of a double workload left little time to prepare lesson plans and I spent nearly every minute of designated prep periods napping in the teachers' lounge. But I toughed it out, trying to steer clear of an assistant principal growing increasingly impatient with my performance. I did plan my schedule well enough to make it to class on time each day until one Monday in late March when I was 20,000 feet above LaGuardia Airport returning from a Sunday night NBA Knicks playoff game in Boston.

"My plane from Boston got stacked up over LaGuardia," I told the school secretary from an airport pay phone after we landed just minutes before the start of my first class. "Mr. Hershey," the assistant principal asked, intercepting me when I arrived two hours late, "you weren't in Boston on school business, were you?" Most days, I thought to myself, I am barely *here* on school business. But I made it through the end of June and by then Plan B had emerged. I had been hired for the 1967–68 academic year by the North Babylon School District to teach high school English and journalism a couple of miles from the *Suffolk Sun* office. I'd sold administrators on the idea that I could be an apt role model—a teacher paid to write about sports.

That game in Boston was not the first sports playoff I covered. In December the *Sun* decided it was too costly to send Pat Putnam to the inaugural Super Bowl in Los Angeles and instead suggested he cover the American Football League title game in Buffalo a week before, on New Year's Day. After Pat told his bosses where they could put that assignment, it was offered to me. I left Newark Airport at dawn for War Memorial Stadium, the ballpark where *The Natural* (1984) was filmed, and watched the Kansas City Chiefs demolish the Bills so badly that frustrated fans pelted Bills' quarterback (and future Republican Vice Presidential nominee) Jack Kemp with snowballs. I flew home after filing my story, saving the Sun the cost of a hotel room.

Boston ten weeks later was a much different experience. The game was surprising—Willis Reed, Cazzie Russell and Walt Bellamy combined for 85 points giving the Knicks their only victory of the series—but that mattered less to me than just being there. I laughed with the other writers as Jerry Levine of the *World-Journal-Tribune* traded barbs with gravel-voiced Celtics broadcaster Johnny Most, whose call at the end of the seventh game of the 1965 Eastern final—"*Havlicek stole the ball!*"—was a signature moment in the annals of sportscasting.

There were more laughs during a late-night dinner in Boston's Chinatown where war stories flowed more swiftly and grew more ribald and less convincing with each beer. An aging New York Times writer recounted this experience in our hotel, the Somerset, fifteen years earlier.

"I was here to cover a Yankees-Red Sox game that night and invited a friend up for a matinee," he said. This was before hotels were air-conditioned, and it was a hot day so the windows were open. B.U. was playing football at Fenway Park and Harry Agganis ran for a touchdown just as we finished doing the deed. So there was this huge roar. I looked up from the bed and said, 'I knew I was good, but I didn't know I was that good!'"

20

Big League

Suffolk Sun sports editor Larry Conroy relished expanding my horizons with assignments that took me out of my element, and I got a double dose during a weekend at the Bridgehampton race course on Long Island's stylish East End where socialites mingled with world-class sports car drivers on the Trans-Am circuit.

Rather than fake sophistication, I embraced the role of neophyte. At least that way I could share a sense of discovery with readers. I accepted an offer from the race promoter to tour the circuit in a racecar at speeds well below full throttle, but fast enough to make me queasy for a story headlined, "Once Around Swiftly Sets Wheels Spinning." The next day a baby-faced thirty-year-old Ivy Leaguer named Mark Donohue won the race in a Lola owned by trucking magnate Roger Penske. Donohue met Penske at the funeral of a driver who died in a fiery crash, something he might have taken for an omen. With a reputation for daring and the scars and fractures to prove it, Donohue went on to drive a Penske car to victory at the 1972 Indianapolis 500 in record time—and took the fast lane in his personal life as well, divorcing the mother of his two young sons to marry a model. Five years later, he died from a cerebral hemorrhage suffered when he blew out a tire on a practice run at the Austrian Grand Prix. He was thirty-eight.

My next stop on Conroy's tour, National Speedway in a dusty middle-of-nowhere town called Center Moriches, presented a far different side of auto racing, attracting thousands of Bud-swigging, Marlboro-smoking men and women watching pairs of cars take off down a quarter-mile drag strip at decibel levels well past ear-splitting. "I think maybe one of them needs a muffler," I joked to the PR man.

He didn't laugh. The souped-up dragsters shared one element with the Trans-Am cars—decals advertising myriad sponsors. But I realized that was where the similarity ended when someone approached a drag racer after he'd won a heat and offered him $50 to affix a logo to his vehicle, even though it had no connection to the advertised product. The driver pointed to an empty space on a rear fender and slipped the fifty into a pocket in his fireproof jumpsuit. "I guess," he told me with a wink, "that you could say I'm just a bucks-down kind of guy."

Another motoring story sent me on a 100-mile auto rally called the Suffolk Safari in a white Triumph driven by a reporter who worked in the women's section. (We were still living in an era when Feature sections could refer to women as "pert" without inviting scorn for gender-based stereotyping.) "I've never done this before," she said, "but that's all right. The navigator does all the work." That was hardly reassuring. I was the navigator! Coded instructions identifying landmarks along the way were masked as clues you might find in a cryptic crossword puzzle. That was one challenge. Another was the need to drive from one point to the next at precisely the prescribed speed for exactly the correct distance on a course deviously (if not insidiously) devised to invite wrong turns and missed checkpoints. Several hours and countless miscalculations later, we amassed 4,371 "error points" to finish 57th of 62 entrants and wondered how five teams could have done worse.

Not every story involved competition. The Whaler's Festival in Sag Harbor made little pretense of being a true sporting event. The festival's ostensible race—oarsmen rowing reproduction whaleboats to honor the town's eighteenth-century whaling heritage—was an excuse for a party. "Try to save this," the harbormaster's wife said, handing me a paper cup as I boarded their yacht. "We run out of cups before we run out of gin." That inspired the headline: *Old Whalers Never Die, They Just Save Their Cups.*

We never left the dock, but I did get a little ways out to sea a few weeks later for a story on a sailing regatta in Great South Bay, and it proved less than pleasant. I went out on the judges' boat and after a couple of hours told the captain," I'm ready to go ashore." He responded with a quizzical expression. "Oh," he said, "have you arranged to be picked up?" He planned to stay on the bay until the last of the sloops completed the race late that afternoon. That was the day I came to understand that you can experience *mal de mer* even in near-calm water within sight of land—or at least I could. Eventually my host took pity on me and ferried me ashore.

I suffered a more tangible injury at a press conference promoting a professional wrestling card at Madison Square Garden. Everyone understood that unlike college and Olympic wrestling, pro rasslin' was choreographed to the delight of 19,000 true believers. "Tell me," I asked 600-pound William (Haystacks) Calhoun, a Texas farm boy and perennial crowd favorite lumbering around the ring in denim overalls, "how do you respond to people who think wrestling is fake?" Big mistake. "Do *you* think we're faking?" he asked and then, grasping my right hand and bending it back, added, "Does this feel like a fake?" My wrist hurt for two days, my pride a little longer.

There were more oddball stories, but they barely mattered in comparison to the bulk of my work. Ready or not, two years out of college I was in the big leagues. Admission to the Baseball Writers Association of America came with my name in black calligraphy on a membership card that was also a pass to every major league ballpark. And when training camps opened in July, I added pro football to my repertoire: A year after standing with a group of summer campers peering through a fence as the Giants practiced, I was inside now, grilling Allie Sherman on his plans for the 1967 season.

The Giants would bounce back from a 1–12–1 record, but only to a mediocre 7–7 in Sherman's penultimate year as coach. In fact, my arrival in the press boxes of New York coincided with an era of futility for all the teams I covered. The Yankees were in steep decline, losing ninety games to finish ninth with thirty-five-year-old Mickey Mantle batting .245. Mets' rookie pitcher Tom Seaver won sixteen games, but with the team still dead last, manager Wes Westrum resigned to escape the ignominy of a firing. The Jets rode Joe Namath's arm to a promising start, but faded from contention in December. And when the Knicks lost twenty-two of their first thirty-seven games, coach Dick McGuire was fired. I wrote a column bemoaning this collective ineptitude headlined "The Big Apple Has Become a Big Lemon."

Covering a losing team can become a challenge. One strategy: focus more on visiting teams rather than belaboring another loss. Another: Ignore the game altogether, as I did the day the Mets brought lovable old Casey Stengel back to Shea. But fans do want to know about their team. So one night I decided to explore the toll that mediocrity was taking on Yankee manager Ralph Houk, the battled-tested Marine veteran who had returned to the dugout from the front office a season before. Our conversation did not go well, but got me a telling story. It was headlined "The Major Won't Answer," which ended this way:

The Yanks had just lost, 8–7 to Cleveland. Houk was leaning back in his chair, a cigar in his mouth. It had not been an easy defeat. That really is the point because to Houk no defeat is easy.

"They say Burke and MacPhail and you will be satisfied with a .500 year," I said. "But that still means you lose 81 times. Is it tough for you to reconcile each of those losses with the total picture?"

"If we get enough guys healthy," Houk answered, "we'll surprise some people." That is not, of course, what the Yankee manager had been asked. He tried to make it clear he did not want to begin assessing season prospects or the manager's personality. To his visitor, though, this seemed the perfect time for a self-assessment, after a tough loss for a man who walked back into the clubhouse last year knowing he faced the kind of frustration he had never put up with before.

"You're 13 and 14," I said. That's almost .500. There've been some bright spots. Are you satisfied with the season so far?" Houk put his cigar down. His face reddened.

"Look," he said, "let's get something straight. I don't give a damn if we're .200, .400 or .800 or 10 hundred. I'm never satisfied unless I'm in first place. And I'm not about to start answering horsefeather questions like that at this time of night. You want to ask me about our season prospects, make an appointment. You want to know something about tonight's game, ask me. I just worry about one game at a time."

The Major smiled at the press this year when he was asked about Mickey Mantle's experiment at first base, about the many errors his infield was making, about a lot of other things that used to send him into fits of rage and had banished more than one sportswriter from his office. He had been peaches and cream.

But Wednesday night, Ralph Houk refused to answer when he was asked how he had accepted mediocrity.

Houk had a point about my timing, one that a young rookie named Bill Bradley reinforced at the Knicks' training camp that summer when I asked how a Missouri banker's son with degrees from Princeton and Oxford could relate to black teammates like Willis Reed and Walt Frazier. "Look," Bradley said, "if you want to talk sociology, let's have coffee some time and I'll be happy to do it. But this is a locker room. Let's talk basketball."

I was as prone to rookie mistakes as the players I covered, with a lot to learn about writing, reporting—and life. But two weeks past my twenty-third birthday I was in the big leagues.

21

Insignificant Others

The big summer news for me was that I could live a semi-normal life before taking a new teaching position in the fall to preserve my draft deferment. That meant more sleep as well as some semblance of a social life.

Two jobs made it hard to find women to date and time to date those I could find. Beyond a few fix-ups—my housemate's girlfriend's best friend and the sister of a teaching colleague—about the only women I went out with were those I encountered along the way. One was a pretty Long Island Ducks hockey fan and another the Suffolk Sun receptionist. I invited her to use one of the two complimentary seats that came with my Jets beat and, since I would be in the pressbox, arranged for my friend Jerry to join her. Jerry and his wife Ellen (who was no football fan) would dine with us after the game. They lived near Shea Stadium so we picked Jerry up en route and that's when it hit me that this scenario meant his newlywed wife had to watch him leave the apartment with my tall, blonde, and statuesque date. It was a long time before I stopped apologizing to her for that.

What I most wanted was a steady girl, not the steady stream of one- (or maybe two- or three-) date wonders I came to call my insignificant others. Instead, that summer produced quite the opposite—a string of escapades.

It started as I drove home late one night and spotted a woman sitting on the curb, head in her hands, blocks from my house. I pulled up to discover her bawling about a breakup and offered her a cup of coffee. We were in each other's arms before the coffee perked. In the morning, she asked to use the phone to call her erstwhile boyfriend

who came to pick her up a discreet distance away. I never saw her
again.

Not long after that I got a last-minute call from a college classmate inviting me to join him on a friend's plane to visit Expo '67, the
Montreal world's fair. After poor weather delayed our return trip,
two of us returned to the fair where we flirted with two women who
knew as little English as we did French, a barrier that only seemed to
add charm to an instant attraction. We wound up in their apartment
in the suburb of Chateaugay for a night that took me places I had
never been.

I made another social debut of sorts after driving to the Catskills
a few weeks later to cover an annual celebrity fundraiser for Maurice
Stokes, a basketball star paralyzed by encephalitis. "Except for a college weekend at Grossinger's, I've never stayed at a resort up here," I
told two Knicks' beat writers and their wives at dinner after the game.
"I have a couple of days off. Any ideas of where I might go?" "You
could try the Pines," one of the wives suggested. "It caters to a younger
crowd. We know the manager. I'll make a call for you." I checked in
the next afternoon and found my way to the swimming pool, where
I struck up a conversation with two women about my age. "We just
checked out," one said, "and we figured we'd hang out for a while
before going home." By nightfall the three of us were hanging out in
my room. It was no *ménage a trois*—I was entwined with the slender
brunette who first caught my eye while her friend drifted off to sleep.
As we walked hand in hand the next morning she posed the classic
Catskills question: "Will we see each other in the city?" Actually, I
dated *both* of them back in New York.

So while my libido had made up for lost time, I still had no girlfriend by Labor Day when I covered the national tennis championships at the posh West Side Tennis Club in Forest Hills where a press
credential included complimentary service in the club's dining room.
"I just might land myself a debutante," I half-joked to Steve Ende.
But all the debutantes must have fled to the Hamptons or Europe for
the ten-day run of the tournament. I wound up with a bright-eyed

University of Iowa student spending a summer in New York as a waitress at an International House of Pancakes. She was moonlighting during the tournament when the tennis club enlarged its staff to serve interlopers like me. We were a couple until she returned to Cedar Rapids and I went back to the two-jobs-a-day grind that kept me out of Vietnam.

North Babylon High was a step up from Macon Junior High in a number of ways—convenient location, manageable classes, ambitious students—but there were new challenges, including standing before a classroom in a school without a dress code when mini-skirts were in fashion. I learned early on to meet girls' glances at eye level to avoid being caught looking down at the veritable peep show several nubile teenagers were offering their twenty-three-year-old teacher. And not all students were engaged in school. In my general English classes those glances were often blank stares from shopping mall rats who sat impassively, rarely connecting with the material.

While Babylon next door was a quaint seventeenth-century fishing village with history and character, *North* Babylon was a nondescript three-square-mile inland byproduct of mid-century sprawl created by developers cashing in on the suburban migration of working-class families. Just 40 miles from Times Square, they might as well have been living in the Midwest. When I took my journalism class on a field trip to Manhattan I discovered that most students only went to the city for family visits. Several said they did not remember ever being there. And those were the bright ones.

The lesser lights were pursuing a general diploma, steered away from challenging coursework much as many of the sons and daughters of blue-collar workers in my own high school days in Brooklyn had been. Two girls in sophomore English were the exception, participating in class and turning in good work. I asked them to stay after the bell one day. "I know you think this is where you belong," I said, "but I can see that you are capable of more. Even a year in classes like this will put you so far behind that if you decide you want to go to college it may be too late. Why not give the academic track a try? You can always go back." They nodded and said they would talk to their parents but in the end they took my interest less for enthusiasm about whom they could be than disrespect for whom they were. "What's the matter, Mr. Hershey?" a friend of theirs who caught wind of my approach scoffed. "Aren't we good enough for you?"

22

Running Uphill

DECEMBER 1967
San Francisco

I did Tony Bennett one better. He only sang about leaving his heart in San Francisco.

I was in the Bay Area to cover a game between the New York Jets and the Oakland Raiders on the penultimate weekend of the 1967 National Football League season. On the eve of the game, Jets publicist Frank Ramos hosted the New York writers for a night on the town as an end-of-the-season thank you. It began with dinner at the upscale Blue Fox followed by visits to bars in North Beach that featured topless dancers Yvonne D'Angers (aka "The Persian Bombshell") suspended on a swing at the Off Broadway and Carol Doda ("The Girl with the Two 22's") putting her prodigious (if artificially endowed) attributes on full view at the Condor Club.

A two-drink minimum at these nightspots on top of cocktails and wine with dinner had us aglow as we walked along Broadway when Ramos, a well-liked twenty-nine-year-old PR guy in the first decade of a forty-year Jets career, decided to have some fun at the expense of the rookie scribe from the *Suffolk Sun*. "Hershey," he said as we passed one of those San Francisco streets that go just about straight up, "I bet you couldn't make it to the top of the hill." I was about to agree with him when two women walked by, one about my age and the other maybe twice as old.

"You're in such lousy shape I bet you couldn't even beat a girl to the top of the hill!" Ramos shouted before he intercepted the younger one, pulled out a bill and said, "If you can beat this guy up the hill, there's $20 in it for you." Before I could say a word, she was running up Kearny Street—and I was chasing after, fighting for breath and traction in my dress shoes. When I somehow managed to pull alongside her ten yards from the top, she gave me a shove and called over her shoulder, "Sorry, I really need this $20!" After we reached the top I stumbled over to the curb and threw up one of the best meals I had ever eaten. Back down on Broadway, everyone was having a good laugh. Ramos handed over the money and told the women he would leave tickets for them for Sunday's sold-out game. I traded contact information with my erstwhile competitor and we went our separate ways.

When I got back to my hotel room the message light was flashing. Gayle, a freshman working her way through college down in San Jose, had returned home to word that her boss needed her on Sunday. She could not go to the game. *Considerate,* I thought, tracking me down so the tickets were not wasted. The Jets had dealt the powerful Raiders their only loss of the season earlier in New York, but fell apart (and out of playoff contention) in the fourth quarter on Sunday. I filed my story and took a red-eye flight back so I could arrive in time for my first Monday morning class at North Babylon High. I was sorting out my expense receipts later that week when I came across Gayle's contact information. *Why not,* I thought. I sent her a bottle of French cologne. "For a good sport," I wrote. Her response arrived on two sheets of orange paper in a matching envelope. "I can't tell you how surprised and pleased I was to receive your present," she started. "I was beginning to think I would never hear from you again. What great taste you have in perfume."

It became a steady correspondence. Mostly I called and she wrote—
intimate thoughts that ran as long as five handwritten pages with intricate illustrations in colored pencil. When I sent a St. Valentine's Day
card and she signed a heartfelt response "Love, Gayle" our unlikely
flirtation seemed to be turning into a cross-country romance. We kept
saying we hardly knew one another, but these disclaimers always gave
way to the intoxicating idea that this was meant to be. "You seem so
real to me when we talk or when I am writing to you or reading one of
your letters," she wrote in March, "but when I wake up in the morning (this morning to be exact), I wonder if it is really what I think it
is—and then I talk to you and know *it is*."

It was too compelling a story to keep to myself. "I hear we played
cupid that night in San Francisco," a witness to our race, *New York Post*
columnist Milton Gross, said with a wink at a Knicks game. I could
tell Gayle was sharing our story, too, because there were giggles in the
background when one of her sorority sisters called her to the phone.
Then I realized that both New York baseball teams would open the
season on the West Coast during my spring break from teaching. I volunteered to pay my travel costs to cover the Mets in San Francisco and
Los Angeles and then stay on to cover the Yankees in Anaheim. Money
was more of a problem for the *Suffolk Sun* than it was for me. I had two
paychecks and little free time to spend much.

"I can't believe you're really coming to see me," Gayle wrote. I
landed in San Francisco on a Saturday and headed south in a rental
car the next morning. When I turned on the radio the first song was a
hot new release by Dionne Warwick—"Do You Know the Way to San
Jose?" Meant to be? To paraphrase Winston Churchill, it felt like fate
wrapped in magic inside destiny. Gayle showed me around town and
we had dinner with her family. I wasn't fazed when we didn't instantly
fall into each other's arms. We had a long way to go in person to match
the passion of those calls and letters.

The country shut down Monday for Martin Luther King Jr.'s
funeral—even the Oscars were postponed—so the Mets-Giants
opener was delayed until Tuesday. Gayle drove to Candlestick with the

friend she was with the night we met, Carol, who was to return to San Jose alone—allowing us time for a farewell dinner and perhaps more. I rushed through my clubhouse interviews after the game—the Mets blew a lead in the ninth inning—and met Gayle alongside the visiting dugout, intending to escort her to the press box where I would write my story. But the look in her eyes betrayed what she was about to say. There, in the near-empty ballpark, it only took eight words to tell me what I should have already known.

"Ed," she said, "I think I'm going home with Carol."

"It's not happening, is it?" I said.

She shook her head. The magic we imagined at 3,000 miles had been what magic often is: illusory. We embraced and walked off in opposite directions. After filing my story, I walked across the desolate parking lot hearing every footstep echo. In truth, it had not been happening for me either, but that hardly made it better. The car practically drove itself to Broadway and Kearny. It was dinner hour and watching commuters trudge home from work and into the gritty row houses that lined the street I realized it was hardly the idyllic setting I had re-imagined in my mind's eye. Back at the hotel I did something I had never done before. I wrote a poem. Then I called Gayle and read it to her.

"I looked up at a hill this evening in search of a person to love," the poem began. It might have qualified for top prize in a bad poetry contest, concluding too many tortuous if heartfelt stanzas later with

> So I left Kearny Street to the souls who live there
>   in their own sad scene.
> They'll never know how close it came to starting
>   a beautiful dream.
> But wasn't there more beauty in those old flats
>   above North Beach?
> Isn't it reality that we are all trying to reach?
> And that's one thing I didn't find.
> Perhaps I just wasn't inclined.

It made me feel better that she was crying, too. A poignant end, I thought, to a story of mutual longing gone awry. But that, too, would prove illusory. Several weeks later I decided to call San Jose one last time just to say that things were all right. I had a lead on a great new job and had secured a place in an Army Reserve unit, obviating my need to avoid Vietnam by teaching. This time there was no giggling. Her roommate came on the line (former roommate, actually, as I was about to discover). "Gayle isn't here," she said. "She's left school. She got married."

I stammered a request for a forwarding address to "send her my good wishes," I said. Fort Knox in Kentucky. I shook my head. We'd talked of running off to Canada together and she had married a G.I. Then I took a closer look at the name. It was her friend Carol's last name. Was her new husband Carol's son? We'd shared a lot of secrets, but clearly not all of them. Several days later a letter with a Kentucky postmark and no return address arrived. "Dear Ed," it started. "My roommates tell me that you called the other night. Vickie said that you wanted my address to write and wish me well. If you write I will find it hard to explain to my husband exactly who you are. So if you wish us well please do it silently and there will be continued peace (if you know what I mean). Everything is fine and I am happily married. Thank you so much. Gayle." I suppressed a sense of betrayal, reflecting instead on how exciting it was while it lasted and what an improbable idea it was to think our bizarre meeting might lead to true love.

23

Chipmunk Pride

A new generation of sportswriters—a wave of impish curmudgeons casting irreverent eyes on the games they covered—invaded the nation's press boxes in the 1960s. Superb stylists like Red Smith and Jimmy Cannon were still there, but they had always been the exception to an old guard of housemen whose work was rarely critical of the home team and generally held to a lower standard than news reporting.

It was Cannon who gave this new breed a name. He called them "chipmunks" to disparage how they sniffed around for stories he saw as pseudo-sociology and armchair psychology. But instead of resenting the label as an affront, writers like Len Shecter of the *Post*, Jerry Izenberg of the *Herald-Tribune*, and Stan Isaacs of *Newsday* adopted it as a badge of honor, separating them from the old just-write-the-game school. They even considered Cannon something of a patron saint. Hadn't he written one of the all-time great leads? "Joe Louis is a credit to his race. The human race."

The goal was to transcend the make-believe world of sports, exploring serious issues without taking themselves too seriously. Isaacs, who once pilfered the Dodgers' 1955 World Series flag from Chavez Ravine because he felt it ought to be in Brooklyn and not Los Angeles, was one of the best, and his exchange with winning pitcher Ralph Terry after the seventh game of the 1962 World Series exemplified the chipmunk ethos. Terry was called away. When he returned to the throng of writers at his locker, he said that his wife had phoned to congratulate him. "What was she doing?" Isaacs asked. "Feeding the baby," Terry responded, to which Isaacs shot back, "Breast or bottle?"

Isaacs was central to another fabled chipmunk story. He, Larry Merchant of the *New York Post,* and Stan Hochman of the *Philadelphia Daily News* enlivened a dull winter meeting of baseball executives by concocting a devilish rumor that the Yankees and St. Louis Cardinals were talking trade: Yogi Berra for Stan Musial, allowing Berra to conclude his career in his hometown and Musial to complete his by pulling homers into the "short porch" in right field at Yankee Stadium. Their fiction quickly spread through the coterie of writers hovered about in search of scuttlebutt. As their deadlines approached and the trio discussed what they would write, Hochman said, "I'm going with Musial for Berra." Isaacs was incredulous. Hadn't they made it up? "You know that and I know that," Hochman said, "but my editor doesn't know it."

I especially admired two purveyors of the new sportswriting paradigm, Vic Ziegel of the *New York Post* and George Vecsey of *Newsday.*

In print and in person Ziegel was just plain funny. A City College grad who started as I had by taking sports scores over the phone, he was a protégé of Shecter, the resident iconoclast of the *Post's* sports section who turned the baseball world inside out collaborating with pitcher Jim Bouton in the tell-all book *Ball Four.* Ziegel lived a couple of doors down from Dustin Hoffman in Greenwich Village and hung out at a pub on Christopher Street called the Lion's Head, which was frequented by writers whose book jackets lined its walls. Clever graffiti on the men's room walls made "the Head" a tourist attraction and its dining area hosted impromptu Irish sing-alongs by the Clancy Brothers, but the attraction for me was constant banter over politics, sports, and events of the day.

The bartenders added to the atmosphere. Nick Browne had a deep baritone voice and wrote well enough to freelance for the *Village Voice* a few feet away on the corner. Silver-haired Mike Riordan was so handsome that a movie director who spotted him on a Rome street cast him without an audition. Don Schlenker was cranky enough to turn misanthropy into an art form. And, with his lilting brogue, pixyish smile and red hair, Archie Mulligan was the quintessential leprechaun. And when a drink order was ready, the bartenders would yell "Jessica!" to summon a drop-dead gorgeous waitress. Soon millions would know her name when she was cast in a remake of *King Kong*. It was Jessica Lange.

If I had an assignment in the city I would stop in before driving back to Long Island, hoping Ziegel was there. I loved the stories he told about himself, like the one about the time on a train in Germany when three youths started snickering and gesticulating in his direction. You could not look much more Jewish than Vic, who was balding and bespectacled, so he assumed the worst. "Finally one called over, '*Sprechen Sie Deutsch?*'" Ziegel said. "I looked right at him. 'Tappan Zee Bridge?' I said."

Middle-aged appearance and self-deprecating sense of humor aside, he fancied himself a cool guy conversant with current tastes, and my ignorance of pop culture made him wince. Once, in the Yankee Stadium press box, he glanced over my shoulder at a lead I had just typed, grabbed a copy pencil, and yelled, "I can't stand it!" I'd written "hep"—as in "hep cat," a term that went out before I was born—instead of "hip," which I surely was not. When he arranged a two-day getaway for us in Las Vegas between the time the Mets left Los Angeles and the Yankees arrived at the start of the 1968 baseball season, I convinced him to forego catching a set by Afro-Cuban percussionist Mongo Santamaria for a show starring the hopelessly un-hip singer Vikki Carr. I also failed as his accomplice in the casino where I dropped $50 about as fast as I could and fled.

Vecsey had a more serious outlook on life and sports. The son of a sportswriter, he and his artist wife Marianne were raising a family on Long Island not far from Hofstra, where he'd gone to college. Vecsey also saw sports as reflective of the human condition rather than apart from it. But while Ziegel favored clever leads and snappy one-liners, Vecsey's work reflected a more profound sensibility and subtle sense of humor. In time, that would lead to one book with Bob Welch, a pitcher who overcame alcoholism, and another (after he left sports to cover Appalachia for the *New York Times*) with Loretta Lynn: the best-selling

Coal Miner's Daughter. He eventually returned to sports to share the "Sports of the Times" column, once the province of Red Smith.

Like Ziegel, Vecsey was a generous and gentle mentor, and on one late spring day in the press box at Shea Stadium, he became more. He bequeathed me his job. "This is not public knowledge yet, so please keep it to yourself," he confided, "but I'm going to the *Times*. There will be an opening at *Newsday*. I've told them, so feel free to apply." I did and for one day in July 1968 I felt like a bride courted by two suitors. Stan Asimov, *Newsday's* editorial administrator (and brother of the noted science-fiction writer Isaac Asimov) called to say the job was mine. Stan had overruled the sports editor who found me brash and unseasoned. It was not an unreasonable assessment, but Asimov considered luring a young talent from the upstart *Suffolk Sun* worth the risk. He did warn me not to expect the level of assignments I'd had at the *Sun* at least to start. I said I was inclined to accept the offer but asked for time to let the *Sun* know.

"I hate to lose you," *Sun* sports editor Larry Conroy said, extending his hand. He alerted higher-ups and that led to a counter-offer. "Pat Putnam is leaving for *Sports Illustrated* to cover boxing," *Sun* editor-in-chief Cort Anderson said, "and we'd like you to replace him." I could become the youngest sports columnist in America. There was also a raise involved. I said yes, we shook hands, and after giving Conroy the news I went back to my desk. But as the day wore on my doubts increased. Was I really ready to be a full-time columnist? And what about the *Sun's* viability? Still hampered by mechanical issues, the paper did not seem to be catching on. Not long before, when Conroy and I were alone in the sports department, he told me, "We're not making it, Ed. Nobody's reading us. We're not getting any letters. At the *Trib* we'd get tons of mail. Here, weeks go by without a single letter from a reader."

One newspaper had already folded out from under me. Even with the increase, my salary as a *Sun* columnist would be $10 a week lower than what *Newsday* had offered me to start near the bottom, an indication of the two papers' financial standing. I called Asimov to alert him to the *Sun's* counter-offer and confess that I was torn. I was not looking for more money from *Newsday*, I assured him, but just wondering what he thought. "You have to think of the future, Ed," he told me, "and frankly it really shouldn't be a very tough decision." I knew he had an ulterior motive, but I also knew he was right. Two hours after accepting the counteroffer, I knocked on Anderson's door to say I was going to *Newsday* after all. The *Sun* folded eighteen months later.

24

Vince and Paul

AUGUST 1968
Green Bay, Wisconsin

I spent my first week at *Newsday* editing copy and writing headlines, a chore meant more for me to get acclimated than as a comedown. Even seasoned sportswriters there worked the desk in addition to covering games, a protocol that optimized staff resources and also gave writers an appreciation of what it took to turn our copy into the next day's sports section. That was one way *Newsday* was different. Another: Baseball writers assigned to cover the Mets and Yankees swapped beats at mid-season. The extra effort to catch up was viewed as more than worth the benefit of limiting relationships that might turn writers into fans or dissuade them from reporting stories out of concern for a player's feelings.

The paper underscored this point by calling us sports reporters, not sportswriters. Our job was to report on the teams we covered, not support or sympathize with them. Close ties to our subjects could threaten to compromise coverage more than a free meal or an extra ticket ever did, although *Newsday* was also ahead of its time on that score, too. To avoid the appearance of conflict, we did not write stories for game programs or serve as official scorers as writers at the other papers did. None of us would ever have to explain to the third-baseman why he had ruled a hot grounder that skipped past him an error. It was a far cry from my days at the *Suffolk Sun,* where the New York Jets and Long Island Ducks flew me to road games.

After a couple of weeks sports editor Ed Comerford called me into his office. He was sending me to Ohio and Wisconsin to cover two of the hottest topics in the National Football League that summer, each involving a legendary figure: the return of Paul Brown as owner-coach of the Cincinnati Bengals, an expansion franchise in the American Football League, and Vince Lombardi's departure from the sidelines after coaching the Green Bay Packers to victory in the first two Super Bowls. Comerford was skeptical about Brown's ability to come back and Lombardi's willingness to let go, and wanted me to discern and report how each of them was adjusting to his new role.

A remarkable innovator who built the Cleveland Browns into a dominant force in pro football after an outstanding high school and college career, Brown devised the playbook, football's version of orchestral sheet music detailing the specific role of each player on every play. He was also the first to study film of opponents' prior games, hire specialized position coaches, amass detailed dossiers on college prospects, and design protective facemasks. The closest visionary pro football had to Branch Rickey (who had designed baseball's first batting helmet), Brown signed such stars as Marion Motley and Bill Willis when few black players were in the league. But after a so-so season in 1963, a new owner of the team he'd founded and bore his name sent Brown packing.

Unlike Brown, Lombardi left the sidelines at the top of his game and on his own terms, remaining as general manager and appointing a trusted assistant to succeed him. And I soon realized these were two different situations in other ways, too. A Bengals' public relations man seemed pleased by my call and said he would arrange for me to stay in a dorm room at Wilmington College in the southeast corner of Ohio where the Bengals were training. The reception in Green Bay was somewhat cooler. No dice on staying with the team at St. Norbert College in De Pere, thirty miles south of Green Bay. The Packers did not let outsiders get that close. Like the other writers, I was welcome at team meals and would have access to players and coaches after practice.

A week later I landed in Dayton and picked up a rental car for the fifty-mile drive to Wilmington. Over the next two days I immersed myself in the training camp and made a point of connecting with writers from newspapers in Cincinnati and Dayton. That yielded some valuable perspective and eventually a jackpot. One of them had recorded Paul Brown's opening talk to 120 prospects on the first day of training camp. I also watched drills, listened to banter, and interviewed players and assistant coaches. But I knew the key interview would be with Brown himself. And that almost became a disaster. Our conversation was uneventful until I started getting to the point, reeling off a series of criticisms of Brown at the end of his time in Cleveland, including the assertion that he was so wed to his once-innovative system he refused to adjust to change. "They said that you'd lost touch with your players," I intoned, ending with a flourish that made me sound too much like the bombastic sportscaster Howard Cosell, "that the game had passed you by."

Brown sat silently for a moment and then said, in a soft voice, "Well, I'll say this for you, young man. You certainly know how to hurt a guy."

Damn, I've blown it! I thought. *This is a giant, a man who created sports dynasties. And I've come all the way from Long Island to insult him. Is this the end of my interview and my story?*

Just then there was a knock on the door. A quarterback injured at practice that day needed permission to see a medical specialist in Cincinnati. Brown excused himself and returned several minutes later when he explained the intrusion and then said, "Now where were we?" It was time for a journalistic "Hail Mary" play.

"Coach, you seemed insulted by my last question and I want to explain," I said. "Now, I know Bill Wallace was here a couple of weeks ago. This is what he wrote in the paper," and I pulled out a clipping from the *New York Times* and read Wallace's words:

"What pro football wants to know is which Brown directs the Bengals—the suave genius of the nineteen-forties and nineteen-fifties or the intractable sourpuss of the nineteen-sixties who lost touch with his players and reality? The answer would seem to be a little bit of both."

"Now, I don't know for sure but I'm guessing you and Bill had a lovely conversation. I know you both go way back. But I would much rather ask the tough questions face to face than avoid them and risk insulting you in print." Brown nodded and said, "Go ahead. Ask your questions."

Our conversation spilled into dinner and he invited me to join him and his wife at his table in the college cafeteria. Then, at ten o'clock that night as I typed some notes, there was a knock at my door. It was Paul Brown. "I thought of something else," he started and then, catching sight of an old *Sport Magazine* clipping about him on my desk, shook his head, smiled, and said, "You really do your homework, don't you?"

I filed a four-part series that received major play in *Newsday* and also national attention twice over—when it was distributed to papers across the country by a syndicate and again when *Pro Football Digest Magazine* reprinted it in its entirety. From the start I tried to focus on what had changed and what had not as Brown began anew at an age when most individuals retired.

At one end of the practice field, quarterback John Stofa called signals, lifted the football from an imaginary center and slammed it into fullback Tom Smiley's gut. "No, no, Tom, you got to slide across there," shouted Rick Forzano, an assistant coach for the Cincinnati Bengals, "You're stopping and starting again. You've got to sli-i-ide."

Stofa and Smiley started back to their positions to try the draw play one more time. A slender, almost slight man in tan slacks and T-shirt greeted them at the "scrimmage" line. Unlike Forzano, he did not shout. What he said was inaudible from the sideline only 15 paces away. Then the man was off again, walking back toward the other end of the field where assistant coaches Tom Bass and Jack Donaldson were drilling their men in how to defense the draw play.

Paul Brown glanced toward the sideline and apparently became aware that his unobtrusive travels around the field had been observed. He took a slight detour. "You want to see something?" Brown said. "Look at the two old gals sittin' up there in the bleachers with their straw hats on. They've been up there every day since we started. You know, just before, one of them yelled down, 'Hey, that man's playing too wide.'"

His friends were always entranced by Paul Brown's charm; his enemies enraged by its effectiveness. It is still there. And so is every other facet of the man who won 11 divisional championships with the Cleveland Browns and was fired five years ago because, his critics charged, the game had passed him by.

That first installment allowed Brown to respond in his own words:

"Did the game pass me by?" Brown repeated very softly. "I guess that's for you to decide. I know they all wrote that. But you know, my last season in Cleveland we had a winning year. I haven't changed. If coaching today means going out and drinking and carousing with your players, then maybe the game has passed me by. A man has to do a job in a certain way. I like to think we developed something in Cleveland that had nothing to do with winning and losing. I think we developed a set of principles. A man's principles don't change."

That set up the second part, which was Paul Brown's elocution of those principles in the talk to his team. Part 3 quoted coaches and players and part 4 assessed the team's chances and how Brown was likely to handle the inevitable string of defeats any expansion team suffers, concluding with an anecdote about a local newsman who called over to him from the sidelines during practice seeking an interview. "Can you stay till after practice?" replied Brown, and when the reporter said he couldn't Brown walked over and spoke with him. "Can you imagine Vince Lombardi doing that?" a bystander asked. "I can't imagine *Paul Brown* doing that," another responded.

And then it was off to Green Bay, where I had a very different approach in mind. My idea was to spend several days watching Lombardi and talking to just about everybody *but* him because I felt he was unlikely to diverge from what he'd expressed in a sheaf of clippings I had. I checked into a motel in Green Bay and drove the 30 miles to St. Norbert. Since it was Sunday there was no practice. An assistant coach I happened upon, Mike McCormick, said that coaches and reporters gathered for a cocktail hour every day at 5 in a dorm that served as Packers' summer headquarters.

By the time I arrived Lombardi was holding court in a corner of the room. Principal topic of the day was not football but golf because the final round of the PGA championship was on a television at one end of the room and his friend Julius Boros was winning. I hung back, pondering whether to say hello. No need. Lombardi had spotted *me*. I watched him whisper to a colleague and gesture in my direction, igniting a chain reaction. One assistant asked another and another until the question reached McCormick, who sent word of my identity back in the other direction. Then I could see Lombardi asking his friend and biographer, the journalist Bill Heinz, about me and getting a blank look. That was when he looked over and said in his familiar boom, "Hello, I don't believe we've met!"

I introduced myself without explaining my exact mission. My presence didn't escape Lombardi's notice again at the training table for breakfast Monday morning at dawn. "Is *he* staying here?" I overheard him ask a press aide. As planned, I did my best to stay out of his view and we did not exchange another word that day or the next two. I interviewed the new coach, Phil Bengtson, as well as quarterback Bart Starr and a slew of Packer greats from a dynasty about to fade, chatted with beat reporters as I had done in Ohio and mingled with locals in town.

Almost everyone agreed Lombardi would find it difficult to adjust to his new behind-the-scenes role, reinforcing what I thought I detected from watching him. When Lombardi hosted University of Arkansas coach Frank Broyles and his staff at practice one morning, the offense was going through a drill. He diagrammed the blocking scheme and then said, "They've put in a new wrinkle this year. They're smarter than I am!" sounding like the don in a gangster movie as the others forced an obligatory laugh. Another day, with the team practicing in a fierce downpour, few fans were there. But a block in the distance I spotted a stolid figure in a rain slicker standing motionless and watching intently. It was Lombardi.

By Wednesday I was ready to head home, armed with evidence that Lombardi was already uncomfortable out of coaching (something affirmed a year later when he left to coach the Washington Redskins before his death at 57 from cancer in 1970). But I stayed for the daily five o'clock gathering. I was just a bit smug about how much I had gleaned without speaking to Lombardi and wanted to thank him for the hospitality the team had extended to an interloper from New York, fully expecting that I would have to remind him of who I was.

The usual coterie of coaches and writers surrounded him and I waited for an opening. The television was tuned to *The Mike Douglas Show*. When Douglas introduced movie star George Hamilton, who was often in the news as First Daughter Lynda Baines Johnson's escort, I heard a voice boom out, "My god, that guy's hair is almost as long as Ed Hershey's!" It was Lombardi's way of letting me know that he was still totally engaged. Far from forgetting my name, he knew what I was up to all along.

25

Pied Piper of Peace

When the phone rang at midnight I might have guessed it was my old college friend Fred Carlin. Fred had awakened me at a similar hour after Bobby Kennedy's shooting two months before to say, "Turn on your television." Now his opener was, "I'm in Long Beach. Can you get over here? There's someone here you ought to meet."

Readers Digest used to run a feature called "My Most Unforgettable Character." Fred would have been high on my list. He led the university's Young Republicans (a club that probably never had a quorum), started a fraternity (when he was not invited to join one) and ran for student body president (amassing a vote total barely cracking double digits). Yet he never seemed daunted or discouraged, so perpetually aswirl in original if implausible ideas that the last one was barely out of his mouth when he started formulating the next. Just after graduation Fred had the last laugh. He was appointed assistant commissioner of the city's Department of Markets, a reward for co-managing one of newly elected New York Mayor John Lindsay's local campaign storefronts on Church Avenue in Brooklyn. Three years later, when Fred was volunteering for Governor Nelson Rockefeller's re-election campaign, he surprised me—and startled my colleagues—driving up to Lincoln Farm Camp in the Catskills in a panel truck festooned with cartoons of fish praising Rockefeller's environmental record. Fred had driven 120 miles just to show me "how cool" the truck looked.

The man Fred introduced to me in 1968 in Long Beach was not a Republican but a Democrat—and not just *any* Democrat. Allard Lowenstein had already made history, turning what seemed like a quixotic exercise into a surge of opposition to the Vietnam War, founding the

"Dump Johnson" movement, aimed at keeping Lyndon Johnson off the 1968 ticket, and recruiting Minnesota Senator Eugene McCarthy to run for president. McCarthy's strong second-place showing in the New Hampshire primary precipitated LBJ's shocking withdrawal and lured Bobby Kennedy into the race. By then Lowenstein was running for office himself, having moved to Long Island to seek the Democratic nomination for an open Congressional seat.

The anti-war campaign was the latest of a string of idealistic endeavors at the time that included undercover work exposing atrocities by South Africa's Apartheid rulers and playing a pivotal role in the Mississippi "Freedom Summer" in 1964, a volunteer civil rights project to register African Americans historically excluded from voting there. But local party leaders saw Lowenstein as an interloper better suited to Manhattan (where he'd sought a Congressional nomination in 1966). They tried to pre-empt him by endorsing a national leader of Reform Judaism who was a vocal critic of the war but Lowenstein persisted. He, his wife Jenny, and their infant son moved into a home a block from the ocean in Long Beach and the race was on. Bobby Kennedy's assassination cast so deep a pall that only the most driven Democrats turned out for New York's primary a week later and Lowenstein won 56% of a low vote. That pitted him against Mason Hampton, Jr., a Conservative running on the Republican line in a deal crafted by Nassau County GOP leader Joseph Margiotta in exchange for Conservative Party support of several of his candidates for the state legislature.

When I arrived an hour after Fred Carlin's call, Lowenstein was slumped on a couch bantering with several young volunteers. He had Coke-bottle thick glasses, spoke in a nasal tone and seemed disheveled, but it did not take long to detect the intellect behind such remarkable accomplishments before his 40th birthday and the charisma that turned him into a pied piper for peace. He was witty and yet self-effacing, intense but disarming, and whip smart without sounding arrogant. With RFK dead, McCarthy's candidacy over, and Hubert Humphrey a damaged nominee in the aftermath of the riotous Democrat National Convention in Chicago, Lowenstein personified the peace movement. Long Island, he told me, was a perfect place to make the case against the war just because it was assumed he could not sway such a Middle-American electorate.

"A liberal," Hampton told *Newsday,* "is a Democrat with his brains kicked out." He dismissed Lowenstein as out of step with the district, which spanned the South Shore from the largely Jewish and affluent Five Towns through predominantly blue-collar Baldwin, Freeport, Oceanside, and Rockville Centre (where the Roman Catholic Arch-diocese was headquartered) to post-war developments in Merrick, Wantagh, Seaford, Bellmore and Massapequa. The race became a phil-osophical showdown and young volunteers who had shortened their hair and shed hippie attire to be "neat and clean for Gene" McCarthy arrived by the busload on weekends from campuses as distant as Har-vard and Notre Dame to bunk in with local families and knock on doors for Lowenstein.

It was inappropriate for a journalist, even a sportswriter, to be involved in partisan politics. I knew that. But with two grievous assas-sinations and the grotesque scenes in Chicago fresh in my mind and war still raging in southeast Asia two years after the Mel Dubin peace campaign in Brooklyn, I opted for what I considered the greater good. "I'll help if I can," I told Lowenstein, "but anything I do will have to be under the radar." He suggested I talk to Nancy Steffen, who had come from California to handle communications. A 1965 graduate of Stan-ford, where Lowenstein taught, Steffen made it clear that she was no wide-eyed groupie but a (modestly) paid staffer. I gave her a rundown on who was who at *Newsday* and reiterated that I could not involve myself in any overt work, which might have been a relief for her given how prone the candidate was to blurt out to people he encountered on the campaign trail that they might help with PR.

Lowenstein insisted on approving any campaign literature, a pro-viso that turned me into his temporary chauffeur one morning in September—a chore that threatened to out me at *Newsday* and nearly caused me untold embarrassment. I had designed a brochure to appeal to moderate Republicans entitled, "There Is No Republican Running for Congress in the 5th District This Year." Lowenstein was returning the next morning from visits to Harvard and Wellesley and Steffen suggested that I pick him up at Grand Central Station and drive him to a couple of kaffeeklatsches so I could run it by him in the car. Lowenstein was in characteristic disarray when I spotted him, carrying a satchel overflowing with $5 and $10 bills he'd collected at his campus stops before sleeping on a friend's couch and catching a pre-dawn train from Boston. We stopped at a restaurant his family owned in Manhattan for him to freshen up. "This is good," he said after scanning my draft as we headed for Long Island. "Let's go with it."

When we arrived at our first stop in Seaford at the eastern edge of the district there was a familiar face in the room, someone Steffen had not mentioned. *Newsday* columnist Harvey Aronson, a favorite of the younger journalists at the paper, would be spending part of the day with Lowenstein. I waited for a chance to take him aside to explain my presence. "Don't worry, kid," he said with a wink and a smile. "I won't say a word." Patrick O'Neal, a handsome silver-haired man of a certain age with a deep voice who seemed to attract more attention than the candidate, was also there. Before we started out for the next stop in Lawrence at the opposite end of the district, Lowenstein pulled me aside. "Ed," he asked, "can you drive down with Patrick so I can spend some time alone with Harvey?"

For the next half-hour O'Neal pontificated on politics, the Vietnam War and civil rights. I wondered just who he was. There were notable names in the campaign, people like Harold Ickes, Jr., son of FDR's Interior Secretary, and Franklin Delano Roosevelt III, whose grandmother Eleanor had befriended Lowenstein. Was O'Neal an ad exec, a book publisher, or some other progressive business leader opposed to the war? Every time we stopped at a light and I was about to ask he was in mid-sentence and then the light turned green and I was back negotiating traffic on Sunrise Highway. So I never got the question out.

When we reached our destination and Lowenstein and O'Neal sat down to engage the women there, I asked Aronson about him. "That's Patrick O'Neal," he said. "I know his name," I said, "but who is he?" Aronson laughed and started reeling off some of O'Neal's stage, screen, and television credits—opposite Bette Davis on Broadway in Tennessee Williams' *The Night of the Iguana*, with Sean Connery, Joanne Woodward and Jean Seberg on screen in *A Fine Madness*, and all over TV. I just about shuddered realizing how close I had come to asking a prominent actor: "And what do you do for a living, Mister O'Neal?"

As the campaign progressed I was frustrated by my limited opportunities to contribute, especially given the sense of excitement building and the focused leadership of operatives not much older than I was, like Kirby Jones from the University of North Carolina, Paul Offner from Princeton, and Paul Tully from Yale. It did not escape me that they were devoting themselves to more useful endeavors than explaining how the Packers might fare without Vince Lombardi. Then, reading a review of a documentary called *Goal!* about England's victory in the 1966 World Cup I had an inspiration. Why not stage a sports event? Lining up some athletes to endorse Lowenstein might be one way to crack the stereotype that a candidate opposed to the war was a wimp.

I secured the rights for a one-time showing of the film and with the campaign's approval booked a theater in the heart of the district. The first player I approached, Jim Bouton of the Yankees, immediately agreed to appear. Then I went to Bill Bradley, who had once lectured me on separating sports and politics. After asking more questions of me than I ever had of him, Bradley said yes and volunteered to bring another Knick, the future hall-of-fame coach Phil Jackson. Attendees said they loved the movie, the players seemed pleased and the candidate was eloquent, but my *Sports Night for Lowenstein* was a bust at the box office. Maybe it was the heavy rain that night, the poor promotion or the lack of wide appeal, but the theater was three-quarters empty. I came to believe that the nature of suburban Long Island as a confederation of separate locales with no core made it hard to lure people from one town to another. Embarrassed for those I had involved and worried that I had frittered away campaign resources, I showed up the next day with a personal check for $250. "At least this will offset some of the costs," I said.

When Humphrey came to Long Island to campaign on the Saturday before Election Day, he rode down Hempstead Turnpike with Lowenstein in a gesture of rapprochement designed to help them both. That evening at Lowenstein headquarters everyone wanted to know what each had said to the other. Lowenstein called their conversation fairly innocuous. Then he started to giggle. "When we reached Hofstra and he saw the ugly dormitory towers, Hubert turned to me and said, 'Did federal funds go to building *those?*'" We all laughed and three nights later we could hardly stop laughing when final returns gave Lowenstein a 3,000-vote victory out of almost 200,000 votes cast, touching off a raucous celebration. Nobody seemed to care that Richard Nixon had just been elected President of the United States.

Lowenstein served one term before losing re-election in a revamped district gerrymandered to defeat him in another deal orchestrated by Margiotta. A number of unsuccessful runs for Congress in various districts followed and the last, in 1976, proved one too many for Jenny, who divorced him. In 1980 a deranged former protégé, who might well have been in the basement the night we first met, assassinated Lowenstein in his Manhattan law office. I was among 2,000 mourners at Central Synagogue in Manhattan where he was eulogized by a spectrum of figures from conservative columnist William F. Buckley to Senator Ted Kennedy, speaking at yet another funeral in the aftermath of an assassination.

"I always thought that, somehow he was too good for this world," Kennedy said, "and in the end the world broke him because he was the last friend left of a man scorned by everyone else." At the end of the service folksingers Peter, Paul & Mary and Harry Chapin sang "Amazing Grace."

26

One Hot Summer

Men walked on the moon. Rockers rollicked at Woodstock. Ted Kennedy drove poor Mary Jo Kopechne off the Chappaquiddick Bridge. Gays rioted at the Stonewall Inn in Greenwich Village, launching the gay rights movement. The Mets won the World Series. And, perhaps most improbably of all in that signature summer of '69, I ran a mile on a broken ankle in combat boots in Georgia in 7 minutes and 35 seconds.

Nearly as ineffective a teacher in the suburbs as I had been in the inner city but still thirty months short of aging out of the military draft, I had signed up for a spot in a U.S. Army reserve unit at Fort Tilden in Rockaway, Queens. It was a long shot. There was a waiting list of 2,000-plus. But in 1968 with their initial six-year commitments fulfilled, almost every man left the unit to avoid exposure to a call-up for Vietnam. Seeking to replenish its force, the unit found that most young men on the waiting list had been drafted, enlisted, found another unit, or aged out; my name was reached in days. After passing a physical I became Private E-1 Edward Hershey, 77th ArCom, U. S. Army Reserve Signal Corps.

That meant spending one weekend a month on a windswept beachfront so bone chilling in winter I wore as many layers under my government-issue khakis as I had for football games in sub-freezing weather. We marched and stood around and marched some more under the direction of two likeable sergeants, one short and Syrian-American, the other tall and African-American, each logging time for extra cash and pension credits. One Saturday the tall one was missing and our first sergeant, a gruff Brooklyn beat cop, made an uncustomary appearance on the drill field. "I have to tell youze sometin'," he said. "Sergeant Fuller won't be here no more. He got caught in a conveyor belt where he worked at the post office and died." Then he walked back to the orderly room in one of the rickety World War I-era buildings dotting the base. "So much for long goodbyes," I whispered to the weekend warrior next to me.

These drills were peppered with reminders that unexcused absences could lead to activation and Vietnam. So when a plane returning me from a Jamaican vacation on a Friday evening was diverted to Miami because of bad weather, I had the airline wire word that I would be late. "They called your name this morning," someone in the ranks said when I arrived. The last thing you ever want to hear in the Army is your name. I assumed it was about my lateness but the orderly room clerk said no, my orders for active duty training had come through. I was to fly to South Carolina on Memorial Day weekend for orientation at Fort Jackson and then up to six months at Fort Gordon in Augusta, Ga., starting with eight weeks of basic training. I informed *Newsday*, gave my landlord notice, and arranged for my mother to move my car twice a week to adhere to alternate-side parking rules.

All that was left was to call Marilyn. "I'll write every day," she promised. We'd met that spring in Florida where I covered several weeks of Yankees spring training to prepare me to fill in when *Newsday's* baseball beat writers were off. The Yankees had traveled from their home base in Fort Lauderdale to St. Petersburg for an exhibition game against the Mets and then hosted a dinner that night at a Cuban restaurant in the Ybor City section of Tampa for writers covering both teams. Back at the hotel I peeked into the bar and spotted her—tall, attractive, and alone. She had been Bing Devine's secretary when he was general manager of the St. Louis Cardinals and followed him to New York when the Mets hired him in 1966. She was also older—33, she said at first, shaving five years. We spent the night in my room, but it was not a one-night stand. Back in New York we picked up where we'd left off. I called her "my Mrs. Robinson" after Anne Bancroft's role in *The Graduate* (1967).

As if I needed a reminder of what lay ahead, one of my final assignments was the Mets' annual exhibition against the cadets at West Point. The week before, the Yankees sent me off in style, flashing this scoreboard message during a game against the Oakland Athletics at Yankee Stadium:

GOOD LUCK

TO NEWSDAY'S GI,

ED HERSHEY

At twenty-five, I may have been the May half of a May-December romance back home, but I would be the old guy in my basic-training unit, a point driven home by a beefy fellow in the next seat on the plane to South Carolina. As we lifted off and banked he clutched my wrist and whispered, "Is it supposed to do that?" He had never flown.

We landed in pitch black and were herded into an Army bus for the ride to Fort Jackson where two shrieking sergeants took turns separating our minds from the civilian lives we'd left.

"Excuse me, sir" one recruit started to ask and got no further.

"*Sir?!*" one of them screamed. "Don't call me 'sir.' I ain't no candy-ass officer!"

The next day we got uniforms, immunization shots, and military haircuts as well as early affirmation of a time-honored maxim about volunteering in the military. "Anyone here speak French?" a sergeant asked. When a half-dozen hands shot up he had his KP (kitchen patrol) detail. This was called "zero week," because it did not count toward the eight weeks of basic training. My first chance to demonstrate how ill-equipped I was for military service—one of many—came that evening when it was my turn to polish the floor in our barracks with an electronic buffer that bucked and pinned me against a wall 20 feet away. "Y'all'll catch on," a fellow recruit said above the laughter after rescuing me. "It's just a matter of maintaining leverage."

On the fourth day, an olive-colored oven on wheels bused us 80 miles to Fort Gordon just over the state line in Augusta, Georgia. At least the clock was ticking now, but for me time threatened to stand still. To complete basic training you had to pass a five-skill physical proficiency test. Each segment—up-and-back arm-over-arm on a row of monkey bars, a run-dodge-jump agility course, a 50-yard man-carry, a 50-yard chin-to-the-ground crawl, and a mile run—was graded on a 100-point scale with an aggregate score of 300 needed to pass. On my first try I scored 112.

That earned me an interview with a captain on the other side of the base who looked down at a form, then up at me and declared, "Private Hershey, I think we are going to have to recycle you." It was the worst possible news because it would add two weeks to my time under the 100-plus-degree Georgia sun. "Sir," I said, "I've never done any of this kind of activity before, but I think I can get the hang of it. If I'm not making progress you can always recycle me in a couple of weeks, but I'd like the chance to try with my unit." Judging from the orderly room sergeant's look back at Charlie Company, no recruit sent off to be recycled had ever returned. And while I would never again encounter the officer who gave me a second chance, I thought of him a lot as I pushed into uncharted territory in the ensuing six weeks.

Our platoon included reservists, draftees, and enlistees who volunteered for three years instead of two so they could pick a military occupational specialty (M.O.S. in Army lingo) that might spare them infantry duty in Vietnam. It was also a relatively egalitarian refuge in a country torn by racial strife, a veritable agglomeration of diversity: West Coast surfers talking Porsche models, Puerto Rico draftees chattering in Spanish, and college grads angling for safe assignments. We reservists were the privileged ones. We would be back home in a few months. We were also the largest group, creating a cultural divide with noncommissioned officers who had little experience with New Yorkers. The funniest example, if anything could be funny about a lecture on rifle safety in searing midday heat, came when a drill sergeant just back from Vietnam sought to jolt us from our stupor with a trick question. "Who likes to eat pussy?" he drawled. Hands shot up. "Now I *know* you're not paying attention." He cackled. "I'll ask again. Who likes to eat pussy?" When a majority raised our hands even higher, he just shook his head.

Two Southern teenagers named Graves were in our platoon. One was ebony, the other whiter than white, but I realized when we took a written quiz one day that they had more in common than a name. Neither could read. Yet when we reached the mechanical portion of the test both Graves boys sailed through and I was the dumbfounded one, unable to make any sense of a display of diagrams. How desperate Uncle Sam had to be for able bodies, I thought, to conscript functional illiterates even as some in our company wondered how I ever passed an Army physical.

The heat could feel almost unbearable but for someone as out of shape as I was it could serve as an equalizer. A fellow next to me in formation lost consciousness with heatstroke and went over like a felled tree. He was a college basketball player and I was the last one chosen for every street game I ever played, but he was down and I was standing. I could eliminate carbohydrates and sugar and drink water and black coffee to shed weight, but increasing my endurance and strength would take more than a change in diet. Two weeks of daily jogs to the rifle range jumpstarted that turnaround. They were easy enough up front, but when gaps opened those of us down the line had to run at full speed to close ranks, often pushing me past a level of exertion I thought possible. By week five, I took another test and broke 260— below 300 but a far cry from 112. Nobody was talking about recycling me anymore.

I checked my ego and did everything I was told, even if my subconscious resisted. Once I awakened from a convincing predawn dream about home only to realize where I was. I trundled off the top bunk, dressed, and walked outside in time to catch the only breeze there would be on another scorching day. "This too shall pass," my mother wrote. I appreciated the encouragement, but my secret weapon was Marilyn, who proved true to her word. She wrote every day (sometimes twice) and was always there when I could get to a phone. "Aw, you're going to make it through," she said in her Midwestern twang,

"I just know you are." When the Mets were in Atlanta to play the Braves July 4 and I got a pass, Marilyn flew down for the weekend. My baseball writers' card gave me access to the field, where I renewed acquaintances with players, writers, and broadcasters. I'd alerted my mother that I would be at the game and she heard Bob Murphy mention me during the telecast. It was the first thing I thought about every time I heard him on the air over the next 35 years.

Back at Fort Gordon I was psyched, running on my own after dinner, losing weight and gaining confidence. Then one morning I stepped into a rut, turned an ankle, and crumpled to the ground. My combat boots offered a level of protection from further damage, but each time I thought it had healed the ankle gave way again, and I worried that it would collapse on the day of the test. A soldier from Atlanta who had studied athletic training volunteered to tape me on the morning of the test, which was mercifully cool and drizzly. Knowing how far I had come, just about everyone in the platoon was rooting for me.

I scored well on the crawl and the run-dodge-jump, but lost ground on the bars when a scorer said I'd released too soon. When I started to protest that he'd shortchanged me, he gave me a weird look and a compatriot pulled me away, lest I be docked for insubordination. You were never supposed to tell the Army it was wrong. The man-carry presented a different sort of injustice. Seven weeks earlier I'd been paired with a fellow my own weight, a bull of a guy from Buffalo. The problem was that he was still that weight and I was down 50 pounds. Somehow, with him exhorting me every step, I managed to carry him the 50 yards without losing ground on the score sheet. The mile would decide, and I ran 7:35, a personal best.

There were two prolonged ovations when the results were announced, one for the lone trainee who maxed the test with a 500, the other for my 308. Even the drill sergeant cracked a smile. Two days before, we had been given the afternoon off to view fuzzy images of an American walking on the moon, on the television in the barracks. It was, I told myself, the second most improbable achievement that week. Only I did not yet know just how improbable. The next morning I went to sick call and X-rays revealed I'd run that mile on a broken ankle. It was already healing, so I was not put in a cast, but bandaged and ordered on light duty with no marching, KP, or other work for the remainder of basic training and two weeks beyond. Some things do work out. Had I gone to sick call before the test I would have been recycled for medical reasons.

I was to report for 16 weeks of signal corps training, which was why we'd been sent to Fort Gordon, home of its Southeastern Signal School, rather than a closer base like Fort Dix in New Jersey. First, though, was another "zero week" for in-processing. That gave me an inspiration. Who would miss me if I flew home to pick up my car? I recruited an accomplice to share the driving and we signed blank leave forms ("basket passes" in military parlance), flew home for a brief weekend reunion with our families, and drove back.

This was at the height of the war and the plane was filled with soldiers. Sitting next to me was a slight bespectacled recent Brown University graduate who had just completed advanced infantry train-ing and after two weeks at home would report to a base in Califor-nia en route to Vietnam. I wondered how prepared he could be. The prior eight weeks had shaped me up but hardly trained me for combat, something driven home the day I qualified for hand grenade use. I had to arm and throw a live grenade from a pit with a sergeant peek-ing over the edge to grade me on pulling the pin, placing my finger on the trigger and tossing the explosive device with a kind of shot-put motion. Suddenly, I had company in the pit. The sergeant dove in as clumps of Georgia clay rained on us. "Your form was good," he said, still shaking, "but you need to throw it a lot farther." He passed me anyway, probably to spare a future scorer from danger. I related this to the Brown grad. "I guess you really get to it in AIT?" I asked. "No," he responded quietly. "Not at all." I often wondered whether he survived the war.

The audacity of forging a weekend pass was more than matched by my next stunt. The day after I returned to the base I heard someone call me and turned to see an unfamiliar figure in a sergeant's uniform.

"I'm Ed Arangio. We were on *Seawanhaka* together at L.I.U. I was a freshman when you were a senior." He had enlisted after college to get an MOS in communications and had a plum assignment as the signal school's public relations man. "If you can get out of your signal corps training," he said, "I can arrange for my captain to have you work for us. Officially, you'd be an OJT clerk. You'd write press releases for eight weeks—that's standard time for on-the-job training—and then go home."

"I may have a way to make that happen," I told him. Because signal corps work involved color-coded wires, color-blindness was a disqualifier. It was rumored that anyone discovered faking the condition would be harshly punished, but two months in uniform had imbued me with a healthy skepticism about Army rumors and I enlisted the help of the fellow testing me after noting the name imprinted above his shirt pocket: G-O-O-D-M-A-N.

"Where are you from?" I asked.

"Brooklyn," he said.

"I lived on Ocean Parkway," I said.

"Ocean Avenue," he said with a wink, adding, "Just say what I tell you to see in these pictures."

So instead of spending four months climbing utility poles I wrote press releases about soldiers who received medals for valor and I returned to civilian life after just eight weeks. The soldiers in my dorm room had recently returned from Southeast Asia or were waiting to go. Neither group was inclined to take anything at Fort Gordon seriously. "When you've been through what I have," one returnee explained, "this is pretty Mickey Mouse. I mean, what are they going to do to me if I screw up, send me to 'Nam?"

That stuck with me, and I suggested a story for the base newspaper about how commanders fostered morale and enforced discipline in such an environment. The four colonels I interviewed were earnest and forthright. "There's hope for the Army yet," I told Arangio, handing him the piece a day before out-processing. That winter I saw him at a basketball game when he was home on leave. "I have to tell you," he said, "you really got us jammed." Higher-ups had pulled the paper from the presses because of my article, and he and his boss were called on the carpet for even raising the idea that it might be difficult to maintain morale or discipline. I told him how sorry I was and thought to myself that I had been too optimistic. The Army was beyond hope.

My mother (left) emigrated from
Belarus with her brother and sister.

My mother's father and the stepmother
who awaited her in Brooklyn.

My father, the bar mitzvah boy,
could be studious to a fault.

My father and aunt celebrating their parents 50th wedding anniversary.

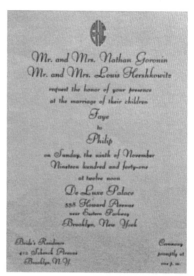

Newlyweds Faye and Philip were still Faygel and Fishel to family.

Proud parents with baby Edward on Ocean Parkway.

Grandma defied arthritis to collect goods for Holocaust survivors.

An unlikely cowpoke on Halloween
at the playground on Avenue P.

Nobody ever called our apartment
house Parkway Terrace.

Phil Hershey was at home
in Coney Island. Faye loved
the Catskills.

I posed a good game but was hitless
in the West Highway Little League.

My sister Nancy's arrival helped
loosen my mom's apron strings.

When the occasion called for it,
my parents dressed up quite nicely.

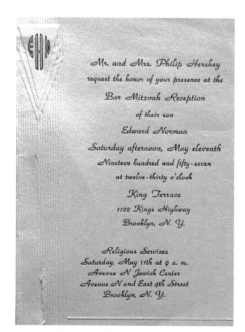

Mr. and Mrs. Philip Hershey
request the honor of your presence at the
Bar Mitzvah Reception
of their son
Edward Norman
Saturday afternoon, May eleventh
Nineteen hundred and fifty-seven
at twelve-thirty o'clock

King Terrace
1122 Kings Highway
Brooklyn, N. Y.

Religious Services
Saturday, May 11th at 9 a. m.
Avenue N Jewish Center
Avenue N and East 4th Street
Brooklyn, N. Y.

A boy's bar mitzvah invitation amounted
to a get-out-of-shul-free card.

Lack of military service hindered
Phil Hershey's civil service career.

Grandma honored by an organization of émigrés from Uscie Biskupia.

Watching Larry Yellen sign a $55,000 Houston Colt .45s bonus contract.

Top right at Ole Miss. That's my roommate Steve Ende in the glasses.

Mel Dubin might have won but for "the wrong Abe Cohen."

Summer campers were nothing like the students waiting in Bed-Stuy.

Suffolk Sun sports editor Larry Conroy sent me on an auto rally.

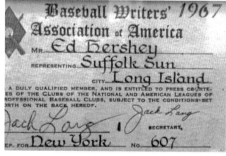

At 23 I had the most treasured baseball card of all. I was in the majors.

Gayle's love letters arrived with intricate designs, adding to the illusion.

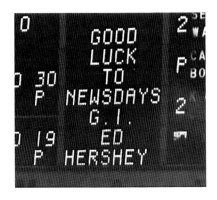

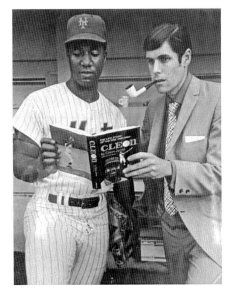

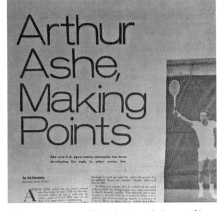

Getting serious: My Arthur Ashe profile was a Best Sports Story of 1968.

My work on the Lowenstein campaign started with a late-night call.

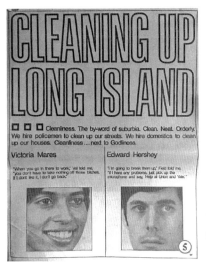

Victoria and I shared a Newsday magazine cover—and much more.

After a rabbi
turned us down
we turned to
a reporter
to marry us.

After a 30-month union campaign
we finally had a contract.

Colleagues welcomed me to Newsday's
Attica team …

… and I went right to work interviewing
guards' wives at a bar in Batavia.

Accepting an award for my ground-breaking coverage of a bus crash.

Trading up: A police press pass replaced my baseball writer's card.

This fishing trip yielded a rare catch— a front-page murder story.

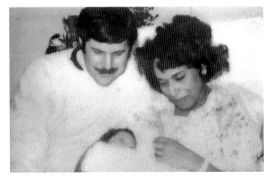

Rebecca 's arrival came with a "front-page" announcement.

Christmas in Wilkes-Barre: This, I thought, is what unionism is all about.

My Newsday good-bye included
a gag gift from Bruce Lambert ...

... and ended with a
tearful embrace with
George Tedeschi.

A story I tried to avoid led to my book with "Hostage Cop" Frank Bolz.

To Ed

Mayor Edward Koch posed with me at Gracie Mansion but really engaged with my daughter Rebecca at a track meet on Rikers Island.

The calls didn't stop just because Rebecca visited my city office.

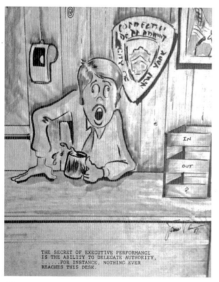

THE SECRET OF EXECUTIVE PERFORMANCE
IS THE ABILITY TO DELEGATE AUTHORITY,
......FOR INSTANCE, NOTHING EVER
REACHES THIS DESK.

The Assistant Commissioner
as Correction Officer
James Vann saw me.

Smiles at Jacqueline McMickens'
swearing-in: A year later I was out.

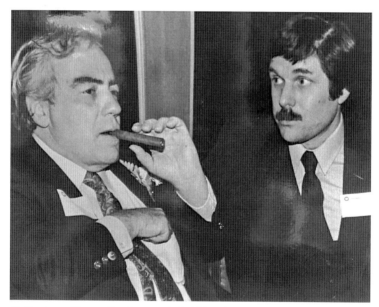

Polk winner Jimmy Breslin puzzled old hands on the J-A sports desk.

PART THREE

The Real World

27

Cleon's Ghost

The call came out of the blue. Two of my cousin Charlie's legal clients needed a writer for a project involving a client of theirs, New York Mets' left fielder Cleon Jones. Was I interested? Would I come to a meeting? How fast can you say yes and yes?

I liked to joke that Charlie Simmons was the white sheep of our family, a successful tax lawyer and dyed-in-the-fleece Republican. Charlie began his career in the U.S. Department of Justice under Attorney General Robert F. Kennedy and loved to tell about the Saturday morning he and a colleague were working on a difficult case and Kennedy peeked in and told them how pleased and impressed he was to see them in the office. "The next Saturday," Charlie said with a laugh, "everyone in the building was at work and Bobby was nowhere in sight."

The importance of being in the right place at the right time was a lesson reinforced for Charlie at a Cornell Law School reunion. He told a school official that he hoped to enter private practice. "In that case, come meet someone," the man said. Charlie was introduced to William Rogers, a Cornell Law grad who preceded Kennedy as AG in the Eisenhower Administration and would later be Secretary of State. Charlie became an associate at the influential New York firm of Rogers & Wells. That was where we met the agents who explained that Dick Schaap, former editor and columnist at the defunct *Herald-Tribune*, was writing a book with another client of theirs, star pitcher Tom Seaver, and was looking for someone to ghost one for Jones.

I was ready even before they said there would be a guaranteed $10,000 advance against royalties, but I had something to divulge first. I was no longer a sportswriter. It had been my dream job or so I thought. But at twenty-five I was barely looking up during Sunday doubleheaders, alternately filling in my scorebook and the *New York Times* crossword. I'd thought about switching to news since 1968 when I met people my age running Allard Lowenstein's anti-war campaign for Congress. *We're all prodigies now*, I told myself, *but in another twenty-five years they'll be running the country and what'll I be? A fifty-year-old sportswriter?* That point came clear in the Shea Stadium pressroom the following spring when I overheard a veteran San Francisco writer sobbing into a telephone: "I just can't do it anymore, boss. I'm sorry. I just can't do it." Red-faced and disheveled, he looked every bit the broken-down drunk after so many years on the road.

Plus, I was starting to produce serious work. I spent two days at the Columbia University football training camp in the Berkshires for a story about how alienated the players felt when other students ostracized them for their opposition to campus protests. Then Mike McGrady, editor of *Newsday's* weekend magazine, assigned me to do a feature on Arthur Ashe at the first United States Open tennis championship. My take on Ashe's metamorphosis as a black man in a white world was included in a juried anthology, *Best Sports Stories of 1969.* Two months later I ventured outside sports altogether to profile a former colleague at North Babylon High. He and his wife had abandoned suburbia to teach and raise their four children on Fishers Island on Long Island Sound, a hideaway for the ultra-wealthy in summer but a desolate outpost of 500 fishermen and caretakers the balance of the year.

Was I ready to abandon sports? Maybe, but it would never have happened as soon or as suddenly as it did if I had not encountered a major obstacle at *Newsday.* Dick Clemente, who had replaced Ed Comerford as sports editor, was scornful of the chipmunk school of sportswriting and seemed to take special pleasure in riding me. "He was the bowling writer," a colleague observed at the time. "What more do you have to know?" I'd been teased and bullied before. I could handle that, but not answering to a supervisor who would never appreciate my work. I went to see *Newsday* editor Bill McIllwain. "I'm not here to complain," I told him, "but with all that's happening in the real world, I'm feeling a little left out. I think I'd like to be a news reporter."

McIllwain leaned back in his chair. "The trouble with y'all up in sports is that you want special treatment," he said in his North Carolina drawl. "That Vecksey," he added, hardening the silent C in George Vecsey's name for effect, "he wanted to come down heah ta be a columnist straight away." I nodded. "Bill, I don't want any special treatment," I responded, "and I'm certainly not asking for a column. If you doubt me, try me." Equal parts savvy editor and unabashed lush, he took me at my word. Four days later I was a general assignment reporter. Had I waited even a couple of weeks I might never have had the chance. My transfer was one of his last acts at *Newsday*. Troubled by his excessive drinking, *Newsday* publisher Bill Moyers arranged McIllwain's departure for a teaching position days later.

Whatever they really thought, Cleon Jones's agents seemed undeterred by my career adjustment, even suggesting it spoke to the seriousness with which I could approach the book and adding that the year I spent teaching in Bed-Stuy would provide empathy for Cleon's experiences as a black athlete from Alabama. "We want this to be more than a sports book," one said, and his partner chimed in with "That's the kind of social awareness we're looking for." Unsaid but understood was that with so few black journalists writing about sports, an empathetic white writer would do.

A number of challenges awaited me. I would have to draw Cleon out and he was not exactly expansive. When people asked why I was leaving sports I'd say, "Now that the Mets have won the World Series what's left for me to see?" But it was as much white lie as glib retort. I'd spent the summer 800 miles away on an Army base in Georgia. I had seen little of the Mets' stunning season. Cleon hit .340 during that year and was in a pivotal play during the series when he took first base as a hit batsman after manager Gil Hodges spotted a scuff mark where the ball nicked his shoe. He even caught the final out of the Series. But he was just 27 with only four full seasons in the major leagues. Was

there enough *there* for a book? Finally, could I write in his voice without sounding stilted or condescending?

I flew to Mobile, where Cleon had flown with his wife Angela and
their infant daughter after the Series. The day I arrived the city staged
a parade for Jones and his hometown Mets teammate, Tommie Agee,
who had added to a local baseball heritage that produced such stars
as Satchel Paige, Hank Aaron, and Willie McCovey. It would have
been Cleon's second post-season parade but he skipped the mammoth
ticker-tape celebration down lower Broadway—taking some heat in
the papers and on talk radio in New York for snubbing Mets fans.
They were spending a few weeks in a small frame home owned by his
grandmother, who raised him there downwind from a paper mill on
Edwards Street in Plateau, an all-black neighborhood three miles from
downtown Mobile. "Mama Myrt" had watched him catch the fly ball
that ended the Series on a television Cleon shipped to her just days
before. This, he explained, was where he wanted to be as fast as he
could get there, with or without ticker tape.

I tagged along after the parade as Cleon reconnected with old
friends and made a few new ones, middle-class blacks who had broken
barriers of their own—Mobile's first black postal carrier and first black
teacher in a predominantly white school. Finally, Cleon declared,
"Let's get some chitlins," and we were all off, down a back road to a
ramshackle bar where he did the ordering. I was hungry and, while I
had never eaten chitterlings, I knew they had something to do with pig
innards. Given that Eastern European Jewish cuisine has its share of
dishes derived from cow intestines, I thought I'd be fine. Wrong. From
a distance the platters of yellowish strands resembled pasta. Close up,
they looked, smelled, and tasted exactly like what they were and I
could barely get a bite down. When I started moving them around my
plate like a kid avoiding his scrambled eggs, the teacher leaned over
and whispered, "Don't worry, honey, I can't stand them either."

I went to the house on Edwards Street with a cassette recorder
the next morning, expecting to begin interviewing. Wrong again.
Two friends had asked Cleon to join them on Mobile Bay for a day

of fishing. I was invited along. The only problem was that, apparently, nobody told the fish. We ate takeout for dinner. When I returned the following morning to finally start work (or so I thought) Cleon was not there. "He went fishing," Mama Myrt explained. Angela had a sheepish grin. It did give me time to chat with her until Cleon appeared with a bucketful of fish. Clearly the only thing wrong the day before had been bad karma from a New Yorker scaring the fish away.

That evening, Cleon finally started talking into my microphone. He said his father had fled town for Chicago after an incident and his mother died when he was in fifth grade. The white kids, when they paid any attention at all, would throw rocks at him and his friends as they walked the streets.

A few weeks later, following another trip to Mobile as well as a recording and photo session at the Joneses' apartment near Shea Stadium, I had the makings of a book. I traced his early career, augmented his recollections of the 1969 season with a game-by-game account a friend had kept, delved as deeply as I could into the history of Plateau and its environs, and even added Angela's recipes for "Cleon's Special Soul Food Dinner"—potato salad, candied yams, hamhocks and greens, corn bread, banana pudding and iced tea (but no chitterlings).

Cleon was published in June to some good reviews. *New York Times* columnist Bob Lipsyte led off his review on a compendium of Mets books this way:

In 1859, according to Cleon Jones, the war-like Dahomeyans of West Africa overwhelmed the peaceable, farming Tarkars and sold them into slavery. The Tarkars arrived in the last-known shipload of slaves from Africa to the United States and were shuffled among plantations and hidden in the forests north of Mobile, Ala., to avoid seizure by Federal troops.

Their owner, Timothy Meagher, was tried for slave trading but found not guilty, for lack of evidence. The Tarkars were eventually settled in what is now Plateau, Ala., and Meagher grew old complaining that he had lost $100,000, which prompts Cleon to write: "That just breaks me up, you know. I wonder how he would feel if he knew that part of his $100,000 wound up helping the New York Mets win a World Series." The book is called "Cleon," written with Ed Hershey of *Newsday* and scheduled for publication next month by Coward-McCann. It never quite reaches such lofty heights of historical perspective again, but it is interesting throughout... Cleon is a traditional sports biography: The hero enumerates in the writer's words and cadences, the accidents and the people who made him what he is today. Such books, when they are as well-crafted and alertly intelligent as this one, are valuable additions to school libraries, appreciated gifts for youngsters and no chore for an adult sports fan to read.

Hershey has found a good mix. The sense of life in a semi-rural ghetto is suggested; and there are some solid pages about batting; the statistical appendix includes several of Jones' wife's "soul food" recipes; and there are some aspersions cast on Wes Westrum, a question of Gil Hodges' "class" in embarrassing Cleon by yanking him out of the Shea Stadium outfield; and blissfully little of the coy inside dope that lets us know that Tom Seaver was the Mets' best bench jockey and adds, "You wouldn't believe some of the things that clean-cut All-American boy said when there was about $20,000 a man on the line."

"Touché," I thought about being tagged for coyness, though the phrase "writer's words and cadences" stung a bit because I really tried to capture Cleon's voice. A few weeks later a second opinion heartened me. *Newsday* baseball writer Joe Donnelly told me he had spotted Mets' equipment manager Nick Torman with the book. "He said 'Joe, I'll say this much. The guy got him. It's definitely Cleon.' So, my compliments."

I avoided overplaying its social significance but tried to write a book that said something about more than baseball. "When I traveled to Mobile to work with Cleon on his story," I wrote in the preface, "I called the *Mobile Press-Register* and asked for permission to examine its file on Cleon Jones. 'I'd like to check the statistics on his high school baseball and football games,' I said. The man who answered the phone asked me to wait a minute. Then he came back on the line. 'I'm sorry,' he said, 'but we don't have a Cleon Jones file. Nothing more I can tell you about Cleon's background.' This book is simply to fill in the gaps."

In "Confessions of Cleon's Ghost," a story for *Slug*, *Newsday's* house organ, I reflected on a different sort of gap, my mis-spent year in a Brooklyn classroom: "If one of those fifty or sixty kids I couldn't teach to read in Bedford-Stuyvesant five years ago has met better teachers since and reads *Cleon* and gets something from it, perhaps I have evened the ledger with one ghost in my past."

28

Left at the Post

JANUARY 1970
Manhattan

I was all over my first news assignment, a suit filed by the New York Civil Liberties Union on behalf of a woman whose daughter's fall wardrobe was deemed inappropriate for failing to adhere to a school dress code barring skirts more than "a fingertip's length" above the knee. The woman said she had spent her social services allotment for back-to-school clothing that was hardly provocative. I interviewed the mother, her daughter, their lawyer, an assistant principal, the school board lawyer, local officials, even the state education commissioner.

By the time I returned to the newsroom my notebook had more angles than a polyhedron. *This is some story to come upon right out of the box*, I thought, as I gave the county editor a full rundown. "Sounds terrific, Ed," he said. "Give us about six inches and make it sing." *Six inches?* Six inches was just a few paragraphs and I was used to writing 750 words about a baseball rainout. *Make it sing?* Just the legal ramifications had U. S. Supreme Court written all over them, and then there was the public policy implication of a dress code and the social stigma attached to welfare in a split-level world with a growing if invisible population of suburban single white mothers on public assistance.

I started to re-summarize with a you-can't-possibly-understand tone when he interrupted. "Yes, I get it," he said, "but we see this as a funny story that needs a light touch. I figured it was just the kind of piece you're used to doing coming from sports. Give it a shot." Four or five shots later he handed the story to Lew Grossberger, a rewrite man known as "the funny machine" for his knack of finding humor in just about any story. He was reworking mine when I left, and there it was on page 3 when I arrived Tuesday, turned into 10 inches of sprightly copy under the headline, "Hicksville Debate: Legs, In or Out?" *The transition to news*, I thought to myself, *might be harder than I imagined.*

I struggled to find my footing and except for a quirk of fate might have returned to sports—at the *New York Post*. Vic Ziegel alerted me that the *Post* needed a hockey writer. When I called the sports editor, Ike Gellis, to express interest he offered me an immediate tryout and told me to call the New York Rangers office to arrange for press credentials to cover three games the following week. I had not thought through what to tell *Newsday*. I surely did not want to give up one job before securing another and was still mulling this balancing act a couple of days later when Ziegel called again. "There's a problem," he said. "Did you write a letter?"

I'd nearly forgotten. During basic training in Georgia the prior July I'd spotted an issue of *Harper's Magazine* at the PX with an article by Jack Newfield of the *Village Voice* decrying the deterioration of the *Post*. The story was headlined "Good-bye Dolly," an unflattering reference to publisher Dorothy Schiff, the inspiration for a character played by Nancy Marchand in the original "Lou Grant" TV series.

Excited to come upon an inside account of New York newspapering, I decided to add my thoughts in a letter to the editor, which ran well after I returned to civilian life. The letter challenged Newfield's more damning assertions, but rereading it after Vic's call I realized that merely joining the conversation was enough to deem me *persona non grata* at the *Post,* a conclusion affirmed by a call from Gellis who said, "Sorry, kid, but I guess all bets are off."

It was unclear how the *Post* connected me to the letter, which was signed "Ed Hershey U.S. Army Reserve, Fort Gordon, Ga." Then I remembered that *Newsday* national editor Mel Opotowsky told me he had seen it. His brother Stan was a news executive at the *Post* and I came to suspect Stan had asked Mel what he knew about me. If that is what happened I am indebted to the brothers Opotowsky. The last thing I needed was to return to sports or leave for the *Post.,* which was becoming a sensationalist tabloid, a far cry from the conscience-driven liberal bible my father had carried home from work under his arm each evening.

In time I took the incident as affirmation that sometimes the best jobs are the ones you don't get. A few days later I walked up to a ticket window at Madison Square Garden, purchased a seat for the 1970 Millrose Games, and felt good handing over the cash. It was the first time I had paid my way into a sporting event since high school. I had interviewed enough sports personalities for my own private hall of fame—Ted Williams and Mickey Mantle, Frank Gifford and Bart Starr, Wilt Chamberlain and Oscar Robertson, Billie Jean King and Pancho Gonzales, Paul Brown and Vince Lombardi, plus outliers like pool shark Wimpy Lassiter, 600-pound wrestler Haystacks Calhoun and race car driver-impresario Bruce McLaren. But days before the meet I was at the Cold Spring Harbor Laboratory of Quantitative Research on Long Island to speak with Nobel Prize-winning DNA pioneer James Dewey Watson about a federal grant to investigate cancer-causing viruses. That, I mused from my seat at the Garden watching Marty Liquori win the Wanamaker Mile, was really the big leagues.

29

That Extra Call

General assignment reporting was like taking a series of one-day courses. You walked in cold and departed eight or ten hours later knowing a lot about an issue you might have never considered before and leaving 500 words behind. "I'm building a body of knowledge a mile wide and an inch thick," I joked to a friend. "I can go two sentences deep on just about any subject, but I might be in over my head on the third sentence."

Then there was the time I was kept after class. "Drop whatever you're doing," the day editor said, intercepting me before I reached my desk late one afternoon, "and get out to Lawrence." A bus full of day campers from the Hillel Jewish Day School on Long Island's South Shore had careened over an embankment in Pennsylvania, killing seven passengers. Editors throw every live body they have at such a story and reporters usually see it as taking one for the team, pitching in on an assignment unlikely to yield much success. This one would change the arc of my career.

Parents and friends milled about the school awaiting word about the fate of the forty-nine children who had set off that morning on a tour of the Pennsylvania Dutch country. They knew seven were dead, just not which seven. "I have been here for five hours and I haven't found out anything!" one parent who said she was a schoolteacher shouted in frustration. A few minutes later she and her husband were ushered inside. It was dusk and I could see into an office where it became obvious what they were told. Moments later she was being helped down the steps screaming, "For thirteen years I never let her out of my sight!" A TV technician lit up the darkening streets and with the camera rolling a reporter pointed a microphone at her before her husband swatted it away as onlookers berated the crew.

The image of thirteen-year-old Randee Lewis's parents the instant they learned of her death was still with me the next morning in the newsroom after I was assigned to seek angles for a second-day story, conferring with our reporter on the scene in Pennsylvania, Drew Fetherston, and calling various authorities. As often happens in the immediate aftermath of such a tragedy, there were more questions than answers, notably about the condition of the bus, the stretch of US Route 22 the driver failed to navigate and, most curiously of all, the driver who was in critical condition. According to the bus manifest his name was Heiber Day, but motor vehicle licensing bureaus in New York and Pennsylvania had no records for a driver with that name.

I took a second look at a wire-service photograph of the bus lying on its side at the base of the embankment and noticed "NJ" next to a number stenciled near the door. Was "Heiber Day" from New Jersey? There is a tenet of journalism so common it has been reduced to a cliché: *Make that extra call.* Mine was to the New Jersey Division of Motor Vehicles in Trenton where a spokeswoman, Connie Cedrone, said she would check the records. "We don't have anyone named Heiber Day," Cedrone told me an hour later, "but we have a Hubert Daye and with a record like his I might consider driving under an assumed name." She reeled off a list of nine accidents, six traffic violation convictions, and five license suspensions, the latest that April.

I drove to an address for Hubert Daye in Montclair, N.J., found his name on a mailbox, and confirmed with neighbors that he was a bus driver. By mid-evening, when several of us met with *Newsday* editor Dave Laventhol for the final go-ahead on my story, he said, "We have this guy better than we have Bebe Rebozo." It was newsroom humor. A *Newsday* team probing financial shenanigans involving President Nixon's best friend had little to show for months of work. My story ran with a tiny copyright line, which has little legal import but signals pride in an exclusive. The headline and lead paragraph were somewhat cautious:

BUS CRASH DRIVER INVESTIGATED
BY N.J., PA. SAFETY AUTHORITIES

By Edward Hershey

Authorities in Pennsylvania and New Jersey are investigating the driver of the bus that crashed Wednesday near Allentown, Pa., killing seven children from a Long Island school. A man, whose name is apparently the same, has a three-page list of nine accidents, six convictions, and five suspensions on his driving record in New Jersey, Newsday learned last night.

The story accelerated quickly with quotes encapsulating its public policy implications, including word that New Jersey's division of motor vehicles had "announced that a full-scale investigation has begun, and predicted it would lead to reforms in the state's procedures for licensing bus drivers."

Within a week the driver was indicted for manslaughter, his wife had died of a heart attack, two federal investigations were launched, funerals were held, records emerged showing an inordinate number of accidents along that stretch of US 22, and parents of teenagers on a cross-country summer tour expressed alarm when a bus owned by the same operator ran off a road in Utah.

The owner of the bus company insisted it had a stellar safety record and the slickened highway was the primary cause of the accident. Federal safety officials eventually ordered the stretch of road grooved and accidents there dropped dramatically. Charges were dropped against the hapless driver and both New York and New Jersey tightened rules for granting licenses to drive chartered buses. And the following spring the Society of Silurians honored my work with an award at a banquet in Manhattan. Years later when a dispute over Pulitzer Prize deliberations led Columbia University to divulge finalists for prior awards,

Drew Fetherston and I discovered that we had been fourth in line for a Pulitzer Prize

More important from my standpoint, the bus crash story brought me credibility and respect, leading to meatier assignments. One was a profile of former U. S. Supreme Court Justice Arthur Goldberg who was seeking the Democratic nomination for governor of New York in an ill-fated run against Nelson Rockefeller. The piece—headlined "Can New York Stay Awake Long Enough to Elect Arthur Goldberg?"—focused on the candidate's aloof demeanor and dull persona. Our most fascinating exchange never made the paper. Sitting with the candidate as we flew to an upstate campaign stop, I asked why the Supreme Court had never considered the constitutionality of the Vietnam War. "Off the record?" Goldberg asked, and when I nodded he said, "Because we'd have had to declare it unconstitutional, a decision we knew the President most likely would have defied. That would have threatened the balance of powers and thrown the country into a Constitutional crisis."

Such assignments had another important effect on my transition from sports to news. They increased my confidence, a benefit that can hardly be overstated in a profession where even seasoned reporters are prone to self-doubt over unasked questions, misquotes, errant facts, and being scooped by the competition. A retiring reporter who was also honored at the Silurian awards dinner drove this home, recounting a story about the break that launched his own career. It was a foggy Saturday morning in July 1945 and he called into the *New York Herald-Tribune* as he did each day before heading in to work as a copyboy to ask if anyone needed coffee.

"You go past the Empire State Building on your way over here, right?" an editor said. "Something's going on over there. Can you check it out on your way in?" When he arrived, firefighters were streaming into the building and he fell in behind them, climbing seventy-eight floors to the spot where a Navy bomber had slammed into the building, killing three aboard and eleven in the building. The copyboy scribbled furiously on a notepad as firefighters worked to extinguish the resultant blaze and evacuate survivors. "It was a scene I'll never forget," he recalled a quarter-century later, "but after a while something started gnawing at me. I looked around and I was the only reporter there. They'd closed off the building just after I arrived but I had no way of knowing that so I wondered why I was the only one. I said to myself, 'It *looks* like a good story.'"

30

Elusive Meets Superficial

SEPTEMBER 1970
Saginaw, Michigan

A *Newsday* rewrite man introduced me to the new woman in the newsroom, Victoria Mares. "You'll have to come over," I said after some small talk revealed that she, too, lived in Hempstead. "Maybe I can cook dinner for you some time."

"That might be nice," she responded, later confessing she was surprised to hear herself say it since she had decided not to mix her professional and social lives. Victoria's presence in the newsroom was itself surprising, given that she had not considered a career in journalism until both *Newsday* and the *Miami Herald* recruited her as part of a concerted effort to integrate their reporting staffs.

In the 1960s newspapers were hard-pressed to cover inner-city riots and other stories involving race with almost no black or Latino reporters. Few minority students were enrolled in journalism programs so they looked elsewhere to find prospects like Victoria. She had majored in political science at Michigan State and spent three years in Vietnam at the height of the war working for a private nongovernmental organization, a forerunner to the Peace Corps called International Voluntary Services, before returning to Michigan to run an anti-poverty center.

This promising resume aside, Victoria checked several boxes in the minds of recruiters: a black mother, Mexican father and aboriginal roots on each side. She was also easy to look at, which was why I contrived to return to her desk not long after our introduction. "Ready for that home-cooked dinner?" I asked, and we settled on that Saturday, but I doubled back later in the week. My friend Steve Ende had called to say that Roosevelt Raceway had offered to comp him, his wife, and two guests at its glass-enclosed restaurant that evening. Victoria agreed to take a rain check on my cooking to experience a suburban phenomenon—harness racing as a night out.

I could tell from the start it was a mistake. The faux glitz decor, middling steakhouse menu and generally obnoxious clientele were the antithesis of her taste—and it probably did not help that we failed to cash a single bet. "I can see you have the makings of a good life … in a superficial way," she said as we drove back to her apartment in my new Plymouth Barracuda. "Ouch," I said and, trying to respond in turn, added, "I'm not sure I can categorize you yet. I find you a little elusive."

That, I thought on the way home, *was your prototypical first-and-last date.* A few weeks later my cousin Charlie called with a dinner invitation. A visiting attorney from Europe was finishing a stint at his law firm and Charlie and his wife Cookie, who taught high school French, were hosting a small farewell dinner at their Upper East Side apartment. Could I come with a companion? Yes, I said, but as the week wore on I could not secure a date. By Thursday, with concern turning to panic, I called Victoria. I don't remember what I told her, but I do remember that she said, "You're amazing" and it was not a compliment. But she also said yes. When Charlie called a few days later to say how impressed he and Cookie were with Victoria, I wondered if it was to reassure me that bringing a black woman to dinner had been acceptable.

Our next date also tested Victoria's limits. I was doing the guest commentary on a local L.I.U. basketball telecast. If she came to the game, I said, we could go to dinner afterward. I drove the long way around to show her some of my old Brooklyn haunts, noting when we passed the New China Inn on Flatbush Avenue that one way to discern a Jewish neighborhood was from its plethora of Chinese restaurants. She'd known some Jews in college as well as at music camp, Victoria said, but was having trouble getting the New York Jewish thing down. She'd covered a protest meeting about the Vietnam War in Long Beach where a rabbi urged attendees to pay more attention to strife closer to home like tensions among white, black, and Latino residents.

"When I got back Dick Sandler (the night editor) asked if the people at the meeting were Jewish," she said. "I told him I didn't know and he sent me over to Lew Grossberger to explain how to tell if someone was Jewish. Lew started to explain and I said, 'Oh, I get it, like so-and-so,' and he said no, that guy was not Jewish and started again and the same thing happened. Finally, they all just threw up their hands."

Victoria was no sports fan, but L.I.U.'s eccentric gym in a cavernous old vaudeville palace with baroque statuary overlooking a basketball court held her attention. As we drove across the Manhattan Bridge into Manhattan after the game I asked her to close her eyes. "Open them now and tell me what kind of neighborhood this is," I asked a couple of minutes later. "Jewish!" she said. "Actually," I responded, "we're in Chinatown!" We both laughed and kept on laughing, sometimes at ourselves but more often at those around us, through an unlikely courtship.

We were enough of a couple by April that when federal postal workers went on strike and some reservists were activated to deliver the mail, I thought I had better put a reassuring note on Victoria's typewriter before leaving the newsroom. "Don't worry," I wrote, "the Red Chinese would have to be on the horizon before they call my unit up." I had to revise it five minutes later when the phone call came ordering me to report to Fort Tilden at 6 a.m. We sat around the base for two more days before the strike was settled and we were deactivated, but not without my averting a near catastrophe.

Several reporters caught up in the call-up had written unsigned stories in other papers and I volunteered to write one, too, but saw no reason for anonymity. My bylined piece—"Mail Mobilization Is Army as Always"—poked fun at the usual military experience of hurry-up-and-wait. It was nearly forgotten when I was called to the orderly room during my reserve drill in May and ordered to drive to 77th U.S. Army Command headquarters at Fort Totten in the Bronx where, after an hour's wait, I heard a captain tell me, "You are a very lucky fellow."

The day the postal strike ended Major General John W. Kaine returned to his home on Long Island, opened *Newsday,* and blew a gasket. If he'd seen my story before our deactivation that afternoon, the captain said, I might well still be on active duty accused of violating protocol for failing to submit it for review. He added that all of the reporting during the week of the mail strike had missed the real story: Military commanders and city officials were agonizing about how to move uniformed troops through city streets without provoking hostility in ghetto neighborhoods. Then he said that I had better not print what he had just told me.

After what she had seen in Vietnam little about the military surprised Victoria. Recruited by the volunteer agency in her senior year at Michigan State, she was attracted by the adventure and thought the experience might jumpstart a diplomatic career, but when she arrived and saw the futility and destruction of the American war effort first-hand, it soured her on diplomacy. She could tell humorous stories. There was the day when her Vietnamese (learned in a crash course before she left) failed her as she taught English to medical students and inadvertently declared someone pregnant. And the night she watched a John Wayne movie at a theater on an Army base when the area came under attack "and nobody knew whether the shots we heard were coming from the screen or outside." But there were more ominous memories, too. Perhaps the worst was when a GI told her that to alleviate the boredom of all-night sentry duty he and his buddies conducted target practice on innocent villagers in the distance.

"We'd hear the shooting all night," she told me, "but in the morning people were walking down the street with their kids and shopping in the market as if nothing had happened. It was amazing." Yes, she added, some fighters might well have been sitting in her class. But she loved interacting with the students and villagers and even signed on for an optional third year, a move that could have cost her dearly. When Hue was overrun during the 1968 Tet offensive, soldiers who captured several IVS volunteers came by looking for her. She'd left for Saigon the day before to treat a hip injury suffered in a motorcycle accident. It was weeks before her family in Michigan learned she was safe. The staffer who recruited her, Marty Clish, had died a year before when the plane he was in was shot down over Laos.

Victoria—she despised "Vicky"— and I came from very different worlds. She was an accomplished violinist with a gorgeous singing voice and I could not find a key, carry a tune, or keep a beat. She spent three years in a war zone I turned my life upside down and inside out to avoid. She saw reporting as a path to helping people marginalized by race and class while to me professional detachment was a point of pride, if not essential to good and fair journalism. She struggled with the idea of dating a white man because it flew in the face of a growing perception in the black community that it was disloyal or, worse, a reinforcement of stereotypes going back to slavery; I considered that aspect of our relationship an extension of societal fairness and equality, not anything I was trying to prove, but something that had evolved naturally.

As the months passed we began to explore each other's worlds and brought them together at a large open house at Victoria's apartment, inviting just about everyone we knew to feast on Mexican food she cooked. Rep. Allard Lowenstein, whose Congressional district included a number of towns on Victoria's reporting beat, was on the invitation list. With the party in full swing at about 10 p.m. there was a knock on the door. Clint Deveaux, a black aide of Lowenstein's

I'd met in the 1968 campaign, apologized that the Congressman was "running late." Later, we laughed at the idea that he had dispatched a black advance man to the party. "Maybe if it was at my place," I said, "he'd have sent a Jew."

"Why not just move in?" I asked in July, thinking as much in practical as romantic terms. Why spend the extra rent? We wound up at my place most nights because it had an air conditioner. And we were already planning to cap a Canadian vacation with a visit to her family in Michigan to coincide with Victoria's twenty-seventh birthday. She thought it was time to introduce me, given that a friend from New York who called her mother let slip that he heard she "was dating some Jewish guy."

Then the trip took on new meaning. We were each pursuing stories for an issue of *Newsday's* weekend magazine written and edited by younger journalists. She decided to spend a week as a domestic worker, hoping to give white Long Islanders a glimpse of what life was like for black women who cleaned their homes. I convinced the Hempstead Village mayor to let me ride with police officers for a week. A white journalist had dyed his skin so he could live as an African-American for a best-selling book called *Black Like Me*. My headline would be "Blue Like Me."

Victoria's project, which included cleaning a large house in a day for $14, was compelling, but mine might have been dangerous. As I left our apartment in my ersatz blue uniform to ride with a patrol sergeant on a hot August night, we embraced and she implored me to be careful. "You really do care about me, don't you?" I asked. When she nodded I added, "Will you marry me?" She said yes. When I opened the squad car door I told the sergeant, "You will never guess what just happened."

When we reached Saginaw, Louis Mares, my future father-in-law, a short, compact man with a thick Spanish accent and very Latin ways, greeted me warmly, but I sensed an undercurrent of doubt. The next evening as we sat in the living room he noticed me watching him pop homegrown peppers into his mouth like peanuts. "Here, Edward," he said, "want to try one?" The sentence was barely out of his mouth when I heard a high-pitched voice from the kitchen. "Edward, don't eat that!" Victoria's mother Katie shrieked. "Louis, what are you trying to do to that boy?" Back home I appreciated what my future mother–in–law had spared me. Victoria's dad had sent us off with a jar of peppers and Victoria sliced just one into a stew. Forget the pepper. I could barely tolerate the heat of the stew.

31

Second Thoughts?

DECEMBER 1970
Stony Brook, New York

"You mean you'd like to see the other side?" the mayor of Hempstead asked.

"I'd like to see it *from* the other side," I said. "I want to walk and ride your streets as a police officer, to know what it feels like to have somebody look at me and think: cop."

To my mind, "Blue Like Me: Running with the Man in Hempstead" did that. But the real blockbuster in that Saturday's magazine was another narrative by my colleague—and new fiancée. Victoria's story, "My Girl Is Here: Working for the Man in Wantagh," exposed the plight of domestic servants, women who earned less than minimum wage to clean Long Island homes and had to hand over a cut of even that to middle men. It revealed a world hidden in plain sight with a well-told story that might have jump-started Victoria's career the way my scoop about a bus accident had propelled mine. Instead, it proved her downfall at *Newsday*.

The foil of the piece was "Mrs. Goodman," a housewife from Wantagh. Victoria spent a day cleaning her fourteen-room suburban manse for $19, minus $5 for Murray the van driver, who had deposited her there to sub for a day worker whom she had befriended. The woman, whose real name was Greenberg, was portrayed in honest if unflattering terms, screaming at her two-year-old son, swearing at her mother in a daylong chain of phone conversations, bemoaning her weight as she wolfed down cookies, and following Victoria around with instructions. If anyone asked about her political persuasion no doubt she'd have replied, "liberal." A letter Victoria spotted on a dresser from Congressman Allard Lowenstein thanked Mr. Greenberg for his "support against the Cambodian campaign."

Howard Schneider and Jim Klurfeld, the young editors in charge of the special showcase for new talent, augmented both our stories with marginalia. They asked three Hempstead cops to discuss their feelings about reporters for my piece and called Mrs. Greenberg for a reference about Victoria's work. This is what she said:

> "She was a very nice sweet girl, but she wasn't a cleaner. I mean she didn't do the bathtub and she didn't do the toilet bowl and when she left I had to mop and wax the floors myself. I mean at the prices we have to pay. She was a replacement for my regular girl. But I wouldn't recommend you hire her. She didn't do any of the cleaning. I had to do the Venetian blinds and windows after she left. I don't know what she did the entire day. As I said she is a very nice girl but she just wasn't a cleaner, you know what I mean? Just not a cleaner."

When we returned from vacation two weeks after the stories ran we learned that Victoria's story included just enough detail for people who knew her to identify Mrs. Greenberg, something Schneider discovered when he picked up the phone and a voice on the other end of the line said, "This is Mrs. Greenberg, Mrs. *Goodman* Greenberg." While Goodman (a name I suggested) was not as identifiably Jewish as Greenberg, it proved Jewish enough to spark angry letters accusing Victoria and the paper of anti-Semitism. "Why didn't you tell me it was a Jewish name?" she asked me. Worst of all from Victoria's standpoint, some *Newsday* editors and reporters made it clear they thought her story amounted to an unfair assault on the paper's core constituency, exacerbating a schism between blacks and Jews that was already widening on Long Island and elsewhere.

The black-Jewish divide hit home for me in a much more personal way. Although they had never met my fiancée, only one thing about the match mattered to my parents and they were not subtle about it. My mother spoke of seeing an interracial couple with a child and "feeling sick to my stomach." My father was less visceral and more clinical. After seeing Victoria on a television panel show, he said she seemed bright but had "Negroid features," making it sound as if he might have been more accepting if my bride-to-be looked a little less black. My future father-in-law's hot peppers would have been much easier to swallow. Who *were* these people?

I resolved to pursue a Jewish wedding, effectively daring them not to show up, and we approached Rabbi Bernard Kligfeld, who had impressed Victoria at an anti-war meeting she covered and me with a eulogy he delivered after the murder of a schoolteacher. After hearing speaker after speaker at the meeting denounce the Vietnam War, he asked why the largely Jewish crowd did not focus more attention on racial and economic injustice in their own community. And at the funeral—the teacher had been strangled by carjackers witnesses said were young black men—he asked mourners to draw lessons from the victim's life, calling her "a reasonable, rational creature with a calmness, a patience, a forbearance." He said her grieving son told him," It would be a complete tragedy if this became an occasion for people to multiply hatred and let anger take over."

"Victoria may well convert to Judaism," I said when we met Klig-feld, "but I have always viewed conversion for marriage as a charade. I want her to do this on her terms, not out of a sense of obligation." He told us how excited he was for us and encouraged, too. "A higher per-centage of Jews are involved in interracial marriages than members of any other religion," the rabbi said. "It is a testament to the sense of fair-ness that comes with a Jewish upbringing." I could sense a "but" com-ing. Reform Jewish authorities would not allow him to officiate. It was the first time I heard the term "silent holocaust." Kligfeld said he could send us to somebody. We thanked him for his time and kind words. On the way out I said to Victoria, "That's that." We asked *Newsday* religion writer Ken Briggs, an ordained minister, to marry us and reserved the quaint Three Village Inn in Stony Brook for a Saturday, not a day Jews can marry. That no longer mattered.

I spent much of that fall covering a three-way U. S. Senate race among Republican incumbent Charles Goodell, Democratic Congress-man Richard Ottinger, and Conservative businessman James Buckley. Ottinger started out favored to unseat Goodell, an obscure Congress-man from Jamestown when Governor Nelson Rockefeller appointed him to succeed the fallen Bobby Kennedy. Far more reserved though no less conservative than his famous younger brother Bill, the star of "Firing Line," Buckley was the wild card. Goodell had swung to the left earning a reputation for independence that included opposition to the war, allowing Buckley to portray himself as the true Republican also likely to attract votes from blue-collar Democrats.

The assignment sounded exciting, but traipsing after candidates delivering the same speech in town after town could be tedious, so it became an inside joke for reporters to find ways to file stories with date-lines from backwater-sounding spots on the day's itinerary. Horseheads and Painted Post were my favorites. Accommodations were also less than glamorous. One night at a motel in Utica where Mohawk Air-lines ("Slow-hawk" to passengers) housed its stewardesses I had to duck under slips, bras, and panties drying on lines in the corridor to reach my room. Another time I joined Buckley's entourage at LaGuardia Airport for a flight to Buffalo wearing a Goodell skimmer from a campaign event in Manhattan. The gag didn't play well and I put the straw hat on a seat. The plane returned to the city that night, but the pilot had to double back. He had flown off with the lone copy of Buckley's morning speech under my Goodell hat.

Buckley seemed to be surging past Goodell, but what of Ottinger? Heir to a plywood fortune, educated at prep school, Cornell and Harvard Law, and an Air Force vet with three terms in Congress, at 41 Ottinger seemed to have it all. What he did not have was good advice from well-paid political operatives, something I gleaned working on a "twin-out" headlined "The Great Liberal Slugfest," with my profile of Ottinger running alongside Waldman's on Goodell. Mine began this way:

> The young woman in Richard Ottinger's Utica storefront could have been left over from the 1968 crusades—man-tailored shirt, blue eyes burning through a scrubbed face, small–town voice. "You know what the rap is on your man down in the city?" she was told. "They say he's a flaming liberal without the flame."
>
> "I campaigned for Bobby Kennedy, too," the young woman said. "He had a flame, so they shot him. Maybe they won't shoot Ottinger."

I called "the young woman" when I was in Syracuse for a Buckley rally and she agreed to drive the fifty miles from Utica to update me. It seemed like a better use of my time than watching another campaign rally. We met in a hotel suite the Buckley campaign had rented for the press and almost immediately fell into each other's arms. It was rapturous but also jolting. The wedding was less than two months away. Victoria and I seemed deeply in love. Every time she sang her voice so melted me that friends would tease me about the beatific expression on my face. And one summer evening as we sat on a bench overlooking the Plains of Abraham in Quebec City after eschewing a restaurant for baguette sandwiches, she turned to me and said, "I have lived in so many places, but I think I've found the place I want to be: Edward place."

But were we ready for marriage? By 1970, there was no stigma attached to living together, but one reason I wanted us to marry—and we talked about this—was because I did not want anyone to think our relationship was about anything but love. And she was acutely aware that black women who dated white men faced mounting social pressure if not outright antagonism in segments of the black community. Were we too concerned with appearances? And what would it say if we put off the wedding or backed out? Would we be seen as caving into my parents' bigotry or reinforcing all those platitudes that started, "Marriage is hard enough..." I chalked off the tryst in Syracuse to a last fling and my second thoughts as pre-marital jitters, but there was another red flag in the weeks before the wedding: Victoria abruptly left *Newsday*.

She had often expressed frustration but her complaints sounded like newsroom gripes I'd heard—and expressed—for a decade, except for one underlying issue: race. She and eight other minority journalists recruited to diversify *Newsday* were uncertain about their roles. Were they part of a genuine effort to make a difference or being used as, in Victoria's words, "niggers at the door?" The issue was so widespread that journalists organized a National Conference of Black News Media Workers in Missouri in June 1970. After suggesting that one or two attend, *Newsday* relented and sent all its minority journalists. That created some dissension from white staffers whose proposed out-of-town assignments had been denied because of budget constraints. The furor had barely subsided when the reaction to Victoria's magazine story about the plight of cleaning women made her feel unsupported. Still, I was shocked when she resigned. Principles matter and so does job satisfaction, but quitting one job without another in your pocket? It made me wonder. Then, out of the blue, Channel 4, the NBC flagship station at 30 Rockefeller Plaza, hired her. It was as if the fates had justified her decision.

Our wedding day dawned cold, crisp, and clear, but I could not see much of it. I awakened with both eyes inflamed by some mysterious ailment that blurred my vision. We laughed that it had to be a form of hysteria. We exchanged vows in front of a crackling fireplace. Victoria sang a gorgeous rendition of Nina Simone's "Black Is the Color of My True Love's Hair" and when journalist/minister Ken Briggs turned to me, Steve Ende stage-whispered, "Oh, god, Hershey's going to sing!" The laughter provided a sweet counterpoint to my spoken expression of love. It was a double-ring ceremony. Hers was inscribed, "To Elusive... from Superficial" and mine "To my favorite place... Edward place."

32

Case Closed

MAY 1971
Manhattan

When *Newsday* editors paired me with John Cummings, a veteran investigative reporter originally from Pennsylvania coal country, for a series that involved months of digging into Long Island's criminal justice courts we seemed like unlikely partners. But Cummings saw himself as my guide and mentor, often regaling me with tales of characters he knew.

And tales was the word for many of the anecdotes Cummings attributed to local courtroom legends like defense attorney Nick Castellano. One time, as he told it, after a witness took the stand Castellano pored over the man's prior grand jury testimony, raising perfunctory objections from his seat until a young prosecutor complained, "Your Honor, would you please ask Mr. Castellano to rise when he addresses the court?" The judge started to wave off this impertinence when Castellano rose. "Your Honor," he said with a flourish, "if I have done anything to impugn the dignity or decorum of this court or offend you or the jury, please accept my humble apology." Turning to the prosecutor, he added, "And you, you little fuck, if you ever do that to me again, I'll pick you up and throw you through that window." By Cummings' account everyone but the red-faced DA doubled over with laughter, even the jurors who went on to acquit Castellano's client.

I bought every word of it, too, until I saw the scene played out by James Stewart and George C. Scott in Otto Preminger's *Anatomy of a Murder*. I did have immediate doubts about another exchange Cummings attributed to Castellano as he tried a case before an elderly Jewish judge. "On what grounds do you object?" the judge supposedly asked and the lawyer responded with a Latin-sounding citation that was actually an Italian curse. "In that case," the judge announced, "your objection is sustained."

The ultimate plea bargain according to Cummings—sodomy reduced to following too closely—was also an old joke, but the nature of the system we were dissecting was often so appalling that we hardly needed to make anything up. Take the day a seventy-two-year-old lifelong grifter named Larry Knapp faced sentencing for swindling an elderly widow of her life's savings. "Your honor, I'm an old man," Knapp protested when the judge gave him twenty-five years. "I'll never be able to do that much time." Unmoved, the judge looked down from the bench and said, "Well, Mr. Knapp, do the best that you can!"

Cummings did not restrict his advice to journalism. One morning after he pooh-poohed an angle I suggested, I told him that supervising editor Art Perfall thought it was worth checking. A quizzical expression crept across his face. "Perfall?" he asked. "You mean he came in here to talk to us?" I said no, I'd sought him out. It was my first extended assignment and I was uneasy about having so little contact with the desk. Cummings rose from his chair and approached me, his expression hardening into a mix of anger and pain. "Ed, I am going to give you some advice that I want you to remember not only for the rest of our time on this project but for the rest of your life," he said. "Wives and editors are to be talked to on a need-to-know basis only!"

The gist of our series, "Justice on Trial," was eye opening for readers in 1971. It ran for a full week and was reprinted and widely distributed in a 28-page special section that summarized our findings in this lead on the front page of the first installment:

> "It is a creaking, crumbling system that dispenses with justice rather than dispensing justice," State Senator John Dunne says. He is among the critics who have identified a brewing crisis in the criminal courts, a crisis that at times seems to mock the legal guarantees that are the cornerstones of American democracy. A *Newsday* reporting team spent four months investigating the Long Island criminal court system and found that

> - The courts are overloaded and undermanned.
> - More than 95% of all criminal cases never get to trial.
> - Bargaining for pleas has been substituted for traditional legal processes.
> - Drug arrests have swamped the system, and in many cases judges have moved ahead of the lawmakers in reducing pleas for minor offenses.
> - Delays in trial proceedings have made a myth of constitutional guarantees, generally at the expense of the poor.

That was civics lesson material, a depiction of the system readers rarely saw because newspapers focused on cases that did get to trial, especially murders tied to romance gone awry like two on Long Island that suggested that some nights the most dangerous thing the unsuspecting wife could do was fall asleep. In one case, a forty-eight-year-old dentist was accused of injecting his wife with pentobarbital and shooting her in the back of the head as she slept in their home in upscale Plandome. The other was what headline writers liked to label a "deadly love triangle." An elementary school principal, also forty-eight, and a twenty-seven-year-old divorced teacher in his school were accused of chloroforming his wife to death as *she* slept in their home in North Valley Stream. The dentist was acquitted. The principal and his paramour, who later married, were convicted of conspiracy but not murder—the sort of compromise verdict divided juries can deliver in search of a middle ground that allows them to escape the confines of the jury room.

Defendants in the two cases had the same attorney, John J. Sutter, a larger-than-life Long Island version of F. Lee Bailey who was also a close friend of Cummings. Most days at lunchtime Sutter held court, so to speak, at a restaurant frequented by lawyers and judges, sipping martinis and expounding on the finer points of his game. Sutter's world was far less about guilt or innocence than conviction or acquittal. "If you aren't guilty," he said he once advised a new client, " 'why would you need to hire me?' " When another raised a glass "to justice," Sutter waved him off with a toast of his own. "Fuck justice," he replied. "To victory!"

Even an apparently humdrum homicide could be intriguing if you dug a little. A twenty-two-year-old telephone operator was found stabbed to death one morning on a street in Freeport. Colleagues at work characterized her as a shy woman who kept to herself, often walking the two miles to and from the office alone. "Extremely quiet," one told me, "Almost abnormally so." Yet neighbors and friends described someone almost the mirror opposite of the young woman co-workers thought they knew, a devil-may-care spirit who frequented discos night after night. "She was the kind of girl who would make two dates for the same evening and go out with the first to show up at her door," one said. "She thought nothing of arriving at a party with one guy and leaving with another." Those who knew *that* side of her speculated that her coquettish ways might have done her in, which I reported under the headline, "A Mystery in Life ... and Death." As it turned out, flirtatiousness played no role in her demise at the hands of a twenty-year-old who was arrested after attacking another woman a week later, convicted the following spring, and sentenced to eight to twenty-five years.

While felonious behavior was relatively rare in the suburbs, New York City was awash in blood in 1971 when police in the five boroughs investigated 144,108 violent crimes, including 1,823 homicides. But the marquee trial in New York that year did not involve any of them. In 1969, after hearing testimony from undercover officers and informants, a Manhattan grand jury charged nineteen members of the Black Panther Party with conspiring to bomb department stores, police precincts, train stations and the New York Botanical Garden, and to murder police officers. Four of the alleged conspirators eluded arrest and two fled the country after making bail, so thirteen defendants were in court when the trial started.

It was a city story that *Newsday* decided not to staff. When I was sent into the courtroom seven months later just as the two sides launched into lengthy summations, it was like walking into a ball game in the eighth inning, surely no way to cover the longest trial in state history. But the national news editor—by our reckoning anything west of Nassau County was national news—said that rather than a definitive account of the case, he wanted a take on the scene as political theater. And with a ruddy-faced Irish-American judge named John Murtagh clashing dismissively with the defendants and their lawyers before a courtroom packed with their supporters, it was surely that.

There were two familiar faces on press row, my old *New York Post* compadre Ralph Blumenfeld (who had also left sports for news) and famed columnist Murray Kempton, who was writing a book about the case. I had seen Kempton at the periphery of a couple of press conferences but never spoken to him. He was as erudite and charming across a table as he was in print. "Catch me up?" I asked them at lunch, earning a laugh. While both men conceded that some of the accused were not people they would be comfortable calling friends, each expressed sympathy for the defense. In fact, Blumenfeld said, his stories were intended for the eyes of the jury, assuming (as most reporters and lawyers did) that they routinely ignored admonitions to avoid coverage of the trial. And the more they talked about the jury, the more I sensed a perfect lead into my first piece on the trial, which began:

NEW YORK— There was apprehension at the defense table and in the gallery on the October day that James Butters was sworn in as juror No. 11 for the conspiracy trial of 13 Black Panthers.

Butters, a stocky Marine veteran and a conservative dresser with a modest hairstyle, did not appear to be the kind of peer whom the Panthers preferred. Yet, Butters was also a schoolteacher, and the defense team, running short of preemptory challenges, accepted him.

That was almost six months ago. Now, with the trial in its closing days, the juror in seat No. 11 seems to be a new man. As the trial moved through autumn and winter Butters' appearance changed. With the passing days Butters wore fewer neckties and his hair grew longer. He now has thick mutton chop sideburns and listened to the start of the defense summation one day this week in an open-throated railroad shirt and blue jeans.

My story, headlined "Panther Jury Gives Defense Hope," quoted several defense attorneys who speculated that prosecutor Joseph Phillips might be misgauging the jury. "Phillips thinks he's got the usual, a dozen Con Ed employees," Sandy Katz, said, "and I really think he expects them to come back in 25 minutes with 'guilty on all counts.'" Gerald Lefcourt added, "At the start I didn't think we had any chance but now I'm hopeful. I think Murtagh and Phillips have underestimated the jurors, alienated them and lost them."

Before sitting down to write I visited an old haunt, the 8th Street Bookshop in Greenwich Village, to bone up on the Black Panthers and made an intriguing connection that I included in my story:

> Among the most expressionless listeners has been jury fore-man James Fox, a black musician-composer in his 50s. Fox left the U.S. for Europe many years ago because he found mini-mal opportunities in this country for blacks interested in serious music. One of his close friends was the brilliant black conductor Dean Dixon, who has been hailed for his work in Germany, Italy, Britain and Australia.
>
> In a paperbound bookshop a few blocks north of the New York Criminal Courts building where the Panther conspiracy trial is being conducted, there is a volume called, "The Black Expatriates Speak." In that book, Dean Dixon, jury foreman James Fox's friend, tells an interviewer that because the U.S. was not ready to accept a Negro conductor, "I kicked myself out of America."

Was the defense on to something or just grasping at straws? Would someone like James Fox be sympathetic to the defendants? The ver-dict came in May when Fox said "not guilty" 156 times. Even the two defendants tried in absentia after fleeing to Algeria were acquitted. Several jurors said they found the undercover officers unbelievable and were so appalled by the judge's attitude that at times it was all they could do to keep from leaping up in protest. In decades to come, the art and science of jury selection would emerge as critical to trying cases with specialists advising lawyers on who in the jury pool was likely to be sympathetic to their clients. "Con Ed juries"—twelve men typical of white, blue-collar utility workers—were a thing of the past. "We were lucky," James Fox told Ralph Blumenfeld. "It was a lucky assem-bly of jurors, a cross-section, who were able to agree.

33

Behind Bars

Eight days after covering the acquittal of 15 members of the Black
Panther Party I was back in the city. This time there was no question a
heinous crime had been committed. Two uniformed officers responding to a false 911 call at a housing project in Harlem were shot from
behind as they returned to their squad car. Joseph Piagentini was white
and from Long Island. Waverly Jones was black and from Manhattan.
Both died.

A group calling itself the Black Liberation Army claimed credit
for the killings. Five alleged BLA members would be charged in the
Jones-Piagentini case with three convicted and sentenced to life in
prison. Unlike the Black Panthers, who were largely a social and political movement whose calls to arms were often more rhetorical than
literal, the BLA was a confederation of thugs and self-styled revolutionaries who claimed responsibility for a multitude of crimes across
the country, including the murder of a police sergeant in San Francisco
and the assassination of two more New York City cops on the Lower
East Side. Those killings, they said in a note, were in retaliation for
how the authorities had ended a standoff at a prison in the far reaches
of western New York in the village of Attica.

Like most Americans, even most New Yorkers, the name Attica
meant nothing to me until the morning of Thursday, September 9
with the first reports that inmates had rioted there, killing a correction officer and seizing hostages. By Monday everyone in earshot of a
radio or television knew about Attica. After a weekend of negotiation
between inmates and a motley array of twenty-nine citizen observers,
Governor Nelson Rockefeller ordered the prison retaken. Counting

the officer who died of injuries suffered at the outset and three inmates found dead later, presumed victims of old scores, forty-three men died at Attica—the largest peacetime death toll on American soil since the Civil War.

For decades, New York's prisons were mostly a matter of out-of-sight, out-of-mind for reporters. There might be an occasional feature or a spate of stories in response to a violent incident, especially if a guard or other employee had been killed or injured. Otherwise criminal justice coverage stopped at the jailhouse door, in part because authorities who controlled access preferred it that way and in part because most prisons were far from population centers. Then on that September morning a group of inmates dislodged an aged steel gate—an apt metaphor for a decaying system—in an area at the center of Attica Prison's four cellblocks known as Times Square.

As if the takeover and its lethal resolution were not enough to make this a huge story, it became even bigger when the newswires jangled with word that autopsies conducted by a medical examiner in Rochester concluded that all 39 men killed during the state assault—28 inmates and 11 employees—had been shot by law enforcement officers. Just before the assault four prisoners had mounted a parapet each holding a knife to the throat of a hostage, and in the immediate aftermath a state spokesman announced that the throats of seven hostages had been slashed. Confronted with the autopsy results officials retracted that account. By then inmate advocates were alleging that members of the assault force had targeted specific prisoners for death.

Six days after the takeover's bloody conclusion John Dunne, a Long Island Republican who chaired the State Senate Committee on Crime and Correction, discussed his efforts to negotiate a nonviolent conclusion at Attica on a Sunday morning television talk show. Prisons throughout the state were still on "lockdown," restricting inmates to their cells out of fear that allowing them to move about could lead to more unrest, and Dunne said he would undertake a fact-finding tour of the prisons starting the next day. I'd never met Dunne, but after clearing it with the news desk that afternoon I called to ask if he was willing to let me join him on his tour.

Most officials on Long Island had home listings in the phone directory but many were there to create the illusion of accessibility and led to answering systems. Not Dunne's. He picked up on the first ring and said he'd be happy for the company. "Just get here by 8," he said. "I want to get an early start. We'll have coffee for you." When I arrived someone else was there as well: the competition. Fred Ferretti of the *Times* had made the same request. "I guess I'm not the only one who watches television on Sunday morning," I said, and we both laughed. Ferretti had been part of such a large contingent of *Times* reporters at Attica during the takeover that the paper rented a house in town. He told this story as we drove off for our first stop, Green Haven Prison two hours up the Hudson in Stormville:

During the siege an official emerged from the prison to brief the horde of reporters and agreed to allow a pool of four inside to access a vantage point where they could see into D Yard, the area under inmate control. "I'll crumple these pieces of paper up after marking four with an X and put them into this hat," he announced. "Pick one with an X and you're in." All the reporters reached in and one after another the winners self-identified. Ferretti was one. It was not until a steel door had closed behind the quartet and their escort that there was a loud yowl from someone still out on the street. Ferretti had penciled his own X, leaving the fourth legitimate recipient out in the cold. "And I thought politics was tough!" Dunne said with a laugh, and I added, "In my country we call that chutzpah."

The warden at Green Haven granted us complete access and we struck immediate pay dirt, encountering several inmates transferred from Attica who described deplorable conditions there—the first word from a source other than the state of what it had been like on the inside during and after the insurrection. Encountering Fred Ferretti at John Dunne's house I had been miffed about losing an exclusive, but then I realized it was still a reporting feat if only the *Times* and *Newsday* had the story. Our accounts each landed on page one the next day and his, two columns wide above the fold, even acknowledged my presence, describing interviews inmates had given to "State Senator John Dunne and two reporters." When we continued on what would be a four-day tour of eight prisons the next morning we had more company. The *New York Daily News* dispatched reporter Bill Federici to catch up with us.

For the next three days we drove from one dot on a map to the next—Wallkill, Napanoch, Elmira, Auburn, Dannemora and Comstock, prison towns where white officers supervised predominantly black and Latino inmate populations, adding culturally driven misunderstandings to the tension inherent in any institutional setting. Prisons had always been welcome additions to depressed economies in these outposts, providing work for suppliers and contractors as well, of course, as employment for guards, jobs often passed down from one generation to the next.

After that first story the most newsworthy part became the tour itself. Republican leaders had always viewed Dunne's independence warily and his willingness to bring us along for this ride was making him persona non grata in Albany. When we reached the forbidding Clinton Prison near the Canadian border, the warden, an aging hardliner, said state officials had told him not to allow us past the administration building, a proscription repeated at our final stop, Great Meadow Prison, even though a Republican who chaired a committee corresponding to Dunne's in the State Assembly was inside. Small wonder my magazine-length profile five weeks later was headlined, "John Dunne: Reformer in the Rough."

Back on Long Island, I barely had time to pack and catch a plane. My reportorial coup landed me a place on a *Newsday* team assigned to do a post-mortem on Attica that might also serve as a roadmap for reform. Led by Albany bureau chief Jon Margolis, it included John Cummings as well as Pat Brasley, who had recently arrived from Rochester where he was so respected the Democrats tried to recruit him to run for Congress; Bob Wyrick, a fierce reporter who knew prisons from the inside having served hard time in his native West

Virginia; and Brian Donovan, one of legendary investigative editor Bob Greene's regulars.

Working from a Holiday Inn in Batavia, the closest city to the prison, we spent weeks gathering facts in the face of stonewalling by authorities, who denied us access to the surviving inmates and, from the governor on down, refused interviews on the premise that a criminal investigation was under way. We tracked down hostages, negotiators, prison employees willing to speak on or off the record, and members of the assault force to create a detailed chronology—a "tick-tock" in newspaper lingo—and explored the genealogy of the takeover and its deadly conclusion. Several other news organizations, including the *Times,* were pursuing similar stories, lending a healthy air of competition to our mission. It took me the better part of a week to identify and locate one of two state police pilots who had dropped canisters of pepper gas into D Yard from Condor helicopters as the assault began. But when I found him, he was more than willing to discuss the experience, provided we agreed not to name him.

Our nine-page special report, "The Many Faces of Attica," began this way:

> In the end, with bullets flying all around them, troopers charging, clouds of gas blurring the prison yard, the convict who held a knife to Richard Fargo's chest did not kill him, but spared his life.
>
> It was just before 10 AM on Sept. 13, and the siege at Attica State Prison was rushing toward its conclusion in a confused melee of gunfire, shouts and blood. "I'm going to kill you, pig," the convict yelled at Fargo, a guard taken hostage four days before. But between his shouts he was whispering, "It's a sham. You're going to be all right, boss... don't panic."
>
> His knife nicked Fargo's side lightly, just enough to draw blood. "Don't tell them I didn't cut you," the convict said. Then he pulled Fargo backward and let him fall to the ground, where he would be better protected against the troopers' fire.

When the rescuers reached them, they found Fargo unhurt. The man with the knife was dead. He had been shot by troopers who had no way of knowing he had been posturing, playing a role forced upon him by circumstance, much as their role had been forced upon them.

Later, Fargo would think about the convict, but he really could not decide what sort of man he might have been. For despite Fargo's 23 years as a guard at Attica, the two had never met before, and Fargo still does not know his name.

Perhaps as well as anything, the incident captures the dominant themes of those five days at Attica. For in large measure Attica was a tragedy of flawed perceptions, of posturing taken as truth. From start to finish, from the desperate convicts to the highest state officials, everyone's ability to settle the conflict was clouded by misunderstandings, stereotypes and fear. Probably because they came from much different worlds, few on any side had any clear sense of when those on the other were bluffing and when they were serious. In that sense it was indeed a struggle among men who did not know each other's names.
—Newsday LLC, ©1971

My most compelling and poignant moments came 50 miles northeast of Attica in a Rochester home where Bob Wyrick and I spent an evening with members of Elliott Barkley's family. Tall, young, bespectacled, and well spoken, Barkley cut a curious figure in D Yard. Older, more prominent inmates like black activists Richard Clarke and Herbert X. Blyden, anti-war bomber Sam Melville, and cop-killer Jerry (the Jew) Rosenberg called him "LD" and often deferred to him during negotiations. He died in the assault, some said targeted by police. Who was he? The answer, retold as the first of the "Many Faces of Attica," was a Kafkaesque tragedy.

For Elliott James Barkley it began 21 years ago in Rochester's Third Ward, an almost all-black neighborhood of shabby stores and houses on the city's west side. A lot of the young men who grow up in the Third Ward find their way to Attica. Their families talk about the prison much as the suburbanites across town in Irondequoit talk about Syracuse University or Cornell. "Yeah," said one man in South Genesee Street the week they buried Elliott Barkley. "I spent some time there. My son's there now. He just got in two weeks ago." Not everyone, of course, goes right to Attica. Some are shunted off first to local jails and others, like Barkley, prep for Attica at Elmira Reformatory.

Among his former West High classmates, Barkley is remembered as a bright, quiet youth whose troubles seemed to start when he began experimenting with drugs. From glue sniffing he worked his way rapidly to heroin, and his scrapes with the law started shortly afterward.

At 16, he was arrested for the first time, on a shoplifting charge that was later dropped. A year later, Barkley and four companions were arrested and indicted on robbery and larceny charges for snatching a purse containing $3. On August 2, 1968, with those charges still pending, he was arrested again, this time accused of cashing a forged money order at a local pharmacy.

A month later, at 18, he was pleading guilty as a youthful offender. The sentence: two and a half to four years at Elmira.

The prosecutor who handled the case, Don DePasquale, says now that he cannot recall the circumstances. There were just too many cases like Elliott Barkley's.

At Elmira, Barkley did a good deal of reading and without the diversions of the street, earned behavior ratings good enough to win a parole. Back home, he enrolled at Monroe Community College and started studying toward a sociology degree. And he took a job, for $100 a week, as a community worker for the Soul Brothers, a federally funded anti-poverty group. Then Barkley's parole officer, a man named Gerald Zeck, told him to quit the job. Under parole rules, Zeck explained, Barkley could not consort with drug users. Yes, Barkley countered, but he was involved in narcotics rehabilitation work; drug users were the very people he was supposed to be helping.

Again Barkley was told to quit, and when he got the order a third time he brought his father, James, with him to try to explain to Zeck. James Barkley remembers the day well.

"He [Zeck] said, 'Did you quit that job?'" the elder Barkley said. "And Elliott said no. He said 'Why didn't you quit that job? Didn't I tell you to quit that job?' Elliott said, 'Yes, you told me to quit.' The man really got nasty. He talked to Elliott like a dog. And Elliott started to cry, right in that man's office. And I told Elliott, 'No matter what that man says to you, you just go along with what he says… [Otherwise] you're going to be violating your parole.'

"Elliott sat there and cried and after a while he couldn't take no more and he started to talk. And the man said, 'Oh you're so smart, we'll see how smart you are.' And he put the handcuffs on him right then and there." Barkley agreed to quit. Repeated attempts to contact Zeck have been unsuccessful.

The next time handcuffs were out on Elliott Barkley they were not removed until he was inside the walls at Attica. The charge: violation of parole. One of Elliott's 10 brothers and sisters had told Mrs. Barkley that Elliott, who had no driver's license, was out driving the family car, Mrs. Barkley said. She called the parole division, she said, "for help."

The "help" it turned out, was revocation of parole. If the call had come seven months later, after a court decision last January, Elliott Barkley could not have been returned to prison without a hearing. Elliott's older brother, Willie, could have testified, as he had since sworn in an affidavit, that he, not Elliott, had the car. But there was no hearing. Elliott (known as "L.D." to his friends) was sent to Attica, and then returned to Elmira to complete his original four-year term.

This time, L.D. did not play the game. Shortly after arriving at Elmira, his mother said, he got into a dispute with a guard over how shiny he had to make a brass pipe. There was a fight and L.D. was subdued and placed in a segregated cell. Word reached Mrs. Barkley that there had been trouble and she went to Elmira to visit him. "I went in and I waited for them to bring him out. When he came out he was dirty, filthy. He had old shoes without strings and he smelled so badly that it made all of us nauseous. He said that he was beaten, that he hadn't had a bath for a week," she said.

Shortly after that, L.D. was transferred to Attica as a result, the Barkleys say, of the fight at Elmira. "The guard supposedly said something like, 'You think you're a smart nigger. You've got a lot of mouth.' And the guard beat him down, over the head, with a Billy club, and he had some assistants come over and help him," Mrs. Barkley said. "And Elliott told me he felt they were going to kill him. And he decided he was going to fight back. And if he was going to be killed, he'd be killed fighting back."

—Newsday LLC, ©1971

34

Disgruntled Vulture

It was a dream assignment: New York City correspondent.

In the three decades since its founding by Alicia Patterson, renegade liberal scion of a conservative newspaper dynasty, *Newsday* had evolved into a suburban juggernaut, a paper willing and able to take chances. It was so dominant a force on Long Island that occasional boycotts by subscribers to protest one crusade or another almost inevitably fell apart in a matter of weeks. Readers had no place else to turn for the ads and did not want to punish the neighborhood kid who had the delivery route. Yet for all the freedom reporters enjoyed as a result of this journalistic and economic independence, there was one drawback. We lacked the prestige and influence of our counterparts in New York City and found it difficult to connect with sources in Manhattan who never saw our stories.

Back in Garden City, *Newsday* editors chafed at the idea that we were less than major league, and it was newsroom lore (attributed to an early editor named Alan Hathway) that if you quit for a job in the city you could never be hired back. So we assumed we'd seen the last of an up-and-coming desk man named Ken Brief who left for the *Times,* but he was back just weeks later. Disaffected by the impersonality he found there, Brief asked for his old job and got it—a handy object lesson that city journalism was no panacea.

"Where there is no vision, the people perish," the biblical motto atop its editorial page declared, but *Newsday's* approach to covering city news was practically myopic. Many Long Islanders had roots in the city and a good number commuted there for work. They could follow sports teams and read Broadway reviews in *Newsday,* yet had to rely on television or New York-based papers for day-to-day city news. We rewrote wire service stories about New York if we covered it at all. This infuriated reporters, some of them reverse commuters who lived in the city. As much as we valued the journalism Newsday allowed us to pursue, many of us saw Long Island as a dull, stultifying sprawl of cookie-cutter homes occupied by white Democrats-turned-Republicans who clogged freeways and shopped in climate-controlled shopping centers, strip malls filled with chain stores, and fast-food restaurants. So when the creation of a full-time city correspondent's position was announced, it set off a veritable land rush of applications, mine included.

I was getting my share of good assignments—a special legislative session in Albany, a takeout on community resistance to Mayor John Lindsay's efforts to site low-income housing in a middle-class Queens neighborhood, and a magazine story about allegations of sex abuse against neoconservative L'il Abner cartoonist Al Capp that took me to Boston. But I was still under thirty and just three years removed from sportswriting, so when editor Dave Laventhol—an émigré from the defunct *Herald-Tribune* who was one of a number of New York expatriates whose names dotted *Newsday's* masthead—called me into his glass-enclosed office, I assumed he would say that I had a bright future even if I was not quite ready for the coveted New York City beat. What he said instead was that I had won the city sweepstakes. "We want you to cover the city as if you were a foreign correspondent," he told me, and that is what I set out to do.

I went after stories that exemplified city life. I delved into New York's ethnicity with one piece on impact of a population surge on Chinatown as a result of liberalized immigration policies and another on efforts to preserve a waning Polish-American enclave in the Williamsburg section of Brooklyn. And portrayed some of its absurdities, chronicling the bizarre experience of a Brooklyn man compelled to have his own insurer pay to fix a car accidentally set ablaze in a repair shop, interviewing an upscale Madison Avenue butcher about the impact of a citywide boycott of meat to protest high prices, and portraying a campaign against quality-of-life crimes by police laying traps for subway thieves and targeting "johns" propositioning a female officer posing as a Times Square hooker. The goal of that one was to publicly shame the customers and it produced a couple of unlikely targets—a bouncer from a nearby bar where near-naked women jiggled for hours on end and a bus driver who had dropped a group of New Jersey churchwomen off in the theater district for a matinee of *Jesus Christ: Superstar.*

I was still trying to develop a rhythm when I got a call from managing editor Don Forst. I was doing well, he said, but he needed me to take a break from my new role for another assignment he said was critically important. "We want you to vultch 'The Heroin Trail,'" he said.

"Vultching," short for vulturing, had emerged from a costly lesson. Of all the times *Newsday* had been accused of libel (including a $48-million suit against me and others by a teen travel camp in response to stories on unsafe charter buses), the paper had been forced to pay just once because a follow-up story on a series exposing misleading claims and corrupt practices by a Long Island charity overstated the original allegations. Because that story was written by a reporter who had worked the original series and thus had a stake in the fallout, lawyers for the charity contended that the paper was motivated by malice, the standard for libeling a newsworthy figure. After that, only reporters uninvolved in the original stories—"vultures"—would be assigned to cover the impact of an investigation.

"The Heroin Trail" was already the talk of the newsroom— and not for the right reasons. The brainchild of chief investigative reporter Bob Greene, a larger-than-life figure in both bombast and girth, the series sought to trace the drug's route from the poppy fields of Turkey into the arms of addicts on Long Island. Greene's guru-like reputation was built on exposing local corruption, diving into public files long before computer analysis became the backbone of such probes to tie politicians to self-enrichment, cronyism and worse. When he ventured into national politics he had come up empty, failing to nail President Nixon's Florida-based friend Bebe Rebozo. Now Greene had convinced his bosses to commit even more time and money—much more—to "The Heroin Trail." It was clear from that first chat with Forst that coming up empty was not an option this time. That would put the vulture into the uncomfortable position of promoter rather than reporter, the very thing the role was created to avoid. And, Forst made it clear, I was the first and only choice for the job.

Armed with a copy of the series and some supporting materials from reporter Tony Marro, who had been pulled from covering the Watergate break-in to lead a stateside team gauging the extent of heroin use on Long Island, I flew to Washington, D. C., checked into the Hilton, and found some workspace up the street in *Newsday's* Washington bureau.

My job over the next month would take me to Capitol Hill, the State Department and various foreign embassies in search of reaction to supposed revelations in *Newsday*. But before I even began, I knew it to be a fool's mission after reading a thin paperback, *The Politics of Heroin in Southeast Asia*, that Marro had given me. Written by a Yale graduate student, the book dismissed the route from Turkey through Bulgaria to Marseille—*Newsday's* "heroin trail"—as old hat compared to a newer path from the Far East. Far more troubling, in a very few pages he summarized what our series called "revelations." In other words, Greene and his compatriots had discovered little that was new. "I know, Ed," Marro said when I raised these issues. "I know. I've told them. They don't want to hear it."

If my vultching efforts ranged from disappointing to disastrous, I did relish the Washington milieu. I hobnobbed at a party at the Georgetown home of bureau chief Joe Albright and his then-wife Madeline, the future Secretary of State, and dined well on the company's dime, making Trader Vic's in the Hilton such a regular haunt that I barely noticed the hubbub one night as the Nixons arrived. When Victoria flew down one weekend we went to a party hosted by George Omas, a member of the University of Mississippi delegation to the L.I.U. urban affairs conference who had landed a position in the Nixon Administration through his Ole Miss classmate, Senator Trent Lott. She broke a heel dancing and had one shoe on and one off when we returned to the hotel, barely staggering through the lobby into the elevator as we laughed—and precipitating a call from the house detective asking, "Is there a woman in your room?" I resisted the Groucho Marx retort—"That's no lady; that's my wife!"—except for the wife part. We understood that interracial couples were still rare in D. C.

On the work side, diplomats said little (with a Bulgarian envoy just about setting a record for one-word answers in an especially bizarre interview), federal officials challenged the accuracy and importance of the series, and politicians practically winked at me as they expressed concern in an obvious effort to placate a powerful newspaper. Feeling dishonest and used, I filed my stories and Forst got his headlines —"Frenchman Immune to Drug Charge?"—"Series Cited in Testimony"—"Wolff Asks for a New Heroin Probe"—and "U.S. Concerned About Poppy Ban."

That last one was especially tough. I spent a couple of hours with a State Department expert who explained why Greene and his team were wrong in concluding that farmers would defy a deal with the Turkish government to replace heroin-producing poppies with more benign crops. He conceded that a minor element of *Newsday*'s premise might have some merit. I noted that in the final paragraph of the story I filed. In minutes, Forst was on the phone. "That last graph?" he said. "That's your lead."

Back in New York I stewed for a few days before making a fateful phone call. After that my career would never be the same and nor, in time, would *Newsday*.

35

Special Persecutor

FEBRUARY 1973
Brooklyn

Police scandals were not new to New York, but the deep and systemic corruption laid bare by a series of revelations in the early 1970s that became the focus of Al Pacino's star turn in the movie *Serpico* outraged even cynical observers and led to attempts at reform. One of these was Governor Nelson Rockefeller's creation of a special prosecutor's office to supersede local elected district attorneys who were seen as tools of political bosses like Carmine DeSapio in Manhattan, Meade Esposito in Brooklyn, and Patrick Cunningham in the Bronx.

There were some smirks at *Newsday* when the governor chose Maurice Nadjari, a former assistant prosecutor in Manhattan who was Suffolk County's chief assistant DA, to lead this effort. Nadjari had developed a reputation among reporters as someone with an air of self-righteousness and a flair for self-importance who was not above cutting corners to advance his ambitions. He said he intended to go beyond precinct-level cops to clean up a system he called rotten from the top down and then soon made headlines by announcing that his office was investigating "more than 20 judges." One morning a year later, his press spokesman, former *Daily News* reporter Bill Federici, sent out a media alert. Nadjari had nailed his first judge, a perjury indictment of 66-year-old State Supreme Court Justice Dominic Rinaldi, who would be arraigned that afternoon in downtown Brooklyn.

Like a lot of obvious stories, this one seemed less than obvious from the moment I walked into the august state courthouse.

Rinaldi's pro forma arraignment had been delayed because the judge assigned to Nadjari's cases, John Murtagh, was having trouble finding a court clerk willing to participate. "I'd quit before I would help them arraign Judge Rinaldi," one told me. Another said, "He's the right kind of people. He's never changed since he was a lawyer here." So Nadjari was the outside reformer and these were locals circling the wagons, right? Well, no, it didn't feel that way. The charges seemed flimsy, and *Newsday* reporter Manny Topol, who had impeccable sources from years of covering Long Island courts, sent word to me that Nadjari had a score to settle with the judge.

Officially, Rinaldi lived in Brooklyn where he sat, Topol said, but he commuted there most days from a home on Suffolk County's south shore. He was no legal scholar but had a reputation as a calendar clearer, a hard-working hands-on judge with a knack for settling difficult old cases, leading court administrators to assign him elsewhere to help eliminate backlogs. One assignment sent him to Riverhead in Suffolk County where an assistant DA—Maurice Nadjari—balked at Rinaldi's proposed terms for settling a case. Exasperated by Nadjari's intransigence the judge took matters into his own hands. With a wink toward the defense table, he offered to conduct a non-jury trial and acquitted the defendant on the spot. Infuriated, Nadjari told administrators he never wanted to see Rinaldi in a Suffolk County courtroom again.

The more Topol and I dug, the more plausible the vendetta angle sounded. We learned that Nadjari had targeted Rinaldi from the start, pulling the records of every Long Island case he ever handled, the sort of inquiry that lawyers call a "fishing expedition." The indictment accused Rinaldi of lying to a grand jury about seemingly minor details of two old cases he could hardly be expected to recall and, besides, if they were fixed why indict him for perjury rather than bribery? The city papers played the story as Nadjari fashioned it—the *Times* ran it across two columns at the top of the front page with a photo of the judge escorted from his booking by a uniformed police officer—but we reported it this way:

JUDGE'S INDICTMENT WHIPS UP A STORM
Some critics say Nadjari is trying to justify
his office by prosecuting an old enemy

By Manny Topol and Edward Hershey

BROOKLYN— A groundswell of controversy among judges, attorneys and court personnel is growing in the wake of a three-count perjury indictment against State Supreme Court Justice Dominic Rinaldi. The indictment, announced in Manhattan yesterday by the special state prosecutor, Maurice Nadjari, was greeted with extreme skepticism by admirers and detractors of Rinaldi alike.

"What they've done is pit the word of a Supreme Court Justice against the word of a prosecutor on a conversation that took place eight years ago and gotten a perjury indictment out of it," said another State Supreme Court Justice who presides in Brooklyn. He himself has been a critic of some of Rinaldi's past decisions. "I'd like to know from Maurice Nadjari what he knows about what he may have said to somebody eight years ago."

Nadjari was used to cheerleading from the press, not stories that took a hard look at his cases. He had developed cozy relationships with several reporters, notably Marcia Chambers of the *Times,* who turned tips he leaked to them into positive accounts of his purported crusade against corruption. Our story on Rinaldi elicited an angry call from Federici, who offered to have Nadjari call me, leading to a frosty exchange.

"I think you understand that if you charge a murderer for stubbing his toe there will be some skepticism," I said.

"Yes," he answered, "but if I know someone is a murderer and all I can get him for murder is stubbing his toe, then I'll do it," Nadjari said.

"The problem with that," I responded, "is that it is very close to saying, 'If I know someone is a murderer and I can get him for stubbing his toe whether he did or not, then I'll do it.'"

"I think this conversation is over," he said, and the line went dead.

Nine months later Rinaldi was acquitted on all charges. After the verdict, Murtagh unsealed a decision on a defense motion that he rendered before jury deliberations, dismissing the charges as unsubstantiated by the evidence. In an extraordinary move, he had given Rinaldi the benefit of exoneration by a jury, lest it appear as if one judge was letting another off the hook.

Stung by several scathing reversals of his decisions upholding Nadjari's hardball tactics, the crusty old jurist began to rule against him in other cases and Nadjari lashed out in response, accusing Murtagh of blaming him for his failure to gain promotion to an appellate court. Murtagh was in his chambers in January 1976 mulling over a motion by another Nadjari target, Bronx Democratic leader Patrick Cunningham, when he slumped over his desk, dead of a heart attack.

By then other reporters had soured on Nadjari, sensing that they—and the public—had been duped. In a lengthy *New York Times Magazine* piece, "The Zeal of Maurice Nadjari," Pulitzer Prize-winner Anthony Lewis characterized his record as one with "too much rhetoric and too little result." After yet another dubious case involving DeSapio, the *Times* headlined a piece by legal analyst Tom Goldstein "Questions on Nadjari: Critics Label Latest Indictments 'Thin' and an Effort to Extend His Tenure." And legendary *Village Voice* muckraker Jack Newfield summed up Nadjari's excesses this way: "The lawyer who might have been the Seabury of this generation, the man who might have been another Archibald Cox, turned out to be another Joe McCarthy."

Rockefeller's successor, Hugh Carey, asked Attorney-General Louis Lefkowitz to fire Nadjari but when the special prosecutor accused Carey of moving to protect his political sponsors, Lefkowitz extended his term by six months and appointed a retired judge, Sidney Grumet, to investigate the accusations. Grumet's 102–page report cleared Carey (and noted that Nadjari had backed off his initial allegations). Nadjari and his staff of 175 had spent $14 million and gained not a single major conviction.

If Nadjari's demise was small comfort to targets damaged by his ruthlessness, at least one emerged unscathed—and became my friend. When I called Dominic Rinaldi seeking comment the day he was indicted he refused to come to the phone, but after our story ran my phone rang. "Mr. Hershey," I heard a voice say, "this is Dick Rinaldi. I want to apologize for not taking your call yesterday but my lawyer did not want me to talk to reporters. I just read your story. I'd be happy to talk to you."

I spent several hours with him and his wife Sydelle that day and we stayed in touch, occasionally lunching at Gage & Tollner, a gas-lit downtown Brooklyn landmark. Rinaldi insisted that his benefactor, Meade Esposito, had a heart of gold, which I took with a large grain of salt. I was uneasy coming down on the side of such Nadjari targets and jumped at the chance to meet a caller who said he had some dirt on Cunningham, the Bronx Democratic leader. But when I met the tipster at a bar near Grand Central Station, his story seemed hard to track. All I got out of the rendezvous was a corneal abrasion when I leaned in to hear him and poked my eye with a swizzle stick. My health insurance covered the treatment, but for a time I mused about filing a very unusual workers' compensation claim.

Ultimately, Rinaldi invited Victoria and me to a dinner hosted by Esposito at his favorite hangout, Foffé's on Montague Street in Brooklyn Heights. The evening seemed pleasant if innocuous. Driving home, I wondered what the point of it all had been. "Don't you get it?" she asked. "They were sizing you up for a job—and you made it clear to them that you weren't interested."

"Oh," I responded with an ineloquence reflecting ambivalence about whether I should view my clueless naïveté with regret or gratitude.

36

Investigative Reporter

DECEMBER 1973,
Long Beach, New York

One morning I arrived at *Newsday* as a line of school-aged children boarded a bus in the parking lot.

"Where to?" I asked one.

"Hawaii," she said. "There was a contest and we got the most new subscriptions."

At first, I was perplexed. If reporters had a hard time getting travel authorization, then how could we afford to send a busload of teenagers to Hawaii? By the time I reached my desk I'd thought it through. The kids who deposited papers in the ubiquitous blue tubes alongside mailboxes made *Newsday* part of the fabric of Long Island. Sending a couple of dozen of them to Hawaii was a small price to pay for that. Stable circulation that came with home delivery meant we could play stories more responsibly than newspapers competing for attention with flashy headlines on news racks and also allow us the luxury of pursuing the in-depth reporting that became a *Newsday* hallmark.

Months of digging by a team of investigative reporters produced some of these stories, but others emerged organically from good beat reporting—the equivalent of police solving a crime with shoe leather—by one or two staffers. One of those came my way after editors assigned me to "the poverty beat" to develop stories about disadvantaged residents of Nassau County and asked George Dewan to do the same in Suffolk County. It was an area of coverage stemming from the "war on poverty" envisioned by President Johnson's "Great Society" program.

The irony was not lost on us when we met at an upscale steakhouse in Huntington to compare notes, dining on the company's dime to coordinate reporting on Long Island's fight to extinguish poverty.

National attention to another war—in Southeast Asia—diminished this effort even before LBJ left office. And with Richard Nixon in the White House, the promise of an infusion of funds to bolster depressed areas was giving way to crackdowns on "welfare queens" accused of bearing more children to increase their allotment and "poverty pimps" suspected of pocketing federal funds. Yet we knew it was important to expose need and neglect festering in impoverished pockets of suburbia.

I'd spent that very afternoon at a ramshackle home in the dilapidated New Cassel section of Westbury reporting a story that would run as a two-page spread headlined "LIFE UNDER 'THE SYSTEM.'" Unlike my first news assignment about a white welfare mother who spent her daughter's clothing allotment on a wardrobe deemed in violation of her school's dress code, no editor asked me to find a funny angle to a story that started this way:

NEW CASSEL— The house at 86 Urban Avenue has a stone exterior and a prominent fireplace and it is the only residence for acres around. Sixty years ago it must have been a farmhouse, a pillar of early-century life on Long Island. Now, the surrounding acres are filled with factories and auto junkyards, and the house has become a different sort of pillar, a crumbling cornerstone of the welfare system.

Mr. and Mrs. Steve White and their six sons live in the house. They are given $7,800 a year for rent, food and necessities. In parts of Long Island, $7,800 a year is the product of many hard days' work, a living wage. Here, it has become barely enough to enable the White family to make ends meet.

The Whites are from Selma, Ala. They seem puzzled when it is suggested that Selma is a historic place. Steve White, who is 22 and the father of his wife's two youngest sons, can neither read nor write. He has been unemployed for almost a year and says he is awaiting placement in an adult training program. Several of his teeth were extracted recently and he has been told that most of the others must go. His wife, Willie, has been suffering from painful headaches since the birth of her sixth son, George, 10 months ago. One of her sons is anemic; another has asthma.

The house is decaying. In the kitchen one small trash receptacle is overflowing. Two windows broken by vandals last summer are still broken. "I'd like to fix this place up," Mrs. White said. "We need mattresses. We have only one dresser in the whole house. But there isn't any money. Toward the end of the month, there isn't even any money for food."

Inadequate housing was a vexing concern in light of a growing phenomenon: the "welfare motel." With long wait lists for public housing and few landlords willing to rent to government-subsidized tenants, hard-pressed social workers were placing families in dilapidated motels until something better could be found. It was a windfall for owners of properties so rundown they were even past the point of acceptability as "hot pillow" joints for illicit liaisons or prostitution, but a devastating indignity for families squeezed into a room with no cooking facilities for months on end at prices that gouged taxpayers. Outraged state legislators had voted to eliminate funding for a family in a motel for longer than six months to pressure localities to curtail the practice but, predictably, failed to fund alternative programs to house the poor.

It got so bad that when a real estate entrepreneur from Long Beach proposed that Nassau County pay him a $25,000 finder's fee to relocate 120 motel families, the county jumped at the deal. Yes, officials said, it had the distasteful feel of a bounty, but it also seemed like a win-win-win. Unless he owned the building where the families were placed, the realtor would earn about $200 plus the standard commission of a month's rent, the county would pay less in the long run, and the family would have an apartment. Then I got an anonymous tip, likely from a county employee, that sent me to the county records office. After three days of leafing through musty files I had my story. The realtor was double- and even triple-dipping, masking his ownership of several buildings so he could pocket the contract commission above the standard commission *and* a landlord's security deposit that was often unreturned when a welfare tenant left.

My revelation precipitated termination of the contract—and led to another more intricate and subtle story. Sifting through files to establish the true ownership of buildings where the county placed families, I realized that two other Long Beach investors were buying old rundown homes left and right. The question was why. By matching real estate transactions with social services records, I established how easy it was for them to manipulate the system and amass a veritable empire of inferior housing with little upfront cash. The piece—subtitled "Capitalizing on Welfare" and running three pages—started this way:

> Two Long Beach businessmen were able to parlay an investment of a few thousand dollars into $900,000 worth of welfare housing in two years largely as a result of local and state social services' department procedures.
>
> A 10-week Newsday investigation into the activities of the two men, Michael Weiss and Rafael Berger, has determined that from 1969 to 1971 they bought 31 buildings containing 77 housing units, paying an average of $2,000 in cash down payments for the properties. They filled almost all the apartments with welfare tenants and received lump-sum advances from the department that frequently matched the initial cash outlay on each building.

An accompanying chart traced the purchase date, down payment, government advance, rent and monthly mortgage and tax payments for each property, showing that even as inspectors from one county agency cited the men for a multiplicity of violations for hazardous conditions and even deemed some units uninhabitable, employees of another agency were moving families into them. After officials and the landlords professed innocence, I found another whistle-blower, a former employee of the realty firm, who detailed instances of their collusion and explained how the landlords avoided returning security deposits.

No one story could reform welfare practices on Long Island, but this one exposed government hypocrisy and underscored that the real poverty pimps were slumlords like Weiss and Berger and that, far from "welfare queens" gorging themselves at the public trough, most recipients were pawns played by others in an endless system that was half cycle, half maze, and totally unfair to them and the public. The experience also whetted my appetite for the sort of investigative reporting making headlines in Washington where a couple of young reporters were delving into a burglary at an office and apartment complex called Watergate.

37

Our Own Watergate

DECEMBER 1973
Manhattan

Covering Albany amounted to a post-graduate education in political journalism. From the dormitory-like apartment *Newsday* rented for us in a townhouse two blocks up from the Capitol building to the conviviality of the communal pressroom down the hall from the legislative chambers, to the talk at restaurants and watering holes where reporters and politicians gathered after hours, it all had the feel of a campus.

The statehouse was not the only place divided along partisan lines. So were after-hours gathering spots, although both Republican and Democratic hangouts did share two elements. Liquor flowed and libidinous activity often followed, a reality tacitly acknowledged in how the Legislative Correspondents Association scheduled the annual spoof that generated funds for journalism scholarships (as well as booze to stash in an old safe in the pressroom that opened at 5 each afternoon just as we began writing our stories). The show played to legislators and lobbyists on Saturday night with a reprise for reporters' families on Sunday. But an earlier performance, a Friday night dress rehearsal, allowed anyone who had made a very special friend during the session to reward her with a ticket in those days when private lives stayed private.

Not every assignation was blatant. One evening a dozen of us decided to eschew the Capitol area for L'Epicure, a restaurant in East Greenbush, which was as far out of town as it sounds. We were just settling in when a Republican assemblyman from Long Island arrived with a female staffer. Their out-of-the-way tete-a-tete was playing out in front of most of the Albany press corps.

And then there was the embarrassing miscalculation of a Long Island Republican Assemblyman at a reception the *Newsday* bureau hosted toward the end of the legislative session. As an inside joke, we invited a woman who led a double life, a single mother supplementing her income by turning tricks. With the party in full swing, she exited with the legislator who was grinning from ear to ear over his presumed conquest. The next day he visited the pressroom to protest that he had no idea the woman was a hooker. "Doesn't he realize," bureau chief Jon Margolis said, "that it only makes him look dumber?"

Another legislator at the party, a Long Island Democrat who rented a flat just below ours, exhibited more deftness. He connected with a comely abortion rights activist in town to lobby for a bill coming up for a vote the following day. The next morning, I was walking out of the Assembly chamber just behind him when he reached the visitors' gallery—and spotted his prior night's companion sitting two seats from his wife, who had come up to see him speak in favor of the abortion bill. He rushed to embrace her and, turning to the lobbyist as if just noticing her, introduced the two women with seamless ease. *Now that*, I thought to myself, *is some politician.* Alas he was soon embroiled in a scandal that ended his career.

Sexual escapades were not news in Albany. Unearthing political hanky-panky on the other hand, was a reporter's dream and I caught onto some in an unlikely place—back in Hempstead in my own mailbox. A circular promoting Bill Baird's Liberal Party candidacy for the State Assembly arrived just before Election Day, calling him a progressive alternative to the incumbent Republican and his Democratic opponent. New York's Liberal Party, chiefly the province of union leaders, had served for years to tug Democrats leftward, offering those it deemed worthy a second line on the ballot. But sometimes the party ran spoilers against Democrats not to their liking and even teamed with Republicans in New York City to elect "fusion" Mayors Fiorello LaGuardia and John Lindsay. The Liberals were not motivated entirely by philosophy. They also garnered an inordinate number of patronage jobs by helping one major party or other gain and retain power.

I had never seen any literature supporting a stand-alone Liberal on Long Island and the pamphlet piqued my curiosity. I called Bill Baird, an early outspoken proponent of legalized abortion, to ask about the mailing, which was signed by Harold J. Relkin of the "Action Committee for the Liberal Party." Baird said he knew nothing about the circular and had never heard of Relkin. After I did a story about the "mystery mailing," *Newsday* political reporter Alan Eysen told me he had heard that similar pamphlets had surfaced on behalf of Liberals in two other districts. All three had mailing labels identical to those normally used by Republican candidates.

We hit the phones and discerned that Relkin lived on the Jersey shore and once held a minor position on the payroll of Perry Duryea, powerful Republican Assembly Speaker from eastern Long Island. Attorney General Louis Lefkowitz said he would look into the mailings, but after President Nixon's landslide re-election helped Republicans retain control of the Assembly, the matter seemed moot even if, as we suspected, it was part of a scheme to siphon votes from Democrats. In just one of the three districts had the Liberal polled more votes than the difference between the victorious Republican and Democrat.

Months later Eysen approached me again. Someone in the attorney general's office had tipped him off that the scheme was bigger than we originally thought. His source was concerned that Lefkowitz, an amiable Republican loyalist with a career dating back half a century, would bury the matter. With guidance from our own "Deep Throat," we pretended to be routinely following up on the original story, asking the right questions to enable us to report that Republicans had secretly aided a dozen Liberals across the state to help retain control of the Assembly and position Duryea to run for governor in 1974.

"If the allegations are anywhere near accurate," Democratic state chairman Joe Crangle declared, "it would appear we have a New York Watergate." Cornered by reporters as he was about to meet with Governor Nelson Rockefeller on other matters, Duryea said that despite a $4,160 expense item reported by his campaign committee for a "Liberal program," he knew nothing of the scheme, adding, "No, no, my God no, this is not Watergate." On Long Island, one Liberal beneficiary of the mailings apologized; in Buffalo another complained that the circular made her seem too liberal, probably costing her votes; and in Rockland County a third said, "I guess after Watergate nothing should shock me, but I'm shocked."

I was waiting with a photographer outside the attorney general's office in lower Manhattan as aides to Duryea escorted Relkin to a meeting with investigators. He lunged at us, screaming, "You stay away from me!" before his escorts steered him into an elevator. The next day Lefkowitz punted, handing the case to Manhattan District Attorney Frank Hogan. Insiders told us privately that this was his way of burying the matter. A Democrat in office since before World War II, Hogan had a crime-busting reputation, but as a product of the Tammany Hall machine had never shown much interest in political corruption. Then fate intervened. Hogan took ill and his longtime chief aide, Alfred Scotti, a career prosecutor with no political ties, assigned a young expert in white-collar crime, Ken Conboy, to empanel a grand jury to consider the evidence.

I camped out in front of the DA's entrance to the Criminal Courts Building hoping to spot key figures arriving to testify but came up empty. Later when Conboy told me that he had arranged for them to evade me by entering through the lockup on the other side, my frustration was mitigated by the delicious realization that some of New York's most powerful politicians had passed through several sets of jail gates en route to the grand jury room. On December 13, 1973, the gates clanged for them. Duryea, Assembly Majority Leader John Kingston, a third legislator, and three GOP strategists were charged with conspiring to misrepresent the source of campaign literature in an indictment that put Duryea at the center of the scheme and efforts to cover it up.

The defendants arrived in handcuffs, but I got a strong hint that the prosecution might be overmatched when their lawyer, Harold Fisher, strode into court in a full-length mink coat. Fisher, the father of an L.I.U. classmate of mine, was a longtime lawyer for the Democratic organization, which controlled judgeships and other political plums as tightly in Brooklyn as the Republicans did on Long Island. Weeks later, an appellate judge dismissed the case. He had no problem with the section of the law the defendants were accused of violating but ruled that another part barring anonymous mailings violated the First Amendment, rendering the entire statute unconstitutional.

But nobody could dismiss the political repercussions of our work. In an accident of timing, Rockefeller resigned to chair a commission on national priorities the day after the indictments—and before serving as Gerald Ford's vice president in the aftermath of Richard Nixon's resignation, making way for his lieutenant governor, Malcolm Wilson. Considered an underdog to Duryea for the 1974 GOP nomination, Wilson was chosen without opposition and went on to lose to Democrat Hugh Carey in the general election. Democrats also captured the Assembly that year, relegating Duryea to the minority leadership before he relinquished it in an unsuccessful run against Carey four years later. The New York State Publishers Association honored our work on the story in 1974, but that was really secondary. The brochure in my mailbox had changed the political history of New York State.

38

Murder in the Court

It was the sort of story you would expect in a TV police drama: the body of the law secretary to a State Supreme Court Justice discovered early Monday morning in his third-floor office at the Nassau County Courthouse in Mineola, a bullet in his temple.

Finding no weapon, police labeled the fatal shooting of Burr Hollister a homicide and as word spread, reporters descended on the courthouse. *Newsday,* barely a mile and a half away, even had its own witness. A security guard at our office was the last person (aside from his killer) to see the victim walking toward the building alone, after exiting his car Sunday evening. He said he did not know Hollister, but the thirty-two-year-old lawyer was easy to recall given that he was a large man with a full red beard.

Angles abounded. Monday was to be Hollister's last day at work before joining a prominent local law firm. Was his murder connected to the job change? Why had he parked 200 yards from the courthouse with space available steps away? Police found his keys on the other side of the building, presumably tossed there by someone needing them to exit the double-locked building door, but if Hollister went in alone how had his killer entered?

Ken Gross, a reporter returning from the courthouse, called across the newsroom, "Ed, you knew the girlfriend!"

"What's her name?" I asked and his response, "JoAnne Brown," rendered me dumbfounded. I did not recall anyone by that name.

"You went fishing with her," he said.

"Fishing?" I said, even more perplexed. "It must be someone else. I don't fish."

"That's not what Linda Leaf told me," Gross responded.

That's when I understood. Linda Leaf was the county official in charge of enforcing a ban on discrimination in rental housing, and my wife Victoria had once served as a tester for a story on her work, posing as the female half of a black couple responding to a rental ad. If a landlord or agent said the place had been rented and an hour later showed it to a white applicant, the county initiated action. The two stayed in touch and Leaf invited us on an annual Labor Day family fishing outing off eastern Long Island.

The fiascos I associated with that day might have been enough to suppress anyone's memory. My problems started when I went below deck to peek at the Sunday Times. "This is just like you," Victoria hissed. "You're embarrassing me—and yourself. If you didn't want to do this, we shouldn't have come." That brought me topside in time to grab a rod and reel as we entered the "Race," a channel named for the rush of bluefish that move through with the changing tides, making fishing for them less a sport than an exercise in retrieval. After pulling up my fourth blue, I began to wonder whether the fish had decided getting caught was preferable to being jammed in the underwater crush. This largesse led to another unfortunate aspect of our day at sea. We stashed our catch in a basement freezer where it remained until the day we caught whiff of a troubling odor. Somehow the freezer had been disconnected. We rushed the spoiled fish into the trash, but it was weeks before the stench was gone.

Another guest on the boat was an attractive African-American nurse, a friend of Leaf's whose name I did not remember. That had to be JoAnne Brown, "the girlfriend." My reporter's instinct took over and I called Leaf. "This is not my story," I told her, "but if JoAnne needs any advice or wants to get something out, I would be happy to talk to her." She said it was good of me to offer and gave me Brown's phone number. I left a message and Brown returned my call. She remembered me from our day on the water. "I'm not looking for a story here, JoAnne," I said. "If you do have anything to say publicly I'd be happy to print it, but I'm really reaching out to see if you need any advice."

She thanked me and said it might help to talk things through, provided I understood that nothing we said would be on the record or even meant for a newspaper story. We met that evening in the home she and her three children had shared with the murdered law clerk. "I'm worried," she said. "I'm afraid for me and my children. I think Burr might have been killed because of something he knew and that his killer may think he shared it with me." She said (as the press had reported) that Hollister had been working on the campaign of a Democratic candidate for district attorney. "I think this all may be political," she said. "I remember that a few weeks ago when we were out together he said he had to go to a meeting in Mineola. I stayed in the car and when he came out he looked very concerned. 'This is big stuff,' he told me. 'The Mafia is involved in this.' He didn't say any more and I didn't ask any more. But looking back and putting one and one together..."

Over several hours that night and the next I never asked her, point blank or otherwise, whether she had killed Hollister or knew more than she was letting on about his death. Accepting her innocence was an implicit basis for our dialogue. We did talk more about her own role as a suspect and she said she had submitted willingly to police interviews and that detectives had been through the house and removed several objects, including a .22 caliber rifle that belonged to Hollister. She said she was home alone the Sunday evening/Monday morning of his death and we agreed that innocent people often don't have alibis. But I noted that the press would make much of it.

"You know, JoAnne," I said before we parted, "based on what you've told me, if I were you I wouldn't talk to me for the record either." That advice notwithstanding, ten days later the phone rang. It was Brown. "Ed, I'm going crazy here," she said, "and I'm ready to talk for an article. Can you come over?" There, sitting in the livingroom with her three small children roaming about, she predicted that police would charge her with his murder and said the suspense was starting to wear on her. "I know what's happening to me," she said. "I just wish it would happen already."

She professed her innocence. "I didn't kill him," she said and then, turning to her middle daughter, eight-year-old Levearne, who had plopped down next to me on the sofa, "Honey, you know Mommy didn't shoot Burr, don't you? And you know what I told you is going to happen and what you have to do?" The girl nodded and as if on cue there was a knock on the door. Two brawny, crew-cut homicide detectives said they had a few questions. "I can't say anything to you without my lawyer here," Brown told them. "It's a nightmare," she said after they left. "I'm being framed and I know it and there's not a thing I can do about it."

I spent the following day catching up on the details of the case with reporters who had been following it and running Brown's comments by the county's chief of detectives who said little for the record, but denied an arrest was imminent. She shared one outrageous detail: In addition to shadowing her and interviewing colleagues at the hospital where she worked, police had broken into her house and left a disgusting calling card—human feces on the floor. I chalked it off to paranoia until a colleague, Manny Topol, told me that it might have actually happened because police were known to try anything to spook a suspect into confessing.

I met Brown and her attorney, Robert Rivers, back at her home that night and brought a *Newsday* photographer along. Rivers, a former assistant DA and one of the few black lawyers practicing on Long Island, was known as a publicity hound and I figured he would allow us to take his client's photo—so long as he was in it. I was right. The story ran on the front page headlined, "Waiting for the Finger to Point."

Eight days later, Brown was pointing a finger—at herself. She walked into police headquarters and confessed. I called Rivers. "We were discussing the case yesterday and she suddenly looked up at me and said, 'I did it,'" he told me. "I said, 'No, you didn't!' and she said, 'Yes I did' and then she started giving me the details." He said clients had admitted guilt to him before. "You advise your client that you do not have a duty to anyone," he said, adding that he took 30 pages of handwritten notes as she calmly described Hollister's murder and when they met at her home that night she again confessed, this time with her daughters in the room. In his office the next afternoon, Rivers said, Brown broke down. "She was crying and screaming," he said. "She said she wanted to turn herself in and if I didn't go with her she would strip naked in front of police headquarters and wait for them to come and get her."

He was laying the groundwork for a defense of diminished capacity if not outright insanity. But that was the prosecutor's problem, not mine, and I had another exclusive the next morning headlined "Lawyer Describes Brown Confession." Victoria had her own scoop that day. After leaving NBC she had signed on at WSNL-TV, a new Long Island station at Channel 67 on the ultra-high-frequency dial, and when she thrust a microphone at Brown as police escorted her back to jail from her arraignment at the courthouse where Burr Hollister died two weeks before, Brown blurted out, "I'm being framed for this! I killed Burr. I'm ready to talk about it. They're trying to make me think I'm sick." The non sequitur about a frame-up aside, "I killed Burr" was the day's lead story all across New York.

When Brown went on trial fourteen months later I was in an unlikely role: a witness subpoenaed by the defense to describe her emotional deterioration between our first conversations and the night she gave me my front-page story. A *Daily News* story speculated that I might be held in contempt of court if I refused to turn over my notes, but that was not an issue. I had not taken notes to avoid spooking her. My time on the stand amounted to role reversal with a full row of reporters, including my friend and colleague Pete Bowles, hanging on every word. When Rivers asked about my impressions of his client's demeanor, the judge halted the questioning, sent the jury out of the room, and asked, "Are you sure you want the operations of Mr. Hershey's mind?" I knew a good quote when I heard one and so did Bowles who was smirking and scribbling. Sure enough it was in the paper the next day.

Prosecutor Stephen Scaring made a hell-hath-no-fury argument that Brown had killed Hollister in a fit of rage over his decision to leave her and her children. Rivers countered that Hollister had already taken steps to ensure her family's economic wellbeing, and thus, Brown had nothing to gain and all to lose by killing him. It was, he said, an utterly irrational act. She was acquitted by reason of insanity and sent to a state mental hospital but freed in a couple of years. If she did not quite get away with murder, JoAnn Brown had come pretty close.

PART FOUR

The Other Side

39

Talking Union

Managing editor Don Forst's order to file what I considered a phony story when I was in Washington "vultching" the Heroin Trail series early in 1973 had jarred me—and so had my willingness to do it. But I already knew from Tony Marro that *Newsday* had invested such extensive resources in the overblown series that any challenge to its credibility would go nowhere. Was it worth risking my career to take a stand? What choice did I have but to acquiesce to the worst sort of sin I could imagine: write a lie?

After stewing for a few days back on Long Island, I decided that I had to do something. I called George Tedeschi, president of Local 406, *Newsday's* back shop union, and said, "I'd like to have an exploratory conversation."

"Sure," he responded, "but it has to be low key. We're negotiating all our contracts now and I don't want the company to feel threatened."

The more Tedeschi and I spoke, the more plausible union representation sounded. Local 406 was part of the printing pressmen's union but represented employees in other segments of *Newsday's* workforce, including delivery drivers and janitors. "You already have the porters," I joked. "Now you'll have the reporters." Humor aside, I was impressed by the local's sense of responsibility. Members of each segment negotiated their own contracts but everyone voted on whether to strike, providing a system of checks and balances. "If anyone asked for something crazy," Tedeschi said, explaining in a Brooklyn accent even more pronounced than mine why there never had been a strike at *Newsday*, "the other members would tell them to go back to the table and be more realistic."

Tedeschi had advanced from "flyboy" to apprentice and then jour-neyman pressman with a union card that virtually assured him of work at any newspaper in the United States. But he understood those days were numbered. Automation, which had rendered Linotyping obso-lete, setting off a series of strikes in New York and other cities by a union resistant to inevitability, would reach the nation's pressrooms. And that was just the start. The electronic newsroom was no longer a futuristic dream. *Newsday* was one of three papers (along with the *LA Times* and *Washington Post*) contracting with a Boston-based company called A-Tek for a prototype that allowed editors to review stories on a computer screen, add headlines, and transmit laid-out pages to the back shop with the push of a button.

These advances meant that soon no strike would prevent a paper from publishing. The best bet for shutting a paper down had already shifted from production to distribution in part because publishers feared hiring replacement workers ("scabs" in labor parlance) to drive delivery trucks would risk property and even lives. This was espe-cially true in New York where the drivers' union was so notorious for its underworld domination that *Newsday* had given Local 406 tacit approval to organize its drivers to steer clear of racketeers.

I'd voted against a union just two years before. That drive, too, was less about meat-and-potatoes issues like wages, benefits, and job security than professionalism. When the paper's new corporate owner, *Times-Mirror,* put newsroom managers in charge of *Newsday's* entire operation, it seemed to portend editorial independence. Yet, perhaps to demonstrate how business-minded they could be, top editors chipped away at the proverbial glass wall between news and advertising, in one instance ordering a real estate columnist to stop critiquing develop-ments and in another assuring advertisers that thematic issues of a new Sunday magazine would carry only relevant—and positive—editorial content.

The Newspaper Guild, which represented professional and white-collar workers around the country, was an obvious possibility. But some of us who had bad experiences in Guild locals elsewhere were pleased when a surprising alternative emerged—the United Auto Workers. UAW president Walter Reuther had pulled out of organized labor's umbrella organization, the AFL-CIO, auguring a level of independence that appealed to journalists. So, too, did aligning with an industrial union given the schism between blue-collar and professional workers over issues like environmentalism, the Vietnam War and affirmative action for racial equity. But after the UAW defeated the Guild in a preferential vote for the right to attempt to organize, Reuther died in a plane crash and his successor, anxious to return to the AFL-CIO, handed the drive over to the Guild, which lost by a resounding 167–90 vote.

Were enough employees still receptive to the original idea of aligning with a blue-collar union? Tedeschi agreed to meet with us if I kept it quiet until he finished negotiating new contracts for the existing units. But after reserving a room at a public library and sounding out some colleagues, I sensed a problem. There *was* no "us" yet and word-of-mouth would not allow me to reach everyone. So I posted what I took to be an innocuous note on the employee bulletin board with the place, date, and time of "a meeting with members of Local 406 to discuss possible items of mutual interest." The next morning Tedeschi appeared at my desk. "We have to talk," he said. I followed him into the hallway. "What did you do?" he demanded, just about pinning me against a wall. "Didn't we say we would keep this quiet? The company's going crazy!"

"I'm sorry," I said. "This was as quiet as I could be. I had to let people know."

The night of the meeting it rained so hard I could barely see out of my windshield when I pulled up to the library. I began rehearsing excuses for why so few of us had shown up. Not to worry. By the time Tedeschi arrived it was standing room only. I was stunned by the turnout—sixty journalists responding to hushed conversations and an oblique note. Answering questions from men and women who asked them for a living, Tedeschi was straightforward and on point. We would have to show enough interest to initiate a campaign, he said, but this turnout on a stormy night was "a very good start."

We formed a committee from all areas of the editorial department and began meeting at a diner a mile from the office. Unions like to preach democracy but our sessions put that notion into practice in ways I suspected Tedeschi had never seen. Trained to discern false or inflated rhetoric, we debated strategy long into the night and parsed every claim of our communiqués to ensure we were not overselling or misrepresenting. "This is nothing," Tedeschi reassured me. "You should have seen what we went through when we organized the drivers."

As we hit the home stretch, one aspect of management's campaign against the union gave us an opening. Managers contended that even if there were reasons to support a union we had little in common with the blue-collar members of Local 406. The argument smacked of snobbery and hypocrisy and we hit back, reproducing pay stubs of pressmen and drivers who were earning more than most reporters and editors. "If we're so much better than they are," we asked our co-workers, "why do they make more than we do? The difference between these employees and us is that they have a union."

At the end of a long day of balloting there were 149 votes for the union and 138 against with 14 uncounted ballots cast by employees we contended should be deemed ineligible to vote because they were supervisors or had access to confidential files. "The only winners tonight," declared Andy Hughes, *Newsday's* attorney, "are the lawyers." After reviewing case law as it applied to our 14 challenges, our attorney recommended throwing in the towel on six challenges and pressing forward on the other eight. The six ballots were counted. All were against the union, leaving the vote at 149–144.

We established that all eight remaining challenged ballots were against the union. We had to convince a federal hearing officer to disallow at least four of them to win. The contested voters testified along with witnesses called by both sides in hearings at the NLRB regional office in Brooklyn. Then we waited for a decision. And waited. Months passed without word. Just before Christmas, my home phone rang. "Ed, it's George," said that familiar Long Island (Lawn-Guyland) voice on the other end. "Are you sitting down? We heard from the board. We won seven of the eight challenges. They'll probably appeal, but as it stands we won." I put the phone down, turned to Victoria and said, "The one thing I always knew was that I wasn't going to let them beat me down." And then I wept.

For reasons I never understood, *Newsday* did not appeal, and in February 1975 Local 406 was certified as collective bargaining agent for 350 reporters, editors, photographers, artists and clerks. We had a union—on paper. The energy and enthusiasm engendered by the campaign had dissipated in the seventeen months since the vote and even then employees had split almost evenly on unionizing. Somehow we had to unify the staff to establish the strength and resolve to negotiate a first contract. Tedeschi was a savvy leader but in his world in the back shop unions were a way of life. He was on new ground and, of course, so was I.

It was time for reinforcements. I turned to two reporters who had led Guild locals elsewhere, Bruce Lambert in Rochester and Brad O'Hearn in Allentown. At the start of our campaign I told them I respected their Guild loyalties but hoped they would give Local 406 a chance. Both endorsed a "yes" vote and now they agreed to join our bargaining committee. Tedeschi arranged for the parent union to assign an accomplished negotiator, Chuck Ellington, to advise us. Ellington was much in demand, often on the phone cementing a deal he'd cut elsewhere the day before or getting the rundown on a problem he hoped to solve at his next stop the following day. He was knowledgeable, good-humored and patient, the kind of person who can speak only once in a daylong meeting and make the most telling point of the day. Just as important, his presence countered the corporate power of *Times-Mirror*, reminding *Newsday* negotiators that we had a large organization behind us, too.

While Ellington also traced his union roots to a newspaper pressroom (in Detroit), his air of gentility and dapper attire (from monogrammed shirts to Bally shoes) complemented Tedeschi's proletarian style. Balding at 39, he took mock umbrage when I introduced him at

a unit meeting as "a man with decades of experience in the labor movement." Later when we sat down to assess the session he said, "*Decades?*
The only members I ever see are fat, old printing pressmen. I finally
get to talk to a room filled with lovely young women and you make me
out to be Methuselah! I could see the look on their faces change right
before my eyes!"

We laughed at that, but were seriously concerned about some of
the basic questions we had fielded, inviting us to reassert why *Newsday* journalists even needed a union. Then two developments turned
that around. First, the paper declared a wage freeze pending the sign-
ing of a contract. Perhaps executives felt the move would turn workers
against us but it had the opposite effect, alienating newer employees
counting on the next bump in an established six-year wage progression
scale. Then when the company met its legal obligation to furnish us
with a salary list prior to bargaining, the disparities we found were little short of shocking. Respected veterans earned less than recent hires.
A few members of our union committee feared releasing the list might
backfire, embarrassing people at both ends of the spectrum. But most
of us saw no choice. "Information and transparency are what we are all
about," I said. "Withholding this would not only send the wrong message; it would *be* wrong."

The newsroom was instantly abuzz. Union dues are not usually collected until a contract is signed, but to gauge our strength and give
members a sense of ownership we created a $25 fee for joining. Gary
Viskupic, a popular editorial artist who had been hostile to the union,
walked up to Bruce Lambert, pulled $25 from his wallet and asked,
"Where do I sign?" By the time bargaining began a few weeks later, well
over half of the staff had joined Local 406.

As talks dragged on, it appeared company negotiators might be
playing out the clock, doing just enough to appear to bargain in good
faith until a year passed and *Newsday* could promote a decertification
drive. We needed a game-changer, and there was really just one card
to play: threatening to strike. We called a meeting of the entire local.
Tedeschi had few doubts his pressmen would support a strike and

even those evaporated when pressroom managers were spotted train-ing supervisors on a large, wooden replica of a press roller, presumably preparing to publish in defiance of a walkout. It practically caused a wildcat strike that day. But would the drivers vote to strike, and would members of our neophyte unit stand up for themselves? The answer was a resounding "yes" with an 87% strike authorization vote.

That ramped up the pressure and, in a strange twist of timing, so did events 250 miles away in Washington, D. C. After pressmen struck the *Washington Post*, the paper's owners announced that they had sabotaged the presses, causing millions of dollars of damage. In fact, the *Post* had secretly vandalized some of its own presses to justify eliminating the union, but *Newsday* executives took the paper at its word. Concerned about similar mayhem in Garden City, they gave ground on a few lingering issues. Just before dawn that Tuesday we had a contract.

40

Just Desserts?

MARCH 1975
Buffalo

For all the numbers—1,200 inmates holding 39 hostages for 97 hours; 29 citizen negotiators; 43 dead, including 29 inmates and 10 hos-tages killed in the state assault; 49 indictments charging 61 inmates, a $100-million lawsuit on behalf of dead and wounded inmates—one man commanded center stage during and after the Attica insurrection: Governor Nelson A. Rockefeller.

A Republican reformer in the tradition of Teddy Roosevelt, Rock-efeller sought to modernize the state's approach to penology just as he had in areas like higher education and mental health. He started with the stroke of a pen, unifying the prison and parole divisions and putting the reform-minded parole chief, Russell Oswald, in charge of both. From wardens to front-line officers, employees in the state's far-flung prison network were insulted by the first of these actions and alarmed by the second. Oswald was not one of them. When he spoke, what they heard was bureaucratic mumbo-jumbo justifying some-thing they despised: coddling inmates. And they had two important allies—state legislators who put "correctional services" well down the list of spending priorities and sheer inertia abetted by wardens who ran remote prisons as virtual fiefdoms. The result, one Attica post-mortem after another found, was that promises to improve conditions led nowhere, feeding frustration and stirring resentment.

When Attica erupted, Oswald rushed to the prison but the gover-nor did not, dispatching five top aides to assess the situation instead. Thus, the largest question hanging over the siege soon became whether Rockefeller would accede to inmate demands to negotiate directly. His refusal was based on larger implications, he explained later to one of two panels he created to examine the insurrection. "One of the most recent and widely used techniques of modern–day revolutionaries has been the taking of political hostages and using the threat to kill them as blackmail to achieve unconditional demands and to gain wide pub-lic attention to further their revolutionary ends," Rockefeller said. "I have followed these developments with great interest and considered that, if tolerated, they pose a serious threat to the ability of free gov-ernment to preserve order and to protect the security of the individual citizen."

These words may sound prescient given that the lethal seizure of Israeli athletes at the Munich Olympics was just months in the off-ing and the larger issue of political terrorism would one day dominate the globe. But in all likelihood the governor's rhetoric was rooted less in high-minded philosophy than political reality. Rockefeller's dozen years in office were noted for a measured consideration of issues based on expert advice. One longstanding joke in Albany was that his media chief, Harry O'Donnell, showed up to every press conference with two prepared statements, one in each breast pocket, ready to explain his boss's decision whichever way it went. But there was not an either/or to the key issue emerging in D Yard. Once twenty-eight-year-old correction officer William Quinn died of injuries suffered at the outset of the takeover, Rockefeller's vaunted brain trust saw no way to grant the inmates' key demand: unconditional amnesty for crimes relating to their insurrection.

The two panels, one focusing on what happened at Attica and another digging into broader issues, each essentially confirmed what *Newsday* reported in "The Many Faces of Attica," our own post-mortem published five weeks after the state retook the prison. The most poignant testimony came from a soft-spoken inmate named Edward ("Boots") Young, twelve years into a thirty-to-life sentence for murder, describing what it was really like for him at Attica. "There were two chow lines, one black and one white," Young said. "I was the only black man on the white line. This young guard said, 'Get over there with the rest of them.' I told him, 'I've eaten right here with these men for two years. I'm going to eat there today and I'm going to eat there tomorrow.' This officer was a big old country boy. He wasn't prejudiced. He was new and he just thought that was the way it was supposed to be." Inmates had a name for areas where prisons were located, Young continued. "We call it the 'Up South.'"

Each panel decried state policies for victimizing guards as well as inmates. "The system appears to be one that will not furnish the needed protection to the public, is not fair or even safe for its personnel, and is not consistent with twentieth-century technology, administration, or standards of treatment for its inmates," one offered in findings accompanied by forty-one recommendations for reform. The other asserted flat out that the governor should have gone to Attica before ordering an assault that took thirty-nine of the forty-three lives lost. But each group's carefully documented report was destined to wind up where eerily similar findings had after deadly riots at Auburn and Clinton Prisons claimed seventeen lives in 1929—aging in state archives.

A third panel—twenty-three grand jurors from Wyoming County, where Attica is located—had more lasting impact. The grand jury met over fifty-four weeks to hear evidence assembled by a twenty-five-member special prosecutorial team established under a state law originally created to deal with organized crime. In the end, although sixty-one surviving Attica inmates were indicted, there was just one trial. Two Native Americans, John Hill, nineteen at the time of the riot, and Charles Pernasilice, twenty, were accused of killing the guard who died when the gates came down at its outset. It was a case the state had to bring to justify the refusal to consider amnesty, leading to the stalemate and assault that took the lives of ten additional hostages and twenty-eight inmates.

The trial, which began in Buffalo in November 1974, had all the trappings of the infamous Chicago 7 case a year earlier with the chief defense attorney in that trial, William Kunstler, joining radicalized former U.S. Attorney General Ramsey Clark to lead a seven-member defense team. As he had in Chicago, Kunstler clashed with an elderly by-the-book jurist who did not shrink from these exchanges. "The government will literally stop at nothing to convict certain defendants for the benefit of political expedience," Kunstler said, railing against heavy courthouse security he saw as prejudicing the jury. "We saw at Wounded Knee…" And with that, the judge cut him off, snapping, "Mr. Kunstler, we're trying this case here. We are not trying Wounded Knee or the Chicago 7 or any other case. We're trying a common-law murder case here." And on it went. This was how I started my first dispatch on the trial:

BUFFALO— "I may refuse to go ahead under these circumstances," William Kunstler said with one arm flailing the air in a characteristic Marc Antony pose.

"I may hold you in contempt, Mr. Kunstler," Erie County State Supreme Court Justice Gilbert King retorted from the bench.

"Then Judge, you may have to hold me in contempt."

That exchange came yesterday over a relatively minor procedural issue.

In the first three days, prosecutors Louis Aidala and James Grable often have seemed virtual nonparticipants while Kunstler, former U. S. Attorney General Ramsey Clark and five other defense attorneys peppered the judge with motions and requests, the two defendants occasionally stood to comment and even the spectators gained a share of attention.

The state's commitment to gaining a face-saving conviction was evident in its decision to hire Aidala, a seasoned private-sector litigator from New York, to try the case rather than assign a lawyer on the government payroll. Plowing forward in a workmanlike style that contrasted with Kunstler's histrionics and Clark's folksiness, Aidala seemed more comfortable in blue-collar Buffalo than either of them. Interest widened as the five-month trial neared its end and the press contingent ballooned from a handful of reporters to a couple of dozen, including three from New York: Mike Kaufman of the *Times,* Clyde Haberman of the *Post,* and me. By then serious charges against Pernasilice had been dismissed after testimony portrayed him as little more than a bit player, but Hill, accused of braining Quinn, a correction officer, with a two-by-four, still faced heavy time.

Buffalo was uncharacteristically free of snow that winter, and when I flew there to hear the summations and await the verdict I did not bring boots. Big mistake. On Good Friday, April 4, when Judge King charged the jurors and ordered them sequestered to begin deliberations, it snowed nearly a foot, turning the long block between our hotel and the courthouse into a cold, wet, treacherous slog. The jury deliberated for much of that day and all of the next before breaking for supper. Buffalo being a church-going city, a court official alerted us that if the jury did not return a verdict by late Saturday, the judge would probably suspend deliberations Easter Sunday. That was our signal to stock up on beer, wine, and liquor in anticipation of a party back at the hotel.

At dinner I realized that our waitress was also serving the jurors seated across the hotel dining room and asked, half jokingly, for any intelligence she could provide. "The state's paying so you better believe they're eating," she said, adding that several jurors had ordered seconds of the dessert special, strawberry cheesecake. "Sounds like they're gearing up for a long night," I observed.

Some reporter! I was oblivious to what was really afoot. Jurors had concluded deliberations and were hitting the taxpayers up for one last big meal. They finished dinner before we did and by the time I made my way back to the courthouse the forelady was reading the verdict. Pernasilice was convicted of a minor crime and Hill of murder. There would be no party. We told the local reporters to divvy up the booze. Two weeks later, thanks to a tip, I wrote a story revealing that the grand jury had also voted to charge a state trooper in the state's attack force for the death of a hostage, but Rockefeller's special prosecutor refused to file the indictment. So in the end, even 23 rural New Yorkers were willing to seek more even-handed accountability for what happened at Attica than the governor and his protectors.

41

Prison Beat

I relished few assignments more than those that took me behind bars. Investigative pieces and scoops were there for anyone to find but what I reported about prison life would never have been public without me. In short, a prison was a place where a reporter could make a difference.

Among the stories I related—women serving life for killing abusive partners now tending to infants born to younger inmates at Bedford Hills, the advent of conjugal visitation at Wallkill, the equivalent of a nursing home for aged and ailing prisoners inside the walls at Fishkill—three stand out.

One focused on a personal transformation, the second a final act of mercy and the third a telling glimpse of how easy it is to get lost in the system. The lead on the first of these pieces was an eye-catcher:

> Last year, the U.S. Jaycees named Roger Whitfield, son of a New York City police officer from Lindenhurst, one of the "Outstanding Young Men of America." This year Whitfield is hoping for a sweeter honor—release from prison on his murder conviction ten years ahead of schedule.

He was convicted at twenty-two of robbing a bank on Long Island and doing federal time in Virginia when a loose-lipped accomplice told a jailhouse informant about the murder of a man who supplied the shotgun used in the robbery. Confronted by authorities, he fingered Whitfield as the triggerman. Returned to New York and convicted of homicide, Whitfield was sentenced to twenty years to life. After some run-ins at Clinton Prison in Dannemora near the Canadian border, he was transferred to Green Haven two hours north of New York City and started on a remarkable path to redemption. His family, including a brother who was a police officer, traced this new attitude to the revelation that he had a son, then ten, who had turned up on their doorstep on Long Island in the arms of his sixteen-year-old mother. The family embraced the boy, who started visiting his father.

Whitfield founded an "alternatives to violence" program connecting volunteer organizations with younger inmates. It proved so effective that when a hiring freeze precluded the warden from replacing the civilian coordinator, he hired Whitfield at an inmate wage of $1.50 per day. Sitting in his own office, Whitfield operated more like a bureaucrat than a killer doing 20-to-life. It was a turnaround almost tailored to attract support for the clemency petition he had filed and it did just that. The list of petitioners urging his release included renowned psychologist Kenneth Clarke, tennis star Arthur Ashe and civil rights icon Bayard Rustin as well as six New York state legislators, five members of Congress, two district attorneys, a pair of New York City council members and a judge.

That spurred some suspicion both inside and out that Whitfield might be at least as much a hustler as a changed man. "There is the feeling," one of his supporters acknowledged, "that he may be overselling, that if he were really deserving, he wouldn't need this big push. Also, Roger comes across a little too smooth for some people, too good to be true. You wonder if he's conning you."

I decided to tackle that issue head on both to assure myself of Whitfield's legitimacy and, if I so chose, make a case for clemency. Our conversation started innocuously enough, covering his program, called Think Tank, and delving into how a child of suburban comfort with a family in law enforcement could go so astray. We also talked about the perception that his do-gooder persona might be more about promoting his own cause than showing younger inmates a better way forward.

Whitfield conceded that he had probably over-polished his image in part because he sensed that if he did not receive clemency this time he might well remain incarcerated for at least eleven more years until his first scheduled parole date. "I'm cutting down," he said. "If everything I do is interpreted simply as an attempt to impress the governor, then I can't accomplish much for now anyway. But I shouldn't be that way. I mean, when I started doing the kinds of things I'm into, clemency was not around. And now there's no reason for me to impress anyone because, very simply, there's no more that I can hope to accomplish in prison. They can't punish me any more than I've been punished and they can't rehabilitate me any more than I've been rehabilitated."

Sounds of guitar strumming and singing wafted into the room. "Some kind of rehearsal for a prison show?" I wondered and he motioned to me to follow him down the hall where four inmates sat around the guitarist. Talk about a double take. It was Pete Seeger, who lived 15 miles away in Beacon where he often docked his sloop *Clearwater*, the focus of a campaign to clean up the Hudson River. Seeger came by regularly without fanfare and engaged inmates—conducting a workshop would be too formal a word for it—to make music. After we returned to Whitfield's office, I shook my head and readjusted my ego. I had considered my prison reporting a sort of journalistic altruism: big-time newshound trying to make a difference. Pete Seeger dropping by on a summer afternoon? *That* was big time.

I could not put off the hard question any longer. "Look, Roger," I started—and somewhere inside me I was asking Cincinnati Bengals coach Paul Brown if the game has passed him by all over again—"if I go back and write this the first thing we'll hear from readers is, 'There goes bleeding-heart *Newsday* again, being soft on a murderer.' And the governor will hear it, too. For this story to help you and not backfire we have to put everything on the table and for that to happen you have to own up to what you did."

Ask an inmate about the crime that sent him to prison and what you almost invariably hear is designed to sound tough yet deny guilt. "I did a lot of bad stuff, but I didn't do what they've got me locked up for." The first rule of incarceration—the one that bought Whitfield a life sentence after an accomplice violated it—was admit nothing. You never knew when the next legal writ might earn you a new trial and the last thing you needed was some snitch cutting a deal in exchange for testimony that he heard you cop to the crime. So I took Whitfield at his word when he said he had never discussed that night on Long Island with anyone, but I persisted.

"You don't know what you're asking," he said.

"Yes, as a matter of fact, I do, Roger."

He paused and then went on. He had accumulated $900 in debt buying clothes from a local department store where he worked and after he was fired the store threatened legal action. His solution: recruit three friends, borrow a shotgun from another friend and hold up a bank. Whitfield said he stopped after that one robbery, but the friends committed more and it made him nervous. What if police found the shotgun and connected it to him? He and an accomplice, Ronald Hamilton, found the fellow who had the gun, Wayne Foster, and asked him to destroy it. Foster refused. "We were riding around," Whitfield remembered. "Ronald and I were in the front and Wayne was in the back. I pulled a pistol and turned around. I was just going to threaten him. But it went off. We started driving to Southside Hospital, but he died before we got there."

He said they dumped the body and federal authorities never connected them to the murder, a state crime. Surely his version of events was shaded to make him seem as sympathetic as possible, but it was what we both needed: a confession. My story ran, and six months later when the governor released his annual pre-Christmas list of clemency recipients Roger Whitfield's name was on it.

TRUE TO MOST BEAT REPORTING, the more prison stories I wrote the more came my way, like the call from Kenny Jackson on the eve of a four-day July 4th weekend. Co-founder of the Fortune Society, an advocacy and support group named for the hit off-Broadway drama, "Fortune and Men's Eyes," Jackson had quietly arranged a prison furlough for Michael Covello, a thirty-four-year-old heroin addict in the final stages of abdominal cancer, so he could die in the company of family and friends. Covello had withered away to 80 pounds and could not speak above a whisper. But after transferring him to a city facility, corrections commissioner Benjamin Ward decided he did not qualify for release. That's when Jackson decided he needed to make some noise, calling me and rallying nearly 100 sympathizers outside the prison.

Covello probably should not have been convicted in the first place. He and two other junkies were already drunk the night he stood watch while they entered a building to scout out a vacant apartment where they could shoot up. When they failed to reappear he went inside and found them both passed out. He told police that he kicked one of the men to rouse him but a woman who saw the incident painted a more violent picture of the kick. After the man died of a heart attack Covello was indicted for manslaughter. A defense lawyer said that case would never stand up, but because of his lengthy record of drug-related arrests, advised him to take a four-year sentence rather than risk far more time.

When I reached Ruby Ryles, Ward's spokeswoman, she sounded like a caricature of officiousness. "Commissioner Ward is aware that this is a terminal case," she said. "But this inmate does not meet the temporary release standard because of the severity of his crime. There is a point system used to determine eligibility and Covello does not have enough points." Jackson responded that a recent change in the law gave Ward precisely the discretion Ryles denied he had. She said she would try to reach her boss to reconcile that with what he had told her before heading off for the weekend. "In the meantime," she said, "I'm standing on our statement."

This confounding and compassionless response so touched one reader—New York Governor Hugh Carey—that he called the newsroom, setting off a flurry of activity among the skeletal crew on a sleepy holiday weekend. Carey was at his vacation home on Shelter Island in eastern Suffolk County. Two of his fourteen children had died in an auto accident and his wife had succumbed to breast cancer. All three were buried on the island, filling his retreats there with

bittersweet memories. Reading about Covello had turned him maud-
lin and—unless the reporter who took his call, Aric Press, had it very
wrong—sent Carey to the liquor cabinet earlier in the day than even
someone with his widely known taste for Irish whiskey would normally imbibe.

Part of a new breed of reporters whose path to the newsroom had
gone through law school, Press took careful notes. "I want you to
understand the dilemma I face," Carey told him. "This is not just a
man convicted of manslaughter. He has a long background of drug
convictions. When we got him in 1976 on manslaughter he had physically beaten a man to death in a fight over a radio. For such a crime
he would not be granted clemency and was not granted clemency." As
Press let him talk, the governor moved on to a second, bizarre justification for blocking the release: Covello needed to remain imprisoned
for his own sake because someone associated with the victim might try
to exact revenge. He knew of no threats of that sort, the governor said,
"but there is a pattern in these cases. The rule is, if he gets somebody,
somebody gets him."

I rushed into the office and had started making calls when Press'
phone rang again and he gesticulated to me. The governor was calling
with word that Covello could be released after all, provided the family would agree to a 48-hour furlough rather than a pardon. "That way
he could be watched for his own protection," Carey said, clinging to
the absurd pretense that any of this had to do with the dying inmate's
safety. Then, tacking to the opposite extreme, added "and for the reason
that with the last ounce of strength, the man is still capable of commit-
ting a crime. He has a history as a career criminal and a vicious criminal. I intervened personally to make sure he doesn't get wiped out and
to make sure this case is not a precedent."

By then Covello was in a hospital prison ward being treated for
internal bleeding. He was freed shortly before midnight and I was in
his sister's apartment when he was brought there by ambulance. "I
thought I'd get out sooner or later," he said in a low rasp. "I didn't want
to die in the joint." He died a week later. "I leaned over and told him,

'Mikey, God will take care of you,' " his sister Rosemarie told me. "He smiled at me and then he was gone." His parents and two other sisters were at his bedside.

TEXTILES EXECUTIVE Burt Schoenbach had no background in prison reform but his interest, coupled with some well-placed political contributions, gained him appointment to a state watchdog panel. One of his pet peeves was the state's refusal to release elderly inmates who required expensive care and presented no threat to society.

Schoenbach called one day to say that he had come upon the granddaddy of these cases, so to speak, and arranged to have Israel Karp released from Clinton Prison in Dannemora near the Canadian border to a nursing home on Staten Island. Did I want to come along on the 650-mile round trip? *Newsday's* editors agreed that it sounded like a ride worth taking and assigned photographer Ken Spencer to accompany us. As we awaited Karp's release after driving up the night before I asked an official if I could see his fifty-one-year-old file and tried not to appear surprised when he simply handed it to me. It made this story on May 3, 1973—my 29th birthday—my all-time favorite:

SENTENCED 1922, RELEASED 1973

Writs and appeals stream from the state's prisons daily, beseeching one court or another to lend an ear to the cause of a supposedly aggrieved convict. But in the first 50 years of Israel Karp's 20-year sentence he did not file one court paper. Yesterday, after 51 years and 30 days, Karp walked out of Dannemora on parole—a 68-year-old anomaly in a system that is otherwise releasing inmates after an average of 22 months in prison.

Israel Karp, 17, one of five children of a Brooklyn woman widowed when he was two, shot and killed one of his bosses March 7, 1922. He was indicted nine days later and pleaded guilty to second-degree murder April 3. Following a report from the "commission on lunacy" Judge Isidor Wasservogel sentenced him to a minimum of 20 years. The commission reported, in part, that Karp "admitted he was off his head, that he had spells when he could not control himself and did not know what he was doing, that he had impulses to kill people ... and that he also hears low voices.

"I suppose everybody knows him," said Robert McGee, the guard who helped Karp pack for the 320-mile ride to his new residence in a nursing home on Staten Island. "He's sort of a celebrity, the man with the longest time in the institution." Karp was walking out of the front door slowly, for the benefit of two television crews. "This man should have been out long ago," said superintendent J. Edwin LaVallee. "He had nobody." Then Karp was in the car heading for the Northway. "It feels wonderful," he said. "It feels like a whole new world."

"As we are transferring James Dougherty to your institution we thought we had better just make out the commitment blank and send this man with him and thereby save extra expense." —an interdepartmental memo from Sing Sing prison to Dannemora State Hospital for the criminally insane, April 5, 1922, explaining why Inmate No. 73655, Israel Karp, had been dispatched to Dannemora after only a day at Sing Sing, without any physical or mental examination.

The man driving the car was Burton Schoenbach, recently appointed to the State Commission on Correction. "I first learned about Izzy two weeks ago from a parole officer named Josea Brown, who'd heard that I'd helped several others like him," Schoenbach said. Karp, who first was eligible for parole in 1936, was declared legally sane last August. In September he was paroled pending placement by the state in a suitable nursing home. For seven months, Brown found that one agency after another had too many cases to take on a 68-year-old ex-convict. "We had no real facilities for geriatric care," Schoenbach said, "and there are any number of men like Izzy who are sitting at Green Haven or Dannemora because there is no place else for them to go."

*"This hospital is for the care and custody of insane male convicts
and your son was transferred here because the prison physician felt
that his mental condition was such that he could be cared for here
much better than at the prison." —note from Dr. Charles Burdick,
Dannemora administrator, to Mrs. Ethel Karp, April 23, 1922."*

"I don't think they'll come to see me on Staten Island," Karp
said of his relatives. "They don't like the idea that I committed
murder. I'm supposed to be the black sheep of the family. But if
they come to see me I'll receive them. My sister, Frances, lived
on Eastern Parkway and somebody must have opened a letter
I wrote to her, because she wrote me that the whole neighborhood found out about me and she had to move."

*"I am beginning to feel he has paid a good part of his debt and that
it is largely a question of whether he is ready for society or whether
he is lost to it. He was a teenage boy when he committed his crime."
—Herman Karp in a letter, August 2, 1922, asking prison officials
to give his brother Israel construction training so Herman might put
him to work when he was released.*

In October 1933, Karp was declared legally sane and transferred from the mental hospital to the regular prison population
at Dannemora. But the following March he was recommitted
to the asylum, eliminating the possibility of parole. "I had a
fight with the psychiatrist," Karp said yesterday. He had told
the doctor what he has told others for 51 years—that he feels
"someone from the next world" is tormenting him. He repeated
the story last Aug. 15. But then, officials decided that Karp had
"no active symptoms of psychosis, but does exhibit some residue
of the previous schizophrenia."

Yesterday, riding down from Dannemora, Karp seemed lucid
and even displayed a sense of humor. "I never fired a gun before
that day," he said, "not even at the shooting galleries at Coney
Island." Then, noticing the proliferation of women drivers, he
said, "I don't think I'll bother with any women now. At my age
'hello and good day' should about do it." Then, reflecting, "I

haven't thought about women for as long as I can remember, except maybe my sisters."

"I wish to discontinue receiving mail from Israel Karp. At present these letters upset me too much and I find I cannot answer them..." — *from a letter from a sister, Mildred Rimov of Berkeley, Calif., April 8, 1956.*

Karp's brother Herman, a former Suffolk businessman now retired in Florida, and one of Herman's sons were eventually the only relatives to keep in touch. Yesterday Karp spoke by phone to his nephew, who promised to visit him on Staten Island next week and to provide any items he may need. But last night the nephew and his wife pleaded with a reporter not to divulge their names. "None of the children know of this man's existence and it would only cause us to be hurt," the woman said.

She said that it was her understanding that Karp had been driven to his crime by a domineering mother, who goaded him after he was fired from his job. Fifty-year-old press accounts indicate the mother told court authorities that her son was not fired, but quit. "But that was 51 years ago," the woman said. "What good would it do anyone for this story to come out now?" —Newsday LLC, ©1973

42

City of Sam

Even in a city with 2,000 homicides a year, this one was unusual. After seeing the movie *Rocky* and enjoying a nightcap at a bar nearby, Christina Freund and her fiancé, John Diel, were sitting in his car just past midnight on a quiet street in affluent Forest Hills, Queens when a man suddenly appeared and shot her point-blank through the passenger side window. The killing was too late for Sunday editions and, as one of a handful of reporters assigned to *Newsday's* new Queens edition, was mine to check out on Monday.

The murder had the earmarks of a hit. Was it the work of a jealous lover or maybe a case of mistaken identity? A homicide detective at the 112th Precinct offered further intrigue. "We're working an interesting angle," he said, "but I can only tell you about it if you are willing to keep some of it under wraps for now." When I agreed he said the shooter had used a relatively rare .44 caliber gun, the same size used in three other recent unsolved shootings that left one victim dead and wounded three others. There was no obvious connection among the cases, two in Queens and another in the Bronx. As much as they rued the thought that he might strike again, if police really were hunting a serial killer they did not want him to realize how distinctive his weapon was because he might abandon it for one less identifiable and eliminate their only strong lead.

Five weeks later when a Columbia University graduate student was gunned down as she walked home from the subway not far from the site of Christina Freund's murder, my police source confirmed that she, too, was killed by a .44-caliber bullet. Again, I omitted that detail in a story headlined "Connections Sought in Queens Shootings," the first to suggest that a serial killer might be on the loose. Within hours, officials decided that the need for public awareness trumped investigative secrecy. Mayor Abe Beame and Police Commissioner Michael Codd held a press conference in Forest Hills to share details of all five shootings they said were almost certainly the work of one "white male, between 25 and 30 years old, between 5-foot-10 and 6 feet, with dark hair combed straight back."

Not since George Meteskey, a disgruntled former utilities worker, terrorized the city for six years in the 1950s by setting off homemade bombs in public places, had anyone created such pervasive fear in New York. But while "the Mad Bomber" injured fifteen, he killed no one. "The .44-Caliber Killer" had murdered three victims and left several others profoundly wounded. Five weeks later, he struck for the sixth time in nine months—his first double murder, an eighteen-year-old girl and her twenty-year-old boyfriend necking in the front seat of a car on a quiet street in the Bronx.

"It's like trying to find a needle in a haystack," the police chief complained, "and we don't even know where the haystack is." A core force of twenty detectives worked the case from a command post at the 109th Precinct in Flushing logging in hundreds of tips a day, a few of them crank calls but most well-intentioned if useless. Then in early June *Daily News* columnist Jimmy Breslin showed police a letter he'd received from someone claiming to be the killer. What they knew (and Breslin did not) was that the assailant had left a letter addressed to the lead detective on the case, at the site of the April double homicide. After determining that the same person had written both, they decided to make the first one public. Here is an excerpt from that letter:

> Dear Captain Joseph Borrelli,
> I am deeply hurt by your calling
> me a wemonn (sic) hater. I am not.
> But I am a monster.
> I am the 'Son of Sam.' I am a little brat.

> When father Sam gets drunk he gets mean.
> He beats his family. Sometimes he ties me up to
> the back of the house. Other times he locks me
> in the garage. Sam loves to drink blood.
> 'Go out and kill,' commands father Sam....

Now we had a new name for the killer: "the Son of Sam." And at month's end he shot two more, a pair of young lovers sitting in a car outside a discotheque in Bayside, Queens. Neither was seriously hurt. Even more fear, fed by myth as well as the stark reality, spread across the city. After inaccurate accounts that the killer shot only at shoulder-length brunettes, some women cut their hair or dyed it blonde. Inspector Tim Dowd, a thirty-seven-year veteran of the force assigned command of the case, tried to balance optimism with frustration. "I don't want you to get the idea that we're standing back and not doing anything," Dowd told me a day after the latest shooting. "We have all kinds of police here, stopping cars, stopping people on the street. Sooner or later we'll get him. People will say it happened accidentally, but it will be the result of good police work."

It turned out to be sooner but took another attack, this time in the Bay Ridge section of Brooklyn where a couple of twenty-year-olds on their first date were gunned down in a car. The woman, Stacy Moskowitz, was killed. There were 75 detectives on the case with 225 more officers canvassing the neighborhood surrounding this latest shooting. Several witnesses mentioned a yellow car they had seen at about the time of the attack. A series of computer checks winnowed an initial list of more than 50,000 to 351, including a Ford Galaxie registered to David Berkowitz, a twenty-four-year-old resident of Yonkers who had been ticketed in April for driving an uninsured vehicle. City detectives asked Yonkers police to check out Berkowitz. In the meantime, they came across a summons issued at 2 a.m. on July 31 to a Galaxie parked at a fire hydrant near the site of Son of Sam's last homicide. It was registered to David Berkowitz.

By the time two city detectives got to Yonkers, police there had amassed their own set of suspicions. Before nightfall on May 10, Berkowitz, aka the Son of Sam, was under arrest. Except for Jimmy Breslin, no journalist was better positioned to jump on the story. I'd been the first to report on the existence of a serial killer and spent hours gaining the trust of detectives working the case. In fact, Marlon Hopkins, one of those in the interrogation room during the initial interview of Berkowitz after his arrest, emerged into a sea of electronic and print reporters, looked around and asked, "Where's Ed Hershey?"

But I was not there. I was in Bermuda. En route to the 109th Precinct a month earlier I stopped at a travel agency. "It's our save-the-marriage vacation," I announced to Victoria that evening. Our laughs were muted. We had not been doing very well. The island proved delightful—breakfast prepared for us in our own cabin, quaint shops, riding mopeds on roads surrounded by fields of gorgeous flowers.

Once home, I jumped back into the story. The aftermath of Berkowitz's malevolent killing spree was bringing out the worst in almost everyone involved in the case, from lawyers to journalists to psychiatrists to a judge and even grieving family members. A Brooklyn lawyer named Philip Peltz was the first to succumb, coming forward at an arraignment to say that Berkowitz had retained him. After two city newspapers reported that Peltz had offered to sell them tapes of his jailhouse conversations with Berkowitz, he admitted that he had crossed paths with the defendant in a court holding pen and asked if he needed a lawyer. He was dismissed from the case and by year's end had been disbarred.

A second lawyer, Mark Heller, did not last long either. Berkowitz's half-sister, Roslyn Rothenberg, told me she had approached Heller for advice on protecting her family's privacy after informing him she had hired two other defense attorneys, Leonard Stern and Ira Jultak, to represent Berkowitz. Heller asked to speak with Berkowitz, she said, "to tell him I was okay" and dictated a letter of introduction for her to sign. In the ensuing weeks Heller alerted Stern and Jultak that he had been hired as their co-counsel and convinced a Brooklyn judge to list him as Berkowitz's attorney of record. He also made a series of pronounce-ments that seemed at cross purposes with defense interests, disavowing preliminary findings by two psychiatrists declaring Berkowitz mentally unfit for trial. Then Heller brought Rothenberg three letters purport-edly from Berkowitz that looked and sounded like nothing he would write. One described terms of a trust fund he wanted to set up for her children and another declared, "Thank you for sending me Mark Heller." When she visited her half-brother—Heller had advised her to stay away—he said Heller had dictated the letters. Exit Heller.

Prosecutors, too, seemed out for personal gain rather than public interest. The shootings had occurred in three different counties and the elected district attorneys in each engaged in a jurisdictional tug o' war before reaching an uneasy truce allowing them to share the lime-light. When those two court-appointed psychiatrists declared Berkow-itz unfit for trial, it appeared that there might not be much publicity to garner, but DA Eugene Gold of Brooklyn engaged a psychiatrist named David Abrahamsen to challenge their finding. He asserted that Berkowitz was fit to be tried—and then set out to write a book about the case. Abrahamsen had last been in the public eye when members of his profession excoriated his ethics for writing a book analyzing the mental state of a man he had never met, Richard Nixon. This time his work had an impact. Dr. Daniel Schwartz, one of the court psychia-trists who initially found Berkowitz mentally incompetent, reversed himself under immense pressure, he later told me privately, from those in a position to make life very difficult for him.

Even the seventy-one-year-old judge assigned to the case fell vic-tim to its almost demonic allure. State Supreme Court Justice John Starkey, handpicked by administrators who considered him reliable, started to sound and act like Philip Peltz and Mark Heller wrapped in judicial robes. After allowing television cameras to record part of Berkowitz's competency hearing, a violation of court rules, and grant-ing expansive interviews to the press in which he discussed various legal theories that might apply to the case, another no-no, Starkey was quickly replaced.

The Son of Sam case was not journalism's finest hour either, thanks largely to Rupert Murdoch's *New York Post*. Murdoch bought the paper in 1976 and immediately turned it into a scandal sheet, replicating the successful formula he had used in his native Australia and England, even importing Aussie and British editors and writers who never missed a chance to sensationalize a story—even if it meant stretching the truth past its breaking point. Steve Dunleavy, who had come to New York from Australia a decade earlier and landed at the *Post*, befriended Neysa Moskowitz, the outspoken mother of Berkowitz's final victim. She surely mourned her daughter, but also seemed to revel in the notoriety that front-page cries for vengeance brought her. When reporters got our first chance to see Berkowitz at the competency hearing, Neysa Moskowitz was on press row, "covering" the proceedings for the *Post* with a press credential supplied by Dunleavy.

After the hearing broke for lunch that day, the garishness of that scene was a topic of conversation. Yes, she was a willing, even enthusiastic foil for Dunleavy, but wasn't it almost unspeakably exploitive, even for the shameless *Post?* The erudite *eminence grise* Murray Kempton, who had returned to the *Post* after writing his book on the Black Panther trial, puffed on his omnipresent pipe and said, "You know, the problem with all these people who suffer a loss like this is that they feel compelled to try to extract meaning from it. And there is no meaning, no logic to any of this. These killings were about as random as if their loved ones had been run over by a car. It would probably be better for them to look at it that way." Only later did I realize how personal Kempton's analogy was. One of his sons, Murray, Jr., had died in an auto accident in 1971.

Beyond the foibles of preening lawyers, compromised psychiatrists and tabloid journalists, the case represented the corruption of the system itself. I never met David Berkowitz, but it was obvious to me that he had always been in a fragile state. What pushed him over the edge and turned him into the Son of Sam? His lawyers thought it might have happened at Fort Knox in Kentucky before the Army sent him home with a general discharge. Berkowitz was drawn to a coven of

Pentecostal holy rollers whose dramatic prayer meetings must have had a profound impact on an adoptee who had never come to terms with his semi-Jewish roots. Did their preoccupation with the devil plant seeds that emerged as a voice sending him into the streets to kill? It was as good a theory as any.

With their client found competent, all appearances to the contrary, his lawyers gave me my last Son of Sam scoop: Berkowitz would plead guilty rather than stand trial. By then one aspect of the case had become personal to me as well. In the fall we learned that Victoria was pregnant. She went into labor shortly after midnight May 8, the day of Berkowitz's scheduled guilty plea. So in between calls to the obstetrician I phoned the desk at *Newsday* to arrange for a substitute for me. Late that morning at Long Island Jewish Hospital, at just about the time Berkowitz was led to court twenty miles away in Brooklyn, Rebecca Clayborne Hershey came into this world. It was exactly nine months from the day I missed covering his capture because we were in Bermuda.

43

Hostage Cop

JULY 1977
Kennedy Airport

The first call came in the early afternoon of the Fourth of July. Someone had hijacked a bus in the Bronx and diverted it to JFK, where it was parked on a runway. The story sounded good and I knew how lucrative holiday pay was. I'd negotiated it. But Victoria and I had

planned a barbecue at a time when whether I valued my work more
than our marriage had become an issue. So I declined the assignment
then and again a half an hour later. The third call was not a request but
an order. Some hostages were dead and the airport was closed, snarling
holiday air traffic. A summer college intern was at the scene but with
others scattered for the weekend, I was the only full-fledged reporter
close at hand.

By the time I arrived the hijacked bus had moved to a distant spot
on the airport tarmac, allowing takeoffs and landings to resume as the
standoff between police and a gunman on board continued. I connected
with the intern, a bright kid from Harvard named Alison Mitchell,
and we drove around the airport perimeter in a futile search for a good
vantage point before rejoining the mass of reporters, photographers and
television crews at an airport office. Shortly before midnight authorities
announced that they had captured the gunman, a young Panamanian-
born Navy seaman, and freed the remaining hostages. After covering
the press conference and calling in details, I drove home thinking that
I'd missed a barbecue for no good reason. Wire service accounts would
have served the paper about as well as Alison and I had. I told Victoria
we would convert my holiday overtime windfall into a night on the
town and thought nothing more about it until my office phone rang
two days later.

The caller, Freya Manston, said she was a literary agent. She had
the stilted voice of someone affecting a British accent, but her resume
was real with a client list that included Katharine Hepburn. She told
me that she was always looking for new projects, and had seen my story
on the hijacking. Would I be interested in writing a book with Frank
Bolz, the leader of the city police hostage negotiating team? At the
risk of mixing a metaphor, this sounded farther out of left field than
the offer I got to do a book with Cleon Jones of the New York Mets
after missing most of the 1969 baseball season on military duty. I had
never met Bolz and the closest I'd come to him at the press conference
at JFK was from the third or fourth row of reporters. Our story did not
even mention him until the last two paragraphs. My guess was that

Manston had been in the Hamptons for the holiday weekend where *Newsday* was the only paper she saw.

The three of us met the following week. Frank Bolz, Jr. came from a very different part of New York than mine, the German-American enclave of Ridgewood along the Brooklyn-Queens border, but it was obvious from the outset that we appreciated one another even if neither of us knew what to make of the woman who brought us together. Katharine Hepburn was about the last person Manston's flouncy and disheveled appearance brought to mind, but she seemed confident she could sell the book. A few weeks later we signed with a small imprint call Rawson-Wade, which was about to make its mark with *The Complete Scarsdale Medical Diet,* a runaway best seller.

Bolz traced his founding of New York City's groundbreaking police hostage negotiating team to three violent events, two of them far from the city. After the 1971 Attica prison takeover and the Munich Olympic massacre a year later, police commissioner Patrick Murphy announced with some fanfare that New York police would deploy a team of trained negotiators to respond to hostage confrontations like the aborted bank robbery in Brooklyn that August, immortalized by the film *Dog Day Afternoon.*

A forty-seven-year-old detective lieutenant who had risen through the ranks in a series of interesting assignments, Bolz was restless in a humdrum training role and jumped at the chance to join Harvey Schlossberg, an officer with a degree in clinical psychology, to help develop a blueprint for the rapid-response team Murphy envisioned. But in the norm for an agency resistant to change, as their proposal trickled through layers of command, the concept was reduced to lip service. The core element of the initial plan, a permanent trained team of emergency responders, was reduced to a short-course for officers from across the city who would return to their home precincts to pass on what they had learned.

Then came the 47-hour siege at John & Al's Sporting Goods Shop in the Williamsburg section of Brooklyn. "Sporting goods" was a euphemism for guns and ammo—enough to send an army into battle—but initially, at least, that was not what four men who entered the store on a Friday afternoon were seeking. They brought their own guns. What they wanted was cash. An owner recognized it as a robbery even before the last of them was in the door and pushed a silent alarm. In minutes two officers in the heavily patrolled high-crime area were outside. One gunman tried to flee through a side door using an owner for a shield, then retreated when his hostage broke free but not before wounding an officer in an exchange of fire. A second officer crouching behind an El stanchion suffered a head wound and a third was hit rescuing his motionless body. The area had become a war zone with police unable to cordon off a safe perimeter until four hours into the incident when they used an armored vehicle to evacuate six officers and sixteen civilian bystanders from the line of fire. By then Officer Stephen Gilroy had died from his head wound. Bolz and Schlossberg rushed to the scene and spent the next two days there. But when commanders asked if their team was ready to help defuse the confrontation, they could only say that there *was* no team.

The siege finally ended when three gunmen surrendered and a fourth, seriously wounded in the initial exchange, was carried out of the store. Murphy and Mayor John Lindsay praised police restraint and skill but the brass knew they were very lucky. Within months, Bolz was training the first police negotiating team of its kind anywhere, with seventy detectives on 24-hour call. Five years later when that Panamanian-born Navy seaman hijacked a bus on the Fourth of July, Bolz was a familiar figure with a growing reputation. He and his team had successfully intervened in a series of riveting hostage dramas almost invariably ending as the Kennedy Airport case had, with a perpetrator in custody, hostages liberated, and Bolz explaining how negotiators had defused the siege without further violence once they reached the scene.

The first of these cases began on a very hot morning in June 1974. An armed fifty-six-year-old diagnosed schizophrenic named Floyd Steele who had done time for killing women in two states was holed up in a City Housing Authority apartment in Queens with the five-year-old daughter of his step-niece. Bolz gauged what was going on behind the door to Apartment 3B, knowing that an odd coincidence of time and place made it imperative to extricate the girl and take her captor alive. A year earlier a white police officer had killed an unarmed ten-year-old black child in this very neighborhood, provoking riots and leading to the officer's indictment in a case that had just gone to the jury. Bracing for more unrest after an anticipated acquittal, police had bolstered patrols. Bystanders had already gathered three floors below the apartment where Steele was inside with the girl, a gun, and (police would learn later) the body of her father. Shooting him even with justification might ignite a riot.

All was dark and quiet inside apartment 3B. After evacuating adjoining apartments, Bolz acquired as much information as he could. The team interviewed the girl's mother, who had tied bed sheets together to escape through a window, researched Steele's background, and used the apartment above to draw a layout of 3B. When the housing authority produced a passkey, Bolz chanced some reconnaissance, sending an officer into the apartment on hands and knees. But at some point Steele sensed he had company. A flash of gunfire sent the officer scrambling to safety, spared by an improbable stroke of luck. The shot glanced off the face of his wristwatch. The size of the hole another of Steele's shots tore through the door told police they were dealing with firepower, which turned out to be a Magnum .357.

It took thirty-three hours for Bolz to talk Steele into surrendering. Along the way he learned much to apply to future hostage situations—a pattern repeated in each incident, adding to an ongoing body of knowledge about what might work and what probably would not. Sometimes simplicity trumped sophistication. After a futuristic listening device supplied by the city water department detected only garbled sounds of Steele's conversation with his step-niece, Bolz went next door, held a glass to the wall, and heard every word perfectly as Steele assured the girl that her father was "only asleep." And when Bolz edged the front door open again to re-establish contact with Steele, his view of the apartment interior came from a toy periscope that would become a staple of many future hostage cases.

Applied psychology was always important. Two housing cops said they knew Steele and volunteered to appeal to him, but it did not take long to ascertain that they hardly knew him at all. Schlossberg (who wrote his own book, *Psychologist with Gun*) explained that this was a predictable pattern in individuals overtaken by a desire to help. Time and again in ensuing cases associates, neighbors or relatives would express an inflated notion of their connection to someone holding hostages. The perpetrator was susceptible to wishful thinking. of a different sort. When Bolz finally established direct contact with Steele and started to gain his trust by sending coffee and cigarettes into the apartment, the armed man took him aback by asking for "some cigarettes for Freddy, too." Could the girl's father still be alive, despite all evidence to the contrary? "Displacement," Schlossberg explained. "He's pushed the fact that Freddy's dead completely out of his mind and he's convinced himself that Freddy's only asleep." This would come in handy in other standoffs when Bolz was able to coax men into surrendering with illogical assurances that their culpability for earlier crimes, even murders, could be mitigated by the goodwill their surrender generated.

Sweet talk did not work as well with another constituency—fellow officers and superiors. Theirs was a macho culture steeped in the use of force and preserving authority rather than stepping back. When the Chief of Detectives Louis Cottell showed up during the Floyd Steele siege, he said he wanted it brought to an end quickly and could barely contain his contempt when Bolz addressed the murderer in Apartment 3B as "sir." Happily, Chief of Operations Mike Lonergan, who was in command, was focused on a bloodless disposition, worried that a violent end to the standoff might spark more violence. The crowd downstairs had grown so large an ice cream vendor was doing a brisk business.

After seventeen hours, Bolz went home to rest. When he returned the next day, Cottell suggested that it might make sense to have another negotiator connect with Steele. "Let me talk to him," a black deputy inspector volunteered. "I'll get him out of there." Bolz relinquished his position at the front door and his replacement immediately launched into a tirade of street-talk, brother to brother. "Hey you mothafucka, you get outta there or I'm going to kick yo' ass!" Steele, who had been calm for hours shouted back in kind, threatening to kill the girl. It was yet another lesson but one that could result in disastrous consequences. "I don't think it's working," Bolz whispered, trying to be gentle with the ranking superior who sheepishly withdrew. "Hey, I turned that thing around," he would joke to Bolz later. "*I got him to like you.*"

In fact, it was easy to like Frank Bolz. His folksy, gregarious nature served him well socially and professionally and proved an asset when he bantered and bartered with customers after he and his wife Ruthie turned a hobby into a side business selling antiques and bric-a-brac at weekend flea markets. Now it was a key element in easing tension and resolving life-and-death confrontations like the standoff with Floyd Steele. With an officer holding firmly onto his belt ready to pull him out of the line of fire, Bolz leaned a few inches into the doorway trying to make eye contact with Steele and start a conversation, even injecting levity.

> *"You from the south, Floyd?"*
> *"Oh yeah, North Carolina."*
> *"What'd you do for a living down there?"*
> *"A lot of things. I worked the railroads mostly."*
> *"Oh, a gandy dancer."*
> *"Nah, I didn't do much track work."*
> *"They were just building the railroads when you were born,*
>   *huh Floyd?"*
> *"Oh, yeah. I remember seeing them set out for the West*
>   *in covered wagons when I was a kid, you know?"*
> *"Just think how far we've come in your lifetime, Floyd.*
>   *Can you imagine how much Tisha's going to see in her*
>   *lifetime? The way we go to California now, these kids*
>   *will be going to the moon and back."*

Monitoring this exchange in the lobby downstairs a detective muttered, "We ain't going to blow this guy away; we're going to bore him to death." And that was almost the point—to keep Steele calm and convince little Avril Letitia Kinsler that the police were no threat. Once when she walked up to retrieve some food left just inside the door Bolz was about to snatch her to safety but just as he started to make his movie she turned and ran back to the man she knew as Uncle Fly and climbed into his lap, inches from the .357.

With little room for error, Bolz wanted to be certain, placing the food she was periodically dispatched to retrieve closer and closer to the door each time. Finally, as she reached for a refill of Kool-Aid, Bolz latched onto the girl's wrist and his backup pulled them to safety. Moments later, Steele surrendered. There were cheers down on the street. "It is quite likely," the *Daily News* editorialized the next day, "that little Avril owes her life to the cool, patient professionalism of New York's Finest." The *Times* covered the end of the siege on its front page adjacent to a story reporting Officer Shea's acquittal, which produced no violent outbursts in a community with renewed reason to be grateful for its police force.

On arriving at the scene of every hostage case, Frank Bolz would start a tape recorder to provide evidentiary material for prosecutors and a training tool for the team. He did not know until Freya Manston brought us together that these recordings would serve a third purpose. They were a godsend for an author. When we settled on the cases to feature I reviewed each tape before interviewing Bolz, often at dinner where I sat with my back to the door so his could be against a wall, standard precaution for an armed cop.

Hostage Cop arrived in bookstores late in 1979. We anticipated that it would appeal to the true-crime market and as a co-curricular text in the burgeoning academic field of criminal justice studies. We were toasted at a publication party in a dive bar near police headquarters. The publisher sent Bolz on a tour and one of Rupert Murdoch's companies optioned the book for a television movie. But in March a news flash dampened the book's prospects. Dr. Herman Tarnower, "the Scarsdale Diet Doctor," was shot dead by a jilted lover, headmistress of a posh girls' school in Virginia. The case was a tabloid sensation and a bonanza for Rawson-Wade, which rushed a new edition of Tarnower's best-selling diet guide into print. Every other book in the spring catalogue, including ours, fell by the wayside in the scramble to cash in. Nothing ever came of the movie option but after he retired from the NYPD Bolz bought the rights to reprint the book and sold it as part of a popular course he taught on hostage negotiation. At the end of each of the next fifteen years he would mail me a modest royalty check, which I treated as a kind of Christmas Club account.

44

Journalism's Finest

DECEMBER 1977
Brooklyn

I returned to my alma mater, Long Island University, each winter to watch basketball. Then in January 1972 I was invited back for another reason: to help select the George Polk Awards.

Established in 1949 by a pair of enterprising administrators who sensed a chance to increase the university's visibility by memorializing a reporter slain in Greece, the Polks had become one of the nation's most prestigious journalism awards. When I attended the awards luncheon in my sophomore year at L.I.U., reporters from the *Washington Post* and the *Washington Star* were honored along with two celebrated authors, James Baldwin for a *New Yorker Magazine* essay, "Letter from a Region of My Mind," and Michael Harrington for his book, *The Other America*. I loved mingling with such figures and when I was named the George Polk Outstanding Student as a senior, its namesake made the award doubly meaningful. The invitation to serve with jurors like L.I.U. publicist Len Karlin, one of the men who had started the Polk awards, seemed like another honor and I dove into the task.

I was in the pressroom at the State Capitol in Albany a week after we made our choices when I got a call from Karlin. He said the awards chairman, my old journalism professor Jacob Jaffe, was uneasy with the idea that three of our eleven winners were from the *Times* and wanted to eliminate one to Joseph Lelyveld, chosen for an insightful series on a public school class. I was furious. It was not just that I had pushed hard for Lelyveld. Sitting there in a room of reporters banging out stories, it felt hypocritical to be so cavalier about an honor named for someone who died in pursuit of a story. "I'm not having it, Len," I told Karlin. "This is not right. If the results don't stand as we voted, I won't be quiet about it." He urged me to reconsider, but I was firm. I went to the awards luncheon to see Lelyveld accept his Polk—and was not asked to judge or invited back to the luncheon the next year.

Three years later there *were* no awards. They were unceremoniously dropped, ostensibly for budgetary reasons although I suspected the decision had more to do with discomfort over Jaffe's proprietary approach. That notion was confirmed late in 1977 by a call from Robert Spector, a revered L.I.U. English professor and alumnus who was leading an effort to restore the awards. The committee he was forming lacked a working journalist, he said, and asked if I would come to a meeting. "I have to tell you one more thing," Spector said. "Professor Jaffe has declined to participate. I hope that won't bother you." *Far from it*, I thought.

For most reporters a Pulitzer was the Holy Grail, but given my L.I.U. connection I'd dreamt about winning a Polk and wondered if I had come close, especially when L.I.U. president Alexander Aldrich wrote to congratulate me on my Silurians award. Yet selecting the awards was an appealing alternative, less a consolation prize like keeping score for Little League games I was too inept to play than a chance to recognize the kind of journalism I valued. Thus, when we convened on a Saturday in January 1978 to sort through hundreds of entries—which had arrived despite a letter-writing campaign by Jaffe to discredit the reinstated awards—I brought a sense of responsibility and humility to what all of us treated as a sacred trust. Spector, Karlin, and Al Landa, vice president of the New School, all friends from their student days at L.I.U., were there along with Martin Tucker, a professor who taught my freshman English class fifteen years before, and writer Sidney Offit, the newly hired awards curator. Tucker, a quiet man with the soul of a poet, later withdrew, leaving five of us, four old hands and me, to form the nucleus of the Polk committee for the next quarter-century.

The selection process could be intense. Narrowing our choices to about twenty outstanding contenders was relatively easy, but reducing that group to eleven or twelve winners meant making tough calls that often engendered emotion. We did not intend for that first slate of winners to serve as a blueprint, but it pretty much turned out that way. Two awards—for stories by Walter Pincus of the *Washington Post* revealing that the Defense Department had buried a budget item authorizing development of neutron bombs designed to maximize human fatalities in a war zone and Len Ackland of the *Des Moines Register* exposing redlining by realtors denying black residents access to some neighborhoods—were true to George Polk's connection to investigative journalism. Two others—to Robert Toth of the *Los Angeles Times* for debunking Soviet government assertions that it was not harassing dissidents and intellectuals and Daniel Lang of the *New Yorker* for exploring contradictions in German attitudes toward the Third Reich—reflected Polk's legacy of in-depth reporting.

Discerning an iconic moment and turning it into a telling report mattered. Our award for still photography that first year went to Eddie Adams of the Associated Press for putting American wars gone awry into sobering focus with gripping shots of desperate and forlorn Vietnamese "boat people" adrift at sea. It was a fitting companion to the award for television reporting to Morley Safer of CBS for his iconic depiction of an American patrol burning down a village to save it—a clip played over and over after Safer died in 2016.

And our own discernment mattered, too. We cited producer Barry Lando for a series of breakthrough reports on CBS' *60 Minutes* rather than the talking heads who mouthed his words, and honored a conservative editorial cartoonist from Richmond, Jeff MacNelly, for illustrating the foibles of doctrinaire liberals. Two winners, sports columnist Red Smith and *Newsweek* book critic Peter Prescott, added class to the roster and two more broke new ground, giving the *New England Journal of Medicine* its first mainstream journalism honor and naming Carey McWilliams, retired editor of *The Nation,* the first recipient of a career award.

In time journalists came to view a Polk the way actors see a Screen Actors Guild award—not as prestigious as a Pulitzer Prize (or an Oscar) but more reflective of achievement within the craft. We were the Un-Pulitzers. Newspapers could finance a blockbuster series and win a Pulitzer but they could not buy a Polk. That took individual enterprise and perseverance along with a touch of the unexpected. "I don't know how you do it, but you guys sure find them," *Washington Post* editor Ben Bradlee said when Offit called with word that Ronald Kessler's exposé of corruption in the General Services Administration had won. The *Post* had not entered it, thinking it unlikely to catch the eye of contest judges, even though Bradlee said he loved it. One of our advisory panelists had nominated Kessler. And unlike Columbia, where trustees could (and did) kill a Pulitzer after the selection committee voted for it, higher-ups at L.I.U. had no say in the process.

In 1980, *Post* reporter Janet Cooke's dramatic account of an eight-year-old heroin addict's life on the streets of Washington, D.C., "Jimmy's World," won a Pulitzer but not a Polk. Then Cooke admitted "Jimmy" was a composite invention. It turned out she had also exaggerated some of her credentials and fabricated others to get her job at the *Post.* This put renewed focus on vetting entries and debunking cover letters with excessive claims about an entry's significance or originality—especially when two news organizations tried to take credit for breaking the same story.

In 1979 I championed an unlikely entry, a series of articles in *The Angolite*, a news magazine published by and for inmates at Louisiana's notorious Angola State Prison. Karlin sneered at the idea but I persisted. "Just read the pieces," I said. "If they were in the *New Yorker* or *Harpers* we'd have already voted them the award. This is raw, it's real, and it is very well written." We called it "special interest reporting" honoring Wilbert Rideau and Billy Sinclair, two lifers originally sentenced to death, alongside the likes of journalists Ed Bradley of CBS, Jack Newfield of the *Village Voice*, and John Kifner of the *Times*. Far from initial concerns that citing such work might diminish our standing, it brought positive attention. "Vivid Portrayals of Prison Life Bring Recognition to Two Inmates," was the five-column headline over a story from Angola, La., by William K. Stevens in the *Times'* national section in March (a step up from the unsigned five-paragraph article in the Metro section two weeks before when we announced the awards).

Seven years have gone by since the two were moved from the solitude of death row into prison life as it then existed at the Louisiana State Penitentiary: brutality and sexual slavery, corruption and terror. And next Wednesday, in New York City, the two convicted murderers will achieve something no other such prisoners ever have. That's the day when the George Polk Award, one of American journalism's highest honors, is to be presented to them...

...Perhaps the two articles with the greatest impact were the ones that won the Polk Award. In both, the authors laced together their own experiences and reporting with voluminous research findings and sociological studies from elsewhere. In one, Mr. Sinclair described life on death row as part of an examination of capital punishment which, he wrote, "is the other side of murder, which is as terrible as murder itself." In the other, Mr. Rideau investigated the sexual mores of prison life. Citing specific examples and case histories he wrote in graphic detail about not only homosexual rape but also prison prostitution and sexual slavery. The prison, he wrote, was divided into the strong and the weak and the strong often bound male "wives" to them under threat of violence or death. Sometimes the strong sold the wives. "Slavery was widespread and human life the cheapest commodity on the market," he wrote. "The pursuit of survival fueled a heated arms race among the prisoners for the superior weapon—a sword over a knife, a broadaxe over a sword, and a gun over everything. Individual disputes, gang wars and factional feuding kept the blood flowing incessantly, keeping the concrete floors stained despite daily moppings."

The inmates could not attend the awards luncheon, of course, but two prison officials who had overseen and encouraged their work did. To my mind, after dealing with bureaucratic subterfuge in my reporting on New York prisons for nearly a decade, they were courageous as well.

If the Angolite was my favorite, an award to Dianna Marder of the *Philadelphia Inquirer* in 1990 was a close second. Assigned to the Camden courthouse across the Schuylkill River in Camden, N.J., she was leafing through civil motions one afternoon when she spotted a four-year-old case about a program the Cumberland Farms convenience store chain used to discourage employee pilferage. Security officials would escort randomly selected employees to interrogation rooms to demand they confess to stealing and fire them on the spot, making examples of them, regardless of what they said. In three decades as many as 30,000 workers—most who had done nothing wrong and some who were coerced into false confessions—were dealt with in this way. The company eventually paid a $5.5 million settlement. Without Marder's digging the public would never have known.

45

A Coal Country Christmas

DECEMBER 1978
Wilkes-Barre, Pennsylvania

It was business as usual at the November 1978 meeting of *Newsday's* union officers. Drivers were grappling with managers (and each other) over bidding for delivery routes and curbs on overtime. Pressmen worried that fewer of them would be needed when the paper opened its new printing plant. Incessant typing at computer terminals was exposing editors to carpal tunnel syndrome. We talked through these issues before reviewing plans for the upcoming holiday party and turning to union communications.

"We have an appeal from a local on strike in Wilkes-Barre, Pennsylvania," president George Tedeschi said, and someone suggested responding in the usual way with a modest donation that combined with help from other locals across the country would provide strikers with a one-shot infusion of cash. "I know something about this strike," I said, "and I think maybe we can do a little more."

"Eddie," a plainspoken driver named Bob Tedesco said impatiently, "we get these requests all the time and this is how we handle them. If we make an exception once, what do we do next time?"

"But this is more than about one local," I responded. "This was a good, profitable newspaper bought by a huge conglomerate. Maybe you've heard of one of their other companies? ABC Television. They provoked this strike. And it's not the first time. They did it in Fort Worth and Kansas City, and if they can do it in a union town like Wilkes-Barre, they can do it anywhere. And so can *Times-Mirror.*"

I knew all this because of my new role as editor of the international union's monthly newspaper, a gig rooted in the union's quadrennial convention in New York City two years before. Chuck Ellington, who helped negotiate our first contract, had arranged for me to serve as a sergeant-at-arms. He said it would offer an inside perspective on how the union operated. I was to report to the New York Sheraton Monday morning, but that changed when he called Sunday afternoon. "Something has come up," he said. "Can you get in here now?"

Our International Printing and Graphic Communications Union had agreed to seek a merger with the United Paperworkers International Union. Like most industrial unions, both were losing members to automation, corporate consolidation, and overseas competition. This would not reverse or even stem the trend, but it could buy time, cut costs, and increase bargaining power. Union staffers were expected to endorse a vote to authorize pursuance of an alliance, even though it threatened some of their jobs. Thus, IPGCU President Sol Fishko was enraged when word reached him that Roy Reck, editor of his house organ, *News and Views,* was bad-mouthing the merger.

Fishko was a multiple anomaly, a Brooklyn-born Jew leading a blue-collar union with roots in the redneck hills of east Tennessee and a man with a high school education who decorated his Washington office with original artwork from the Madison Avenue gallery his wife owned not far from their Manhattan penthouse. He had not gotten where he was by going easy on anyone who crossed him. Summoned to Fishko's hotel suite, Reck apologized and started to explain, but Fishko waved him off and ordered him to pack his bags. Then he called Ellington and said, "Can you get your guy in here?"

Standing where Reck's career had effectively ended hours before, I assured Fishko that I could write about the convention for *News and Views* without my reporter's skepticism. I needed to clarify that because the last time we'd met, months before in Washington, it was I who had been called on the carpet with Tedeschi to explain why we had approached printers at *Newsday* about leaving the International Typographical Union to join Local 406. It soon became clear that Fishko would do all the explaining that night, too. He said that whatever sense luring members from the beleaguered ITU made to them or us, it violated national agreements and told us to stop. "Well,"

Tedeschi said as we walked down the corridor to the hotel elevator, "I guess that's that."

Tracking the convention was a little like covering the state legislature. However contentious floor debates were, the real business was conducted behind closed doors and in restaurant booths. Hanging with Ellington, who knew how to count votes and wheel and deal for more, gave me a backstage look most delegates never saw. The merger authorization (which would eventually lead nowhere) was the centerpiece of the convention, and a couple of weeks later I flew to Washington to pull together a special edition of *News and Views,* capturing the flavor and color of the convention but, true to my word, not a whiff of its behind-the-scenes politicking.

It also amounted to a successful audition. Reck took early retirement the following spring and Fishko hired me to write and edit the paper on a freelance basis. If the convention reminded me of covering a legislature, my trips to D.C. were more reminiscent of getting the college paper to press. I would arrive one Friday a month to review material assembled over the previous month and check into a hotel a block from union headquarters where I would spend Saturday and Sunday alone except for the constant whir and clicking of an IBM mainframe computer spitting out tens of thousands of hole-punched cards in a weekly update of membership data—a task that would take seconds now but then lasted all weekend.

After writing stories, headlines and captions, cropping photos, and laying out twelve pages, I flew home Monday. And that is how I knew about the strike in Wilkes-Barre. A broadcast chain that acquired the paper in Fort Worth in 1974 along with radio stations, CapCities had targeted unions there and then in Kansas City after it purchased the *Star* in 1977, renouncing provisions on job security, seniority rights, pay scales, and retirement plans that organized labor saw as basic to any agreement. That was also the stance CapCities took when it bought the *Wilkes-Barre Times-Leader* in 1978. But this was not Dallas or Kansas City but anthracite coal country in northeastern Pennsylvania with a strong union heritage.

The company's tactics provoked a backlash in the community, emboldening unions to embark on a strategy of their own. They would publish a substitute newspaper during the inevitable strike. It was a throwback to the earliest days of the American labor movement. When they set up picket lines on October 6, 1978, security guards sprayed them with fire hoses. A couple of nights later, strikers and their supporters retaliated, breaking dozens of windows in the building and trashing the company's fleet of vehicles. CapCities did not publish for ten days and when the presses finally rolled, circulation was down from 69,000 to 5,000. Boys and girls refused to return to delivery routes, newsstands would not stock the *Times-Leader*, and employees of local businesses refused to cross the picket lines. Bolstered by this community support, on October 9 union workers turned out the first edition of the *Citizens Voice*, with members of all four striking unions working in every area of the operation.

The problem, I explained at our meeting, was that they were drawing minimal salaries, using second incomes and limited savings to stay afloat during a long winter to fight a deep-pocketed conglomerate, going into debt to feed families, heat houses, and pay mortgages. "If they can beat us in Wilkes-Barre," I repeated to what was now an attentive audience, "they can beat us anywhere."

Now the question was not whether we would do more, but what we could do. Cash was important, but so was buoying the spirits of families taking a stand for all of us. I glanced at Jack Graham, a large, affable driver who played Santa Claus at our union party each December, and asked, "Do you think we can have our Christmas Party in Wilkes-Barre this year?" The answer was that we could and should. I wrote to members detailing the issues and toys and cash started arriving. Although the IPGCU members at the *Times-Leader* worked in the back shop, a majority of donations were from journalists at *Newsday*, reinforcing important ties between professional and blue-collar members of our own local.

We drove to Pennsylvania in a caravan, barely escaping a snowstorm in the Poconos, and arrived in time to tour the *Citizens Voice* plant. Most who went were Local 406 officers and families, including my wife Victoria and 7-month-old Rebecca (who was fitted for her first pair of leather shoes at a store around the corner from our motel). There was a party Saturday afternoon at the local American Legion hall and then a potluck supper that night where I presented the money we had raised in the form of a ceremonial check rounded up from our local treasury to $10,000, a figure approaching four times that in today's dollars. That brought a collective gasp and then a roar and a lot of tears. Even that much money would go only so far, but what it represented to the workers in Wilkes-Barre—and to us—far exceeded its dollar value. This, I thought, and still do every time it comes to mind, is what unionism is about.

46

Switching Sides

DECEMBER 1979
Manhattan

A few months after Son of Sam struck for the first time, New York's attention was diverted by a different sort of crime, a spree of looting and vandalism during a power blackout that damaged 1,616 stores; sent firefighters to 1,037 fires, including 14 multiple-alarms; led to 3,776 arrests—the most resulting from any event in city history—and caused over $300 million in damage (about $1.25 billion today) in a city on the brink of insolvency.

There had been theft and destruction during a 1965 blackout, but nothing close to what transpired after the lights went out at 9:30 p.m.

on July 13, 1977. Joe Treen and I set out to discover why and after two weeks of reporting, we had an answer. In 1962, the NYPD stopped requiring officers to reside in the city and fifteen years later a large majority commuted from the suburbs and even exurbs (with more living in rural Orange County than Manhattan). It took time for these off-duty officers to reach the city's outskirts where an ill-conceived plan routed them to the stationhouse nearest their home and hours more for buses to transport them to the battle zones. Thus, it was nearly dawn before commanders had enough reinforcements to quell the lawlessness ravaging 31 inner-city neighborhoods.

"We really nailed it," Joe said when we completed our story, and a year later a city report would confirm our findings. But the next day myopic *Newsday* editors nailed *us*. They decided our story was not relevant to Long Island readers and it only ran in the fledgling Queens edition, reaching barely 20,000 readers. We might as well have been writing for a small-town paper.

"If you have a scoop that nobody gets to read," I asked Joe the next day, playing on philosopher George Berkeley's treatise on trees in the woods, "does it make a sound?" I was stunned, then angry, and finally resigned to the idea that my union organizing had taken an irreversible toll. I had covered the city for several years so I knew the turf, but I also knew that was not why I was among a small contingent of reporters tapped to staff the new Queens edition. If my selection as city correspondent four years before had been a "plum," this assignment was a punishment.

Still, I did not consider leaving until a surprising job offer came my way. In August 1979 Mayor Ed Koch named city housing police chief Ben Ward city corrections commissioner after his predecessor, Bill Ciuros, opposed a plan championed by Koch to sell the city's sprawling Rikers Island jail complex to the state. The idea was to build jails adjacent to courthouses so the city would no longer have to transport inmates detained for trial from the island for court appearances. These detainees—the vast majority of its 12,000 inmates—would enjoy easier access to lawyers and visitors. The state would use Rikers for prisoners nearing the end of their sentences to give them a far better chance to make community ties than they could from remote upstate prisons.

It sounded like a win-win and, as I noted in a *Newsday* profile the day he was appointed, Ward had helped develop the plan as state corrections commissioner. A month later his first deputy called to ask if I was interested in becoming Assistant Commissioner of Correction for Public Affairs. Paramount on the agenda, he said, was closing the deal in the face of growing opposition in neighborhoods near Rikers Island.

From the day I walked into the Lafayette High School newspaper office twenty-one years before, journalism had been my life, as much a belief system as a profession. Becoming a PR guy—a "flack" in newsroom terminology—meant crossing a line. When a journalist switches sides there is usually no going back. No matter how worthy the underlying mission, part of the job involves getting some stories into the press that do not belong there and, worse, keeping some that do from ever seeing the light of day. Was I really ready to walk away from reporting?

That was one issue. Another was a requirement that, unlike police officers and most other employees, municipal executives had to live in the city, which meant selling our house in Hempstead. But Victoria saw this as a plus. Our years on Long Island had convinced her that the suburbs were no place to raise any child, let alone a girl of mixed-race parentage. She appreciated my passion for the work. She had lived it with me and sometimes even had to compete with it. But she had also watched my frustration mount. "I know this is hard," she said, "but it may be time."

Finally, what about the union? My role involved more than negotiating contracts and settling grievances. Twice I had interceded to save the jobs of veteran reporters. "This is it," *Newsday* managing editor Tony Insolia said when he called to say he was firing a woman with a history of alcoholism after her latest binge. "We have given her enough chances." I contacted Dan Meenan, a radio reporter who had started a support group for journalists, and he rushed to her side. She returned to work a week later and to my knowledge never took another drink. Another time a journeyman reporter who had covered everything from sports to cabarets suffered a psychotic breakdown in the newsroom and was escorted out by a security guard. I worked with his wife, overcoming her own denial, to convince him to seek therapy for a midlife crisis stemming from a sense of underachievement. He, too, recovered and resumed his career. But as essential as such work was, others were ready and willing to do it. Victoria was right. It was time.

Beyond a grandiose title my new position came with a silver shield, a pager to signal me to call in to respond to a press inquiry or an unusual incident, and a 15th-floor office atop the Criminal Courts building in lower Manhattan. That presented a second line to cross—from union leader to manager, supervising a staff of seven and dealing with the Correction Officers Benevolent Association. In theory, COBA should have been an ally in efforts to secure resources for the agency and raise the image of correction officers to the level of public esteem enjoyed by police and firefighters. In practice, we were adversaries. Much of this was fed by two dynamics. First, officers—we *never* called them guards—resented reforms mandated by the settlement of a federal lawsuit or undertaken to relieve tensions that had exploded at the "Tombs" jail in Manhattan in 1970 and Attica Prison in 1971. They felt such measures challenged their authority. Second, with their ranks diversifying, white union leaders sought to stave off minority challengers by projecting militancy.

To avoid defaulting to the union as a news source for the press, I had to respond to reporters openly and expeditiously even when the underlying facts made us look bad. "When in doubt, beep me no matter the time," I told the central communications staff. Whether it was an inmate suicide, a successful or foiled escape, a cellblock disturbance, or an incident involving an off-duty officer, my goal was to assemble the facts, run what I thought we should say by Ward, and get the word out.

It did not take long to discover tricks to the trade, ways to minimize a negative event, an art Richard Nixon's Watergate-era press secretary Ron Nessen called "damage control" and spin-conscious image builders are now calling "reputation management." For example, when a security breach on Rikers Island went on the police blotter, alerting reporters to a story that might alarm local residents, I tried to diminish the threat and even find a positive. "A sharp-eyed correction officer was routinely checking the louvered windows in the Adolescent Center when she discovered a cut in one of the frames," I might say. "Two inmates managed to slither through but that just got them into a yard surrounded by a high fence bedecked with razor ribbon and enhanced by a microwave security system that has just about eliminated forced escapes from the island."

A suicide always reflected badly on us, but even then there were ways to reduce culpability, deflect blame and create the impression that it was not an important story. I had to wait until a chaplain notified the victim's family before releasing details and that gave me time to assemble the facts. In time, I developed a template that in retrospect seems manipulative enough to affirm journalists' worst impressions of "flacks."

• Detail the press to death down to the specifics of the act, the precise times and places of the inmate's final hours (but not the names of employees).

• Describe our suicide-prevention program including inmate classification, mental health procedures and CPR training, and then, if the victim has a criminal history, add in a regretful tone, "Regardless of all these efforts history suggests that when an experienced inmate decides to do away with himself and really means it he will succeed some of the time."

• If the victim had an extensive rap sheet and/or dim prospects of beating his case, use that to advantage without seeming to justify the act. We avoid referencing an inmate's criminal history to avoid prejudicing his case, but just as you cannot libel a dead man you cannot impact his chance for a fair trial. Say something like, "Look, I can't say this for the record, but while we don't want anyone to commit suicide on our watch, this guy wasn't exactly a first offender facing a DWI charge."

• In the relatively rare instance of a suicide by someone young and/or facing a minor charge, consider several tacks as the facts allow:

> Put the courts and mental health system on trial by declaring he "should never have been in jail in the first place but was put there as a repository of last resort."

> Stress that the victim gave no indication to anyone, listing various opportunities he had to cry out for help.

> Speak forlornly of the fact that the young man had no visitors or had received dreadful news over the phone (something we learned after the fact).

• Indicate that while the suicide will trigger several routine investigations by the city and state including our own "to determine if there was anything we could have done, anything we should have known," the facts appear fairly obvious. Sound genuinely frustrated and moved, if not exasperated. Note that while we have had X number of suicides in the past year they have occurred in five of our 13 facilities and do not appear to constitute an epidemic or a trend.

• Attach the suicide to the victim's problems or prospects rather than jail conditions and cite the numbers—10,500 inmates in custody works out to 3.8 million inmate-days a year, meaning that eight suicides translates to one for each 480,000 inmate-days.

• Try to limit the shelf life of the suicide as news by releasing the information so it misses the 11 pm TV news and morning papers or morning drive-time radio and then subtly mention to those who inquire once the matter is public that it happened "yesterday" with a line like, "Oh, you're just catching up on that? We released it to the wires last night. What else do you need?"

- And always sound sad.

THE SPOKESMAN'S ROLE provided a measure of visibility. My name was in the newspapers—I was quoted twenty-three times in the *New York Times* that first year—and my voice was familiar on both of the city's 24-hour news stations. And while I tried to stay behind the camera—spokespeople can appear evasive and awkward—I had my share of video sound bites, too, and heard from people I had not seen in years, even a Hebrew school classmate. "It really goes to show you the power of television," I told my wife, who needed no convincing given her own time on camera. "All those years writing stories I thought mattered and hardly anyone knew my name. Now I stammer a sentence or two on TV and I'm a celebrity."

47

No Buddy of Mine

JUNE 1980
Brooklyn

Whatever the story—from a boycott of court appearances by inmates angered that lawyers would not travel to Rikers Island, to the escape of an accused cop killer who sawed his way out of a "high-security" area to the unusual 26-weekend sentence of a once-powerful politico in a corruption case—I tried to respond in a way that improved the correction department's image.

When the escapee's body washed ashore two months later, for example, I underscored a time-honored perception that, like Alcatraz in San Francisco Bay, our own prison island had been rendered nearly escape-proof by forbidding river currents. And inquiries about former Queens Democratic leader Matty Troy allowed me to demonstrate that he would not be afforded special treatment except in the interest of his own safety. "Mr. Hershey said there were about 1,400 inmates in the mostly dormitory-style prison," the *Times* reported. "Mr. Troy, he said, had been assigned a one-man cell which is usual for prisoners of his 'past notoriety' as a politician to keep him from becoming 'a target' for other inmates."

The inmate court boycott provided an opportunity to score points. "We are asking our men to try to coax the inmates, to tell them it is in their best interest to see their cases in court," I told a *Times* reporter, "but we do not want to do anything that might escalate what is essentially a nonviolent situation." He asked to speak to protestors but Ward said, "Absolutely not!" To his mind it would embolden the inmates, giving them a platform when our goal was to wait them out. So I said that security issues prohibited an interview but tried to characterize their concerns. "Because they can't afford private counsel they just feel like they're being given short shrift," I said, citing the proposal to replace remote detention facilities on Rikers with jails adjacent to courthouses. The story in that Sunday's paper cemented this link:

> Correction officials refused to allow the boycotting prisoners to meet with a reporter yesterday, but Mr. Hershey said the inmates were protesting what they called discrimination against black and Hispanic inmates in bail proceedings, as well as difficulties in meeting with their lawyers.
>
> He said inmates complained that court-appointed lawyers "buttonholed" inmates in holding pens before court proceedings

or conferred in the courtroom, rather than meeting with them in private interview rooms on Rikers Island.

Mr. Hershey said the court-appointed attorneys were in turn reluctant to take the time to visit prisoners on the island, which is in the East River near La Guardia Airport. It contains 2,200 prisoners in three buildings. The jail is a 25-minute drive from Manhattan, with trips by public transportation taking much longer. In addition, he said, a typical visit takes up half a working day.

A new detention center would be built in lower Manhattan, near the courthouses at Foley Square, under a proposal to be considered at a Board of Estimate meeting on Wednesday. Under the proposal the state would take over Rikers Island for $200 million under a 99-year lease, and that sum and $151.3 million in city funds would be used to build eight new jails on five sites.

It was a small coup, but there was big trouble ahead. It began when my pager went off on the final Saturday in May. "Commissioner," the communications center officer on duty said. "We have a report of an escape from the Brooklyn House of Detention."

"Oh, no," I thought to myself, "not another one." We had barely recovered from an escape in March when three young inmates managed to make it into the parking lot outside the Rikers Island adolescent center, hot-wire an officer's car, and drive over the bridge to Queens, flashing something metallic at two security checkpoints that less than eagle-eyed officers took for a shield.

As my caller continued I realized that this was not just another escape. "The escaped inmate is Howard Jacobson...J...A...C..."

"Wait a minute," I interrupted. "Are you telling me that we've lost *Buddy Jacobson*?"

"It looks that way," he said.

Howard (Buddy) Jacobson, a prominent forty-nine-year-old thoroughbred horseracing trainer, had been convicted of murdering a drug dealer after a beautiful young model who had been living with him moved in with the dealer just across the hall. Jacobson had been held to await sentencing on the tenth floor of the Brooklyn House of Detention, an area outfitted to hold inmates deemed our most danger-ous and escape-prone. How had he escaped? We had opened the front door for him.

When a man in a tweed suit who said he was Jacobson's lawyer showed up and asked to confer with his "client," the two were shown to a tenth floor conference room. They traded outfits and Jacobson left the room, rode the elevator to the ground floor, turned in a visitor's badge, and walked out onto Atlantic Avenue. There was not much spin in this one. We looked like fools, plain and simple. But I did the best I could, noting that "in the old days" only Jacobson's attorney of record would have been allowed to meet with him but expanded inmate rights had liberalized procedures.

The following day a deputy warden retraced the escape for Ward and me. When we reached the sally port near the front of the jail, with gates on either side that cannot open simultaneously, Ward asked whose post it was. "The officers on either side share it," the deputy said. Ward shook his head. "That's where this escape happened, Ed," he said. "When you put two people in charge of something, then nobody's responsible for it."

Jacobson was recaptured in California after forty days and returned to the tenth floor in Brooklyn, but he was not through embarrassing us. My phone rang the following Sunday night. It was Wolfgang Saxon, the *Times* reporter who had been covering the story. "Mr. Hershey, I've just had a series of phone calls from a man who says he is Buddy Jacob-son," Saxon said. "After several minutes the call cuts off and then he calls again. Can you confirm that it is really Mr. Jacobson calling me?" I said I would and asked if he needed to know anything else. "Yes," Saxon said. "If it is Mr. Jacobson, can you tell me why he is allowed to make so many calls?"

Security measures had been tightened after the escape and jail offi-cials concerned that the other inmates, a fearsome bunch, might blame

Jacobson and exact retribution. So they moved all the inmates to one side of the tenth floor and put Jacobson on the other. A phone on each side was available for one call a day for each inmate with an automatic cutoff after several minutes. Normally the number of inmates divided by the time available made that limit a self-enforced stricture obviating the need for an officer to monitor the phone. Jail officials failed to realize that isolating Jacobson would allow him to use the phone on his side of the tenth floor at will. That stopped about three minutes after Saxon's call.

Nobody was prepared for the story we inherited on Tuesday, December 9, 1980, when the world awakened to the news that John Lennon had been shot dead outside the Dakota, his apartment house on the Upper West Side in Manhattan. His accused killer, a twenty-five-year-old misfit named Mark David Chapman, was delivered to us in the court pens fifteen floors below my office. To call press interest over the next several days a media feeding frenzy would understate the level of attention. Our phones rarely stopped ringing and Chapman's court-appointed attorney bowed out of the case, overwhelmed by the barrage of inquiries. By then the defendant had been arraigned and remanded to our psychiatric facility at Bellevue Hospital Center in Manhattan.

I was kept informed of every aspect of Chapman's detention so I could serve as a sort of pool reporter, passing along details to reporters, and I went to Bellevue where I rode an elevator up to the prison ward with him and a correction officer. "You okay?" I asked and he nodded. There had been dozens of death threats. Later that evening my sister Nancy, a twenty-four-year-old law student, called to say she had seen me on television. "They said everyone was wearing a bullet-proof vest," she said. "What were you wearing?"

"A smile?" I answered. A day later we quietly transferred Chapman to a cell in the hospital ward on Rikers Island. He had shown no signs of being suicidal but family members reported some prior suicide attempts. With five inmates already lost to suicide in 1980 the last thing we needed was for the most famous detainee in the world to become No. 6. But that hardly turned out to be the problem. Instead, Chapman showed every sign of wanting to survive. Spooked by a death threat scrawled on a wall near his cell, he fasted for two days for fear of being poisoned and ate only after we allowed his new attorney to watch as his meals were prepared and delivered.

The moment during that week that I treasure came in the lobby at 100 Centre Street with Chapman awaiting arraignment next door in the court pen. Mike Pearl, a reporter for Rupert Murdoch's *New York Post*, stopped me and said, "I've got a great story. The other inmates are singing Beatles songs to him in the lockup." I told Pearl I would check it out. "No, please don't do that," he said.

"Don't worry," Mike," I said. "I won't tell anyone else. This is your story."

"No, that's not it," Pearl replied. "You'll knock the story down and I'll have to print your denial." I never knew if he concocted the story out of whole cloth or just heard someone make a joke, but it was clear Pearl assumed it was untrue.

48

Hostage Cop Redux

JUNE 1980
Brooklyn

Three years after we wrote *Hostage Cop* Det. Capt. Frank Bolz retired. While some high-ranking officers dismissed Frank as a headline hunter, those who knew him best on the force or in his police fraternal activities admired and respected him as a standup guy who elevated the work they did. Thus, the conviviality at his retirement dinner was real, and his roasters—including Frank's protégé and successor, Bob Louden—found just the right tone.

Three days later Louden handled his first major case in that role—and by chance I was in the middle of it. A thirty-four-year-old inmate named Larry Gardner overpowered two correction officers in an elevator at the jail unit of Kings County Hospital, seized their firearms, and shot one in the arm. Then he fled through a series of basement corridors to a locker room where six hospital employees were hanging out at noon on a Thursday. He took five of them hostage and sent the sixth out to tell authorities that he was ready to talk.

I was in my office at 100 Centre Street when we got the call. I checked out an unmarked departmental car and with an assistant along for the ride headed to the scene with a magnetic red emergency light flashing on the roof. By the time we arrived Louden was going through the protocol I knew so well. In the ensuing hours negotiators would discover that Gardner was scheduled for sentencing the next day to the remaining seventeen years of a 25-year term for a parole violation. He said he accepted that, but wanted to be sent to a federal and not a state prison because he had a reputation as an informer. And not just any snitch. His information led to the arrest and conviction of state correction officers for smuggling narcotics to inmates. He figured that once back inside he would have no place to turn.

Alice McGillion, my NYPD public relations counterpart, arrived at the hospital not long after I did, and we both soon realized that there was a third person on the scene interested in press communications—Larry Gardner. He asked to speak to *Daily News* reporter Bella English and in turn asked her to go on the radio and relate his story about onerous conditions in state prison. Over time Louden extracted the release of three hostages in exchange for blankets, cigarettes, food and coffee, but his contact with Gardner on a jerry-rigged speaker was sporadic. The standoff went on through Thursday night and all day Friday. Unlike most hostage cases, there really was something to negotiate in this one. Gardner was not asking for a flight to Cuba or

$5 million. His central demand was doable. But he had to be convinced that authorities could deliver on any commitments they made in exchange for his surrender.

As time passed, McGillion and I became part of a second negotiation. "Ed, I'm not sure you need to be here," she told me. "This is our story now." Technically, she was right, but I was seething. Years before when she was an inexperienced spokeswoman for a special state prosecutor, she had turned to me for advice that I readily gave on several occasions. Now she was pulling rank. "I'm just trying to protect our interests," I replied. "You can do all the talking to the press." I stayed but remained far in the background, mostly chatting with reporters and cops I knew.

Well over thirty-six hours into the siege, there was a breakthrough. Louden told Gardner that he could serve his time in federal prison and police sent for his lawyer to make the deal official. Then absurdity took over. First, the lawyer could not be located. He had taken pains to hide his Friday evening whereabouts in the name of discretion. Then, at about 2 a.m. Saturday, there was a loud squawk over the speaker. "You're trying to poison me!" Gardner screamed. "The deal's off!" After two days, someone in the police contingent decided to switch from regular coffee to decaf. Contrary to television ads declaring that it tasted like the real thing, Larry Gardner could tell the difference. By daybreak Gardner had calmed down, his lawyer was on the scene, and things were back on track. With a resolution imminent, I did leave, figuring my presence might remind reporters about the embarrassing circumstances two days before.

Someone had driven the departmental car back to Manhattan so I walked the mile and a half to our row house in Flatbush, and the cool autumn morning served to clear my head, allowing me to take stock. The proposal that first drew me to the correction department, selling Rikers Island to the state, was dead, a victim of political expedience fed by misplaced fears. Still, I enjoyed the job. Dealing with the press was sometimes precarious but often exciting. "Try not to let anyone see what a good time we're having," I would joke to colleagues during a crisis. I had also gained new perspectives on my first love, journalism, occasionally with mixed emotions. I never sought to mislead a reporter but felt no obligation to volunteer damaging information and more than once when the very next question, an obvious one I thought, would yield an embarrassing admission, I was surprised it was not asked. I'd hang up relieved for the sake of our reputation but embarrassed for my profession.

Two other aspects of the work—positioning the department for positive press and strengthening community outreach (or should I call it in-reach?)—were gratifying. We brought performers into the jails and also promoted inmate talent, even arranging for a co-ed Christmas show that played all of the jails and was reviewed favorably by NBC television critic Pia Lindstrom. After the final performance at the Brooklyn House of Detention, we had a cast party. I can still see the startled faces of officers there when I brought in take-out from Burger King. I also convinced coach Lou Carnesecca to bring his highly ranked St. John's University basketball team to the adolescent center on Rikers for a practice. "Hearing the gates clank behind them," I told him, "will do more to reinforce the idea that your players need to steer clear of wayward temptation than any locker-room speech." What really spooked them—and Carnesecca, too—was how many inmates they knew from the "nabe." Another sports celebrity who came to Rikers, boxer Hector ("Macho") Camacho, needed no object lesson. He had done time there.

And as unlikely as it sounds, positive press was there for the taking. We promoted a feature story on the potter's field cemetery on Hart Island where inmates buried the unclaimed dead; launched a collaboration with Cornell University Cooperative Extension to establish a farm on Rikers, allowing inmates to produce some of their own food; and worked with the New York Road Runners Club to stage a track meet on Rikers that attracted Mayor Edward Koch. Perhaps anxious to balance his law-and-order image with a touch of humanity, each Thanksgiving Koch would bake cookies and deliver them to inmates at a city jail with reporters in tow. "Well, what do you think?" the mayor asked a detainee at the Bronx House of Detention one year. "Too much shortening," was the response. Talk about one question too many!

Sometimes people approached us seeking to engage with inmates. One morning, a woman with an accent called to ask how one went about volunteering. It was Bianca Jagger, recently divorced from Mick and just starting the work that would make her an iconic human rights figure. More often my contact with the public involved their desire to stay as far away from our jails and its inhabitants as they could. When the plan to sell Rikers Island to the state and build jails adjacent to city courthouses fell by the wayside, one downtown facility remained on the drawing board, a second jail just off Canal Street next to the newly renovated Manhattan House of Detention. But business interests in Chinatown opposed it, hoping to develop the site. On the day city officials were due to approve the plan, I looked down from my 15th floor window to see traffic at a halt and lines of people—police estimated there were 10,000—on every street, workers in Chinese-owned garment factories freed from their sewing machines to march on City Hall in protest. Eventually a compromise allowed the jail to be built in a way that reserved street-level space for commerce.

Another time, when the department decided to resurrect part of an old jail on Hart Island so short-term sentenced inmates would not have to be transported by bus and ferry twice weekly from Rikers to bury the indigent or unclaimed dead, we had to contend with opposition on City Island, an idyllic bit of New England off the Bronx with boatyards, seafood restaurants and even one of Jacques Cousteau's research facilities. The only way to get to Hart Island was through City Island and merchants feared the idea was a harbinger for a full-scale jail. I arranged to attend a chamber of commerce luncheon with a colleague where we made a strong case that no such plans were practicable and, in fact, our enhanced presence on Hart Island would actually reduce traffic and improve security. We were so persuasive there was a vote to endorse it, leading to an embarrassed call later that day after we departed. While the chamber would not oppose our proposal, those at the luncheon had decided that formally supporting it could alienate some members.

Such outreach always had the potential to divide communities. Take our efforts to improve relations with the "Atlantic Antic," a popular annual Brooklyn street fair with food and craft vendors along Atlantic Avenue from Flatbush Avenue to New York Harbor. One problem was that our block-long "House of D" was in the middle of the route, creating dead space. I proposed gathering art produced by inmates for a fence show that would brighten up the block and show-case some of the department's positive work. Dignitaries like Koch and City Council President Carole Bellamy were delighted, but you can't please everyone. Just as we put the finishing touches on the show, an elderly woman walked by. "Art, they give them art," she muttered disdainfully and spat at the building.

A different work of art brought us national attention. Al Jenkins, warden of the prison on Rikers that held men serving sentences of up to a year, discovered that a large painting hanging in the officers' lunchroom was the work of the celebrated surrealist Salvador Dali. Years before, unable to keep an appointment to visit because he was ill, Dali dashed off the spare, abstract crucifixion scene and sent it instead. The revelation garnered national press, and I brought the painting to the annual inmate art show in Albany. Heading upstate on the Taconic Parkway in the only department vehicle large enough to hold the Dali, an official blue and orange departmental van, I noticed other drivers were afraid to pass a marked law enforcement vehicle. The line of cars in the rear view mirror made me feel like a mama duck with her babies trailing behind.

I also liked my boss. Ben Ward retained the blunt gruffness that was with him when he began his journey from cop on the beat through law school to a series of high-ranking government positions. This, combined with his overall presence—he was the size of a defensive lineman and often spoke with fierce resolve—could intimidate oth-ers. Yet I came to see a softer side to a man who had made it up the hard way. Ward reminded me of a tough managing editor. He kept a parking meter on his desk, a trophy of his days as traffic commissioner under Mayor John Lindsay, to time meetings. And then there was a jar of honey to remind him, he said, "that you can catch more flies with honey than a fly swatter."

Ward would hear me out on every issue and offer a plausible explanation when he disagreed, affording me a degree of respect essential for any productive relationship between chief executive and chief spokesman. "I hired you," he told me once, "because when I was up in Albany you scared us to death you knew so much." But he cautioned me that knowing too much could lead to disaster in my new position, especially when he felt I was too quick to respond to a reporter. "You usually get it right," he told me once, "but I don't know how you know some of the things you say, and one time you're going to get something wrong and you're going to be in real trouble—and I'm not going to be able to help you." That did not happen, although over time I earned a reputation in City Hall for serving the department's interest ahead of the mayor's—something that did not worry me because just about the last thing I wanted was to become a political mouthpiece.

My route home that morning after the hostage crisis took me past a Western Union office where, as a teenager, I once dropped off my copy following a high school basketball game I covered for the *Journal-American*. So much had changed for me, for journalism and for the nation in those twenty-two years. What I did know was that I had been awake for fifty hours. Just about the time Larry Gardner walked out of the locker room back at Kings County Hospital, I nodded off—and slept for the next twenty-four hours.

49

Et Tu, Edward?

SEPTEMBER 1984
Miami Beach

In my years at the city correction department I continued to produce the International Printing & Graphic Communications Union newspaper. While the extra cash came in handy in a single-income household, the endeavor was as much about fulfillment as remuneration. It also led to a second extra gig. I was at the 1980 IPGCU convention at the posh Sheraton Bal Harbour when I got an offer to teach journalism. In need of an adjunct instructor on short notice, the English Chair at Baruch College called my fellow George Polk Awards juror Al Landa, assuming he could suggest a teacher at the New School, where he was a vice president. Instead, Landa recommended me.

Like volunteering for the Polk Awards, teaching provided a link to news reporting, although it was a somewhat tenuous tie. Baruch had no journalism major and offered my course as an elective. "The easiest way to cheat in this class," I quipped the first day, "is to read the *New York Times* and write just like that." But the joke fell flat. Whether they enrolled because they were interested in current events or sensed a chance for three easy credits, few students had the ability to convert the ambling style of themes and essays they were accustomed to writing into crisp, concise news stories. This crystallized for me the day a student came up after class clutching her C+ paper and, near tears, announced, "This could kill my chance of getting into medical school."

Yikes, I thought, *I don't want to ruin anyone's career.* So I devised a solution. Students would continue to report and write news stories that we critiqued in class but I would craft a final exam to measure quantitative retention rather than qualitative performance. Comprising half of the exam were short-answer questions, while the other half asked students to explain how they would report on several scenarios, with each correct step earning points. It worked well and I extracted a slight measure of satisfaction with one trick question designed to underscore a journalist's need to attend to detail: "Melvin Mencher is (a) a famed reporter, (b) a lawyer specializing in freedom of the press, (c) a journalism professor or (d) a publisher." The answer was (c). Mencher, a prof at Columbia, wrote the textbook we used. When we reviewed the test, students howled in protest. "You've spent a whole semester reading this book," I responded. "Why wouldn't you know who wrote it?"

Newsday was in my past, but the union remained important to me. I'd put out the monthly newspaper since 1977, occasionally turning my trips to Washington into brief family vacations. Two of those outings were memorable for unusual mishaps, both on the New Jersey Turnpike.

At a Polk Awards luncheon one year, *New York Times* Washington bureau chief Bill Kovach asked if the poster commemorating the work that had earned his staff an award could be shipped to the bureau. "I'll do better," I said, not thinking through the logistical complications of properly handling the 3x5 foot cardboard slab. "I'm coming down next week. I'll deliver it." I managed to get the poster home on the subway but discovered it would not fit inside our car and secured it to the roof. "Secured," though, turned out to be a relative term. At 70 miles per hour on the turnpike, I heard a thwack and glanced up at the rearview mirror in time to see the poster lodged in the grill of an auto behind us. Thankfully it was an old car driven by a man with a sense of humor. The worst of it turned out to be my apologetic call to Kovach.

On another trip down to Washington we suddenly lost speed close enough to an exit in south Jersey to coast off the turnpike. "Accelerator rod," a mechanic explained. "I can have one here Monday." When I explained we needed to reach Washington that afternoon, he sent me down the street to a five-and-dime for some twine, which he ran through the floor where the accelerator pedal was and tied it to what was left of the rod. Every time I wanted to increase speed, I yanked on my end of the twine and that is how we got almost all the way to D. C. When the twine snapped I jerry-rigged it to come through the driver's-side window. Then I found a dealer in Virginia who installed a new rod. I can still see all the mechanics doubled over laughing as I drove in.

That convention in Florida even played a role in prolonging my marriage. Mike McNally, a goodhearted gravel-voiced secretary-treasurer, had overbooked the hotel. "Why not bring your family down?" he asked. Only days before, the latest set of frustrations had devolved into talk of separation, but after Victoria flew in from New York with Rebecca in her arms for a long weekend, we had such a wonderful time there was no further discussion about parting for years.

But as another convention loomed in 1984, IPGCU President Sol Fishko and his counterpart at the rival Graphic Arts International Union, Ken Brown, were negotiating a merger that would eliminate my connection to the union. One factor making these unions a good match was their complementary strengths. The IPGCU had a stronger national field operation, but the GAIU owned a building in Washington and had a communications department that rendered my service unnecessary. "Remember that photo of Nikita Khrushchev voting himself out of the Politburo?" I asked my friend Chuck Ellington. "Well, that's about how I feel." After pitching the merger in the run-up to the first joint convention of the new Graphic Communications International Union at the Hotel Fontainebleau in Miami Beach, I helped choreograph the event and wrote both an accolade to Fishko and his farewell address as president.

It was my final act as a union consultant but not my last contact with Fishko, who had a new title, President Emeritus, allowing him to remain in New York except for occasional meetings. He also arranged for a perk he had coveted for years, a seat on the 35-member national AFL-CIO board of directors, but that never came to pass. The same imperious approach that turned so many of us off also made Fishko unpopular among his peers in organized labor's circle of leadership and the AFL-CIO informed the GCIU that it, not a merger agreement, determined who sat on its board. "I was double-crossed," Fishko told me one day at his favorite restaurant in Chinatown where we met occasionally for lunch.

Angered by what he considered shabby treatment, he outlined a ploy he hoped to use to regain leverage on the new GCIU board. But another snub was on my mind—one Fishko had perpetrated. Ellington, his loyal aide for so many years, was in line for a union vice presidency, but Fishko used what influence he retained to prevent it, quite likely because he was put off by how easily his protégé had transitioned into the new regime in Washington. I tipped Ellington off about Fishko's plan and the merged union's leadership was ready for it. Then a GCIU staff attorney got an idea. Under federal law nobody could hold an office for life so, as odd as it sounded, Fishko had to run for the position of president emeritus. Ellington recruited a veteran local leader from Chicago to declare for the office, pledging to resign and thus eliminate it once elected. That would save operating funds without costing Fishko anything, since as a retiree he could draw pension benefits about equal to his salary. What it *would* take from him, was his last vestige of power.

I crafted the campaign announcement and Ellington gave it to GCIU President Ken Norton to spring on Fishko at the next board meeting. "It's done," Norton related to him the following day. "Sol is going to resign and retire the office." One thing puzzled Norton. When he saw the letter, Sol said, "I know who wrote this." Ellington just shrugged in response to his quizzical look. Sol Fishko and I never spoke again.

50

Mad Sam

In November 1983, New York Mayor Edward Koch made history—
and changed the dynamics of my own job. He appointed Ben Ward
as New York City's first black police commissioner, paving the way
for Ward's second in command at the correction department, Chief
of Operations Jacqueline McMickens, to become the first former line
officer to rise in the ranks to commissioner.

I took pride in Ward's appointment because how well I had protected his public persona played a part in the promotion, an observa-
tion reinforced when publicized aspects of his behavior began to catch
up with him as police commissioner, including a report gleefully spread
by the police union that he had urinated from a helicopter flying him
to his upstate country home at taxpayer expense. But when a couple of
reporters said they assumed I would be heading two blocks south to
One Police Plaza with Ward, I told them it was not in the cards. My
refusal to put Ed Koch's interests above Ward's or our department's
made my loyalty suspect at City Hall and, besides, the mayor had
moved Alice McGillion to the police department from his PR staff in
1980. So I stayed on, and for a time little changed.

McMickens' successor as the top uniformed officer, Gloria Lee, was
also a trailblazer as the first female in charge of a male facility. A large,
stern black woman who could have been a female version of Ward, Lee
dropped one of the best lines I heard at correction. When an inmate
secreted himself in the bottom of a bread truck leaving Rikers Island
after slithering through a space that did not look wide enough to be
anyone's outlet to freedom, I could not help feeling a touch of admiration for the ingenuity, cunning and patience it must have taken to plan

and execute that escape. The man studied the comings and goings of officers to time his move after painstakingly cutting through a bar over days if not weeks. "It was like a plot from *Mission Impossible*," I told a colleague. "You'd think a guy like that could make it big on the outside if he had the chance."

But late one afternoon six weeks later when I was chatting with Gloria Lee we got word that he had been captured—in the apartment of a known girlfriend. "In his girlfriend's apartment?" I said in disbelief. "I'd have been light years from here by now. I thought he was more street-smart than that."

"Guys like him," she deadpanned, "are very limited. They're only 'street-smart' on their own street."

A few days later McMickens called me in to say she appreciated all my efforts but felt it was time she had a spokesperson of her own choosing. She said I would have all the time I needed to find a new job. I asked her if there was anything specific that led to her decision. I'd been all over the press the prior week responding to inquiries about our latest star inmate, Bernhard Hugo Goetz, the "Subway Vigilante," who became an urban folk hero three days before Christmas when he shot four black teenagers after they pressed him for $5 on an IRT express train in lower Manhattan. No, she said, it was a decision she had come to over time. "I wanted to wait until after the first of the year," she said, "because I didn't want to ruin your holiday."

Right. Merry Christmas. I tried to be philosophical. It was probably time to move on anyway. Five years of 24/7 responsibility with a pager attached to my hip or on the night table was getting a little wearisome. There was the morning I awakened only vaguely aware that United Press International had called in the middle of the night to check on an escapee. "I only heard your end of the conversation," Victoria confirmed. "You said, 'If he's not in then he must be out,' and hung up and came back to bed." Then there was the day I conducted an interview on a pay phone under a water ride at the Six Flags amusement park in New Jersey, timing my responses between the spray intermittently landing on my head. And the night I was alerted to an escape when we were visiting friends around the corner. The missing inmate's address was on the next block. "If you see someone running by," I joked before heading out to Rikers Island, "tell him to please go home."

It really was time for a new posting, provided I could find the right one—or any one. Ours had been largely a single-income household for years so any period of unemployment would be challenging, if not catastrophic. I mused about returning to journalism perhaps as an editor. I'd learned a lot in my time dealing with so many news organizations and, odd as it seemed, my union work negotiating contracts and dealing with grievances had provided significant insights into newsroom management. But as people liked to put it in Brooklyn: *fuhgedaboutit!* The news business was consolidating and besides, publishers were not likely to hire a union organizer.

Among my calls was one to Al Landa, the New School vice president who had recruited me to teach at Baruch College. Landa said he'd be on the lookout and suggested I compare notes with someone else he knew who was conducting his first mid-career job search. It was hardly an encouraging conversation. "At the beginning you send out about a dozen resumes and sit back and wait for the offers to roll in," he said with a wan smile at lunch, "and then you wait and wait. And wait."

Landa was behind the call that led to my next job. Sam Hartstein, longtime PR director at Yeshiva University, needed a second in command. On the subway to Washington Heights in upper Manhattan for my interview, I realized that I had lacked an essential element of attire—a yarmulke. I raced all over the neighborhood and found one at a store catering to Yeshiva's "modern orthodox" undergraduates who spent mornings in Hebrew classes and studied secular subjects in the afternoon. The job had been Roy Campbell's for the taking but Campbell, a large, affable red-bearded Baptist from Arkansas who was as savvy at PR as anyone I ever encountered, had no designs on advancement. The aggravation that would come with reporting directly to Hartstein, he confided the day we met, was not worth the raise. "You have to understand," he said more in resignation than rancor, "that Sam is a mad man."

It was a charitable description. *The New York Times* appointed one student at each college in the city to serve as a campus correspondent, and in his undergraduate days Hartstein fulfilled the role so well at Yeshiva that the *Times* hired him after graduation. Six months later, he was back in Washington Heights. Homesick for Yeshiva, he returned to take a PR job there, and 52 years later he was still at it, a little man walking around the office with an unlit cigar, making a stream of pronouncements out of the side of his mouth and trying to keep his minions in our place.

I showed up one morning with a big smile. I'd seen a story about a sportswriter from Dallas embarking on a national basketball idyll, reporting on a different college game each night all season long. I called him. "Yeshiva?" he drawled, but I soon had him intrigued. "We're opening a brand new gym," I said, "and where else will you ever see five players running up and down the court with yarmulkes pinned to their hair? One of our stars is even black, the son of an African-American rabbi from Pittsburgh." He covered the University of Kentucky's season opener in Lexington on a Friday night and then flew to New York to watch the Yeshiva U. Maccabees crush the Bard College Raptors, filing a story that made the papers all across the country. "So you're a hero for four hours," Hartstein snapped. "Get to work!"

Yeshiva's bread and butter were "locals," news releases about students sent to weekly and biweekly Jewish newspapers in their home towns across the country. They led to stories and photos that helped recruit new students, connect with alumni and support a proactive fundraising enterprise. Development officers used extensive research to identify wealthy targets and exploit their likely philanthropic interests. Had the prospect lost family to the Nazis? How about a course on Holocaust studies? Had a loved one committed suicide? Discuss initiating a joint program between the Yeshiva's Wurzweiler School of Social Work and Albert Einstein College of Medicine on clinical depression.

My favorite example of this shameless penchant for avarice involved the dedication of the new gym, the Max Stern Athletics Center. Heirs of Stern—who made his fortune building the Hartz Mountain pet food brand—walked proudly past a handsome sign bearing his name at the front of the building on opening night. Three nights later when we named the basketball court in honor of a somewhat lesser donor, workers discreetly uprooted the Stern Center sign, creating the impression that the building—and not just the court—would honor the second man. That seemed audacious even for Yeshiva, where Sam Hartstein would carefully arrange publicity photos so the least significant participants were placed on the outside—and would be cropped out of all copies of the picture except those sent to them or their local papers.

Such cynicism aside, my new job had other drawbacks, starting with the long commute from Brooklyn that was made all the worse because my first chore each day was to meet with Hartstein to fulfill a single imperative. He wanted me to ask a meaningful question related to the work. "Just one question," he said. "Show me you understand what's important." This was instructive and even Talmudic, perhaps, but demeaning to a fault, and on many mornings I was still struggling minutes from the office on the Harlem River Drive or the uptown IRT, trying to figure out what to ask when he folded his arms and said, "So...?"

The extent to which the operation was all about Hartstein was underscored for me one day, several weeks into my tenure, when I asked Campbell about the number-coded files of releases on shelves surrounding the office. Each file had two numbers like 3–105 or 26–10 or 48–202. What was the code? "Oh, haven't you figured that out yet?" he replied with a laugh. "It's pretty simple. The first number represents the year in Sam's time here and the second is the number of that year's release. So the releases I filed today—52–148 a through h—are eight different versions of the 148th release we have sent out in this, the 52nd year of Sam."

Al Landa came to the rescue yet again. David Steinberg, an erstwhile New School colleague of his, had just been named president of our alma mater, Long Island University. "David has hired a VP for development named Ray Soldavin and they're looking for a PR guy," Landa told me. "I explained to them that you just started at Yeshiva, but you could help them define what they need because you know both the news business and L.I.U. So expect a call."

Of course, that was not Landa's real agenda. Steinberg and Soldavin were impressed with my grasp of the position and offered it to me just as he expected. Hartstein said he understood and so did Yeshiva's president, Rabbi Norman Lamm. After all, it was a top position and at my alma mater. "Just don't steal any of my people," Hartstein said. So I hired away the second in command of his graphics unit to lead my design department at L.I.U. I never spoke to Sam after that, but if I had, the first thing I might have asked was whether *he had a question for me.*

51

One More Rabbit

MAY 1987
Cambridge, Massachusetts

My position as Long Island University's first Director of Public Relations meshed with the new president's expressed desire to unify the university in the public eye as well as in the eyes of its students and faculty. With three disparate and barely related campuses separated by geography, history, and identity, L.I.U. had no center. In fact, just about the only thing the gritty flagship Brooklyn campus, C. W. Post College in Brookville on Long Island's lush North Shore, and the tiny

Southampton College on the Island's stylish East End had in common was that more often than not each struggled to survive.

L.I.U. Brooklyn—known simply as L.I.U. in my days as a student there—had been a bootstrap place since its founding in 1927, a "Second Chance U" attracting many students who did not qualify for the tuition-free City University, or who transferred after starting college out of town. When CUNY established an "open admissions" policy for all city high school graduates in 1970, some thought L.I.U. was doomed. But it survived, helped by government grant and loan programs that made it affordable for lower-income applicants and by aggressive marketing. L.I.U. timed its academic calendar to competitive advantage, starting weeks after most peers to maximize its recruitment window and even lure students who enrolled elsewhere and were having second thoughts. I'm not sure if recruiters really tried to poach applicants from long lines of CUNY registrants as I'd heard, but I know the late start protected L.I.U. when classes were delayed by a faculty strike because it was too late to enroll elsewhere.

C. W. Post, founded in the 1950s, was the wrong place at the right time, never matching projections that it would thrive with Long Island's population explosion. The leafy campus had been an opulent estate purchased from breakfast cereal heiress Marjorie Meriwether Post (as in Post Toasties) and named for her father in a clumsy and futile attempt to garner a large donation from her. It was too remote to compete with centrally located Long Island competitors like Hofstra and Adelphi and far more expensive than colleges in an expanding state university system. Plus, the college never did establish an identity, unless it was as a safe harbor for well-to-do white suburbanites who did not want to work very hard.

If launching C.W. Post was a bad guess, accepting an invitation from community leaders to establish the Southampton campus a decade later proved a worse one. University leaders expected to leverage three perceived strengths—a growing interest in marine science, the area's reputation as a center for writing and the arts, and connections to the super wealthy who made the Hamptons a summer playground—and all failed to materialize. Marine science may have been a trendy major, but many students that Southampton attracted did not have the academic strength to stay the course. At the same time, students majoring in English or the arts found the isolation and harsh winters too much to take. And those rich summer people? Few identified with the place.

My friend and mentor Al Landa, as close to a college marketing guru as anyone, offered a fourth drawback. "No walk-ins," he told me. Pardon? "Think of a trendy bar," he explained. "It can be crowded on Friday and Saturday nights, but if you take a close look at the books you'll see it still needs people in there the rest of the week, locals from the neighborhood. Nobody markets to them. They just walk in. Colleges are like that, too. And Southampton will never have any. With almost no year-round population to draw from, the admissions people have to go out and recruit every student they get."

David Steinberg had impressive credentials, but they did not make him a likely choice to try to make sense of this trifurcated dysfunction or identify with the middling students all three campuses attracted. The son of a rabbi who led the Park Avenue Synagogue, Steinberg's curriculum vitae was an academic showcase—Phillips Andover Academy, Malvern College in England, Phi Beta Kappa and magna cum laude at Harvard, University of the Philippines Fulbright scholar, Columbia University Woodrow Wilson fellow, Harvard M.A. in East Asian studies and PhD in history. He taught at the University of Michigan and then joined Brandeis, where as a favorite of retired founding president Abram Sachar he had the inside track to the presidency. But the trustees went outside when he made his move in 1983, choosing Brandeis' first female president, Evelyn Handler of Hunter College. In that sense, L.I.U. was David Steinberg's Second Chance U, too.

Steinberg started his unification campaign by trying to flip what seemed like an anachronism, affirming that the borough of Brooklyn really was part of the island of Long. People always wondered why anyone would name an institution in Brooklyn "Long Island University." Wasn't "Long Island" east of the Queens County line? Yes and no. Geopolitically, maybe, but geographically Brooklyn and Queens were *on* Long Island, separated from Manhattan by the East River but attached to Nassau and Suffolk Counties. We would seek to reclaim that heritage, starting with a new university-wide logo.

I soon realized that efforts to coordinate the communications operation faced considerable internal resistance. Faculty and administrators on each campus saw the other two as unworthy and all suspected any change would impinge on their prerogatives and reduce their power. Creating the new logo added to these perceptions and taught me something else. For anyone in PR, logo is a four-letter word in the worst sense of the phrase, its development and rollout an invitation to scorn and ridicule, especially from individuals closest to the institution usually identified in the process as "stakeholders."

We conducted research and engaged a type designer to create a version of the words "Long Island University" that would mesh with my art director David Grupper's emerging visual design and become ours alone. Steinberg recruited designers he knew to review our work and told me he expected several different "takes" for this group to consider, something that spooked Grupper. "I think I have what we need," he said, "and I'm prepared to go back and tweak it. But you've seen how much time has gone into just one design." He dashed off a few alternatives, including a rainbow-colored silhouette of Long Island linked to the new logotype that was reminiscent of a tourist postcard. It was also clear and away the first choice of the committee, which dismissed Grupper's favorite. Steinberg warmed to the map logo and started chattering about how well it would work "on the bias." I assumed this was design lingo he'd picked up along the way. I had no idea what it meant and I was not certain he did either.

We unveiled the logo to almost universal disdain. Thus, the hard lesson: Six months or a year after its debut, a logo is acceptable to your internal audience—if it is noticed at all. But at the outset, reducing any organization to a single icon is akin to telling constituents how they should feel about the place and that is a hopeless task. Hire a consultant and the new logo is attacked as a waste of money that should have been poured into the core mission. Use internal designers and it is labeled the work of amateurs. In our case some of the most vicious critics were members of the art faculty in Brooklyn who labeled the silhouette of Long Island "the running rat."

Logo aside, some aspects of our new approach showed signs of working. Campus administrators began to appreciate the help we could provide, and we learned to factor their ideas into what we produced. I hired Jane Finalborgo, a talented former *Newsday* colleague, to set up a viable PR operation in Southampton and after a rough patch established a good rapport with the PR staffs at Brooklyn and Post. Working with a New York City studio and an award-winning photographer on the Post faculty, we produced a 60th anniversary video that was part of a celebration on the Post campus honoring such notable Long Islanders as Roy Campanella and Murray Kempton. And I arranged to broadcast a live telecast into the gym in Brooklyn when the basketball team made a surprising run into the NCAA tournament.

Sometimes, as in my days at the city correction department, the goal was to keep from making news. "We may have a problem," Finalborgo told me when I arrived at Southampton for commencement. A student from Maine had dropped out in the middle of her sophomore year. She waited tables to pay her share of the rent and never told her parents she was not in college, timing trips home to correspond with the academic calendar. All through what would have been her senior year friends urged her to disclose the subterfuge, but she demurred. The day before commencement her mother came to her door "I think I had better tell you something," her roommate said. She had not seen Nicole for a day. Her mother immediately asked for directions to the Southampton police station. At that moment, the young woman was slamming her car into a tree across town. It was not the first story I managed to keep out of the press, but surely the most heartbreaking. As graduates marched across a stage in Southampton, her mother was accompanying Nicole's coffin home.

As it turned out, my real problem was not on the campuses. It was just down the hall. Ray Soldavin, the development vice president Steinberg hired before I came on board, was discovering what every predecessor had for sixty years. It was hard to raise real money at L.I.U. And he was also realizing that for all my attributes, I had no experience in fundraising. We met for a drink one evening in January. "This just isn't a good match," Soldavin said, trying to keep it clinical. A quarter-century after hearing Buck Lai's time-honored freshman orientation warning about how many students would be gone in a year, I was living the adult version. When I got home that night, I didn't have to say a word. Victoria saw the look on my face and said, "Oh, no. Not again!"

As lame ducks go, I had a splashy six months. I was home for a week convalescing from minor surgery when David Grupper visited. "I have to ask you something," he said. He and our advertising director had spotted a blind ad for a job that sounded a lot like mine. Back at work I brought them together and told them it was important that word not spread. "If people think I'm history nobody will pay attention to any of us," I said. "So while I'm still here, it makes sense to keep this a secret." Al Landa was furious. "They say they need someone who is savvy about marketing," I told him. "They're very foolish," he said. "You're just what they need. You're a space grabber," his term for a good publicist. I began applying for my next job, but poured myself into my current one, appearing to everyone around me as if I intended to spend the rest of my working life at L.I.U. Placing story after story, I felt as if I was shoving every one of them down Soldavin's throat. It was liberating.

There were some near misses on the job front. I applied for the newly created position of commissioner of the Northeast Conference, L.I.U.'s sports league, and came within one vote of getting an offer. And when New York Governor Mario Cuomo appointed Fordham Law Dean John D. Feerick to form a special ethics commission in response to the latest scandal in Albany, I applied to be his spokesman and had the best interview I could imagine. A few days later, Soldavin stopped by to say he had provided a glowing reference and added, "It looks like you've got it." So I waited for the phone to ring. When it finally did one morning a few days later, it was not Feerick on the line but a friend. "Take a look at the *Daily News*," he said. Feerick had hired a former CBS news vice president recently let go from Fordham. I never even got a note.

That afternoon I got another call, from Earl Smith of Colby College in Maine to tell me I had made the first cut there. "We're bringing twelve people in over two days," he said, "but rather than have everyone trek all the way up to Maine, the search committee is coming down to Cambridge. Are you still interested in the position?" I'd forgotten that I'd applied. "Sure," I said. "Hey, I go to the racetrack every once in a while and I've hit a 12–1 shot a time or two." He laughed before I could think to myself, *Why on earth did you just say that?*

When Smith mailed me an information packet I noticed the college had a modern new logo with Colby spelled out in cursive script. *Maybe*, I thought to myself with a rueful smile, *that's why they're looking for a new PR director*. Dick Whitmore, Colby's basketball coach and athletic director, was on the search committee so I asked Bill Huffman, the sports information director at C. W. Post, to hunt up a dossier on him. Huffman called the night before my interview. "Sorry it took so long," he said. "I don't have much, but I'll tell you one thing. He's all Maine."

I arrived early for the interview at a hotel overlooking the Charles River and walked along the banks. "Wish me luck," I called to a mama duck swimming by with five babies. I needed it. Soldavin had just identified my successor and I had no irons in the fire beyond this long shot. After a futile experiment in public education—a so-called gifted program at P.S. 139 in Flatbush that crammed 30 second-graders into a classroom—Rebecca was attending Brooklyn Friends School. Where would her tuition come from? For that matter, what about the mortgage money? Having flirted with a career as a cabaret singer, Victoria was into watercolor painting. She was good at both, but unlikely to make a living with either.

Betraying even a hint of desperation would make me less a 12–1 shot than a nonstarter. So I was thinking not of horses or ducks but rabbits—all those I'd pulled out of a hat my entire working life. There was the call from a college buddy that revived my journalism career by landing me at the *Suffolk Sun;* the Army Reserve spot that came out of nowhere to spare me from the military draft; the press box chat that sent me to *Newsday* barely a year before the *Suffolk Sun* folded; the appeal to *Newsday's* editor shortly before his departure that extricated me from sports and put me in news; the call out of nowhere that led to the city correction department; and, when it was time to leave there, the offer from Yeshiva that led me back to L.I.U.

Earl Smith was a soft-spoken man with large owl-like eyes and a kind smile. Cal Mackenzie, who chaired the search committee, was a political scientist on temporary assignment as vice president for development. The others were Bonnie Bishop, the design director who reported to Smith, and Whitmore, a successful coach who seemed uncomfortable in this setting belying a reputation for intensity that Huffman had relayed. From what I could tell, Colby's prior PR man had been dismissed not for developing that logo, but rather for being low-key to a fault. I decided that I was likely the outlier in the field, but someone in the room had seen enough in my background to bring me this far. I had to validate that judgment and intrigue the others enough to emerge as a serious if unorthodox choice.

"What makes this a great opportunity in my eyes," I said, "is that Colby is an institution of undeniable quality and yet you're aspirational, seeking to be seen as the equal of peers like Amherst, Williams, and Middlebury. That's a great combination for someone in my field. You have something to sell and are willing to sell it. I suspect there are sensitivities involved in all this, especially on your own campus. I'd guess that the faculty at Colby is no different than faculties everywhere. Professors assume when they show up each September and see all those students in front of them, it's because word of their stellar reputation has spread."

When that drew a laugh, I felt reassured. "Public relations, let alone marketing, is beneath them," I continued, "but we know better. And if you think Harvard doesn't market itself then I've got a bridge back home in Brooklyn I can sell you. Look, I'll bet that your new logo drove some people crazy, but what it shows me is that you are willing to take a chance or two. And I find that intriguing."

I told them that some important parts of college PR were often viewed as mundane, like sending local releases to students' hometown weekly papers. "Take COOT (Colby Outdoor Orientation Trips sending freshmen off for a few days of bonding prior to their first semester)," I said. "Weekly papers are desperate for news, especially good news. Send them a photo of a smiling student from their hometown in a beautiful backdrop and they'll print it. No, it's not the *Boston Globe*. But consider this. That student's parents will be gratified. Colby alumni in the area will be proud. And maybe the local high school will feel good about Colby just when the next crop of seniors is applying to college. What better time for positive reinforcement?"

I was on a roll. "This reminds me of a story I did at *Newsday* about Bayside, Queens," I continued. "Shopkeepers along Bell Boulevard were up in arms because cops were ticketing their customers and they demanded a meeting with the precinct commander. 'We've had burglaries up and down the street,' they told him. 'Why aren't your people out solving those cases instead of harassing our customers?' He heard them out and said, 'I can tell you one thing and I'll be frank about it. When my officers are writing tickets at least I know they are out there working, visible, not hiding in a squad car behind a building somewhere. And you and your customers benefit from that presence. It's not a matter of either/or. We'll solve those burglaries or at least try as hard as we can, but I want my men writing those tickets and not for the money they bring in.' I feel that way about college PR. Yes, by all means let's shoot for national publicity, but the more we're out there with students and faculty doing the bread-and-butter stuff, the more likely we are to run across stories worthy of a larger audience."

All through this as others asked questions, Whitmore sat silently. Finally, with the hour drawing to a close, Mackenzie turned to him and asked, "Dick, do you have anything you want to ask Ed?" He asked, "Do you think you can go from writing about Blackbirds to White Mules?" Those were the nicknames of the L.I.U. and Colby teams. I took a short breath. "Is it true you once got so angry at a ref during a game that you turned around and ran up to the top of the gym and back down again because you didn't want to get a technical foul?" I asked, and then waited a couple of beats as his face reddened and the other three nearly fell off their chairs laughing. "I think I can work very well with anyone who has that kind of passion and presence of mind."

Earl Smith called a week later. "We'd like you to come up to Waterville, take a look at the campus and meet some people, including our president, Bill Cotter, before everyone gets scarce for the summer," he said. The campus was New England gorgeous and the daylong series of interviews, including an audience with Cotter, seemed to go well. I had assumed that this was the second of several rounds, especially given that the field had only recently been narrowed from 12. But the look in several sets of eyes told me something else. When Smith drove me to the airport he asked how I felt the day had gone. "I'm not sure I should say this," I responded, "but I get the feeling you are going to offer me a job."

"Well I guess I had better tell you then," he said. "We planned to narrow the field to four and bring them all to campus, but when we shared our lists driving back to Waterville you were at the top of everyone's list. So we checked with Bill and he agreed we ought to short cut the process if we could. We would bring you to campus and if he and everyone else liked you, we would offer you the job. My phone rang a few times while you were making the rounds and from what I heard, it looks good."

On the way home I did the math. All things equal (and happily for me they clearly were not in this case) the chance of someone coming up first by two people who interview a dozen candidates is 1 in 32. No. 1 on three scorecards is one in 1,320. The odds of finishing first on all four were 11,880 to 1. *Forget about playing the horses,* I thought to myself. *I ought to concentrate on the lottery!*

A week later, I had the job.

Catching You Up

They tell this story about the days long before computers and cell phones when sportswriters had to leave the press box during the game to phone in or take a call and, on returning, would peek at a colleague's scorebook and ask, "Catch me up?" A young writer received a call that his draft notice had arrived and went straight home. After military service, his career took a different path. Back at the ballpark many years later, he stopped at the press box. "I used to be a sportswriter," he told the attendant, who invited him to take a look around. He spied an empty seat next to the very writer alongside him the day he had departed. So, of course, he sat down and casually asked, "Catch me up?"

In that spirit, here is what has happened to some of the individuals and organizations you have encountered on these pages.

PART ONE: The Parkway

1. Horn & Hardart **Automats** are long gone, as are **Mays** and **S. Klein on the Square,** but **1440 Ocean Parkway** still stands and so does **P.S. 238,** now the Anne Sullivan School. When my sister Nancy became a federal bankruptcy judge in 2013, the school's honor guard and chorus performed at her swearing in.

2. When **Adlai Stevenson** died of a heart attack in London in 1965, it felt like losing a loved one. I met Senator Adlai Stevenson III at Joe and Madeline Albright's townhouse in Georgetown in 1973 while on assignment for *Newsday*. "I'm probably blowing my journalistic cool," I told him, "but your father was my Mickey Mantle."

3. An auto accident in 1958 left **Roy Campanella** paralyzed below the neck. Elected to the Baseball Hall of Fame in 1969, he was a beloved Dodgers goodwill ambassador for his remaining 35 years. When he was honored by L.I.U. in 1987, I told Campy about the day I saw (most of) his game-winning homer at **Ebbets Field**.

4. When **Washington Baths** closed in 1969, outlasting boardwalk neighbors **Raven Hall**, which burned in 1963, and **Steeplechase Park**, which went dark in 1964, my parents switched to trendier **Brighton Beach Baths** (which held out another quarter-century before giving way for condominiums) before retiring to Florida in 1975.

5. The name **Hershkowitz** was consigned to history when my father shortened it in 1948, a fate that seemed destined for **Hershey** after my daughter married. But with the birth of their third child—and first son!—in 2013, she and her husband reclaimed the name Hershey. So if my grandson Ellis has heirs, the line will survive.

6. In 1956, I traded in my **West Highway Little League** scorebook for a bat and glove. True to form, I went hitless in ten at-bats and was no star in the field. In a moment I have tried to forget for sixty years, a pop fly that should have ended a game in victory bounced off my mitt as our opponents scored the tying and winning runs.

7. Research for this book led to the realization that some erstwhile contemporaries are gone. One, according to alumz.com, is my 1440 Ocean Parkway nemesis **Victor Dubitsky**, Lafayette High School Class of 1958. With no other information, I can only muse about what kind of life "the bully in 1F" led.

8. Web searches unearthed some early heartthrobs, including **Sandy,** the baker's daughter, but not **Corinne,** the girl who set my heart afire on my first night at camp. **Alan Chagy** became a Los Angeles anesthesiologist. I'm guessing he has no recollection of the ping-pong match that was the high point of my athletic career.

9. Pat Summerall became a popular sportscaster specializing in golf and football with an appealing low-key style. He went public about his battle with alcoholism in 1992 after rehabbing at the Betty Ford Clinic and in 2003, following a liver transplant. When he died in 2012, every obit recalled his kick that beat the Cleveland Browns.

10. After **Dick Clark** banished **Pat Molittieri** for ties to a fan magazine, she recorded a Paul Anka song and appeared in a Connie Francis film. Back in Philadelphia and married with two daughters, she suffered a seizure in 1975 and was gone at 32. **Steve Aiello** served in the Carter White House, was president of the New York City Board of Education and enjoyed a successful public relations career.

11. I found **Tyrone Pannell's** name on panel 3E row 18 of the Vietnam Veterans Memorial in Washington, D.C. Whenever I think back to the Vietnam era, the first image that comes to mind is the sight of Pannell breaking the tape in the 60-yard high hurdles at the armory in Washington Heights that long-ago December afternoon.

12. On vacation in the Berkshire Mountains in 2015, my wife Leah and I spent an evening at the Williamstown Theater where we saw **Glynn Turman** play Audra McDonald's father in *A Moon for the Misbegotten* fifty-four years after my Lafayette High classmates and I watched him on Broadway as the little boy in *A Raisin in the Sun.*

13. Jerry Glazer and I remain good friends, see each other when we can and speak often, especially when we are watching the same telecast of a ballgame 3,000 miles apart. I still call him every June 10—the anniversary of the night **Rocky Colavito** hit those four home runs.

PART TWO: The Big Leagues

14. L.I.U. opened a new gym in 2005 and a decade later began restoring the **Brooklyn Paramount Theater**. As the **Lower East Side** gentrified, just a few relics of its past remain, including **Katz's** deli, **Yonah Schimmel's** knishery, and **Russ & Daughters**, whose fourth-generation owners opened a stylish restaurant a few blocks away.

15. Paul Zimmerman was the nation's pre-eminent football writer at *Sports Illustrated* and author of *The Thinking Man's Guide to Pro Football*, a companion to Leonard Koppett's guide to baseball. In 2008, the first in a series of strokes rendered him unable to walk, write, or speak. He was the subject of a moving ESPN portrait in 2014.

16. Bill Birenbaum left L.I.U. in 1967, fired by a conservative chancellor (who was ousted a year later), spurring a student strike. He was a key figure in RFK's visionary Bed-Stuy Restoration Corporation; led Staten Island Community College and Antioch College; and wrote an influential book on higher education. He died in 2010.

17. Mike Scott, the journalist-candidate who ran with **Mel Dubin**, wrote *The Crafts Business Encyclopedia* and started a successful magazine, *The Crafts Report* (now *Handmade Business*). When I arrived in Oregon in 2005 I regaled his son Tim, a longtime Portland-based cellist and baroque musicologist, with tales of the wrong Abe Cohen.

18. Angry parents forced **Harry Levine** out at **Macon Junior High** after my year there. When a woman whom I met in Maine in 1990 learned that I once taught school in Brooklyn, she said her father was a dedicated principal who was vilified by racist activists. His name? Harry Levine. I never let on. *Everyone*, I thought, *has her or his own truth.*

19. New York sports fortunes improved and in 1969–70 the Mets won the World Series, the Jets won the Super Bowl, and the Knicks were NBA champions. Strangely, the perennially powerful Yankees did not reach the World Series again until 1976. By then **Ralph Houk**, who resigned after the 1973 season, was managing the Detroit Tigers.

20. When the *Suffolk Sun* folded, **Larry Conroy** joined *Newsday*. Separated from his wife, he spent a Christmas Eve with us before seeing his three children in the morning. Doctors could not tell if his fall from a bicycle in 1975 caused a cerebral hemorrhage or resulted from it. He never regained full consciousness and died five months later. He was forty-three.

21. I have proposed marriage to three women. Two said yes. **Carol Kemp** declined. She returned to New York the summer after we met and we dated. She was about to return for her senior year at the University of Iowa when I panicked. Would I ever find the one? Why not her? She knew better. She sent me a sweet note the following year. It was our last contact.

22. Preparing to tell our story in 2015, I found **Gayle**. She and her second husband own a popular restaurant and bakery in a town on Monterey Bay, where she was elected mayor. They wrote a cookbook I found at Powell's bookstore in Portland. "Well, well," her response to my email began. I sent her a video of the story. "Loved it," she wrote back.

23. The adaptation of *Coal Miner's Daughter,* one of **George Vecsey's** dozen books in a celebrated career, won Sissy Spacek an Oscar. **Vic Ziegel** became sports editor of the *Daily News* and later a columnist.

His death in 2010 evoked an outpouring of affection for, as the *Times* put it, casting "a wry eye on the sports world in nearly half a century."

24. I had breakfast with **Paul Brown** the day the Bengals' first season ended in New York with a 3–11 record, a day the Packers edged the Bears to finish 6–7–1 in **Vince Lombardi's** last game as GM. In 1969, he coached the Redskins to their first winning record in fourteen years, a resurgence that led them to the 1972 Super Bowl two years after he died of cancer.

25. **Allard Lowenstein's** assassin was deemed legally insane and spent twenty years in mental institutions before his release, which was opposed by state officials but not Lowenstein's three children, all by then in public service careers, one a champion of eliminating capital punishment.

26. Covering a story about a drug treatment center on the old Mitchel Field air base on Long Island in 1970, I heard someone ask, "Remember me?" I could not place him. "**Fort Gordon**," he said. He was the gratuitously nasty mess sergeant in basic training. Addicted to heroin during his tour in Vietnam, he was trying to kick the habit.

PART THREE: The Real World

27. I saw **Cleon Jones** again at Shea Stadium at the tenth reunion of the 1969 team. Dumped by the Mets after an arrest in Florida over a tryst in a van, Jones was out of the game. "I had a lot of bad vibes within me because of the way I thought I had been mistreated," he said. "Every time I thought about baseball, it kind of brought out the demon in me."

28. Big indoor track meets at Madison Square Garden slowly fell out of favor and attendance dwindled. The last of them, the **Millrose**

Games, left in 2012, two years short of its centennial for a new home—the refurbished **Washington Heights armory** where I covered my first track meet fifty-two years before.

29. An op-ed essay I wrote about the agony of **Hillel School** parents almost came back to bite me after a teen tour group filed a $48-million libel suit over later stories on unsafe buses, contending it showed that I was emotionally involved enough to misread the facts. The suit was dismissed on merit, but taught me to maintain detachment.

30. Someone reading the fine print discovered that **Army Reservists** activated during the postal strike were entitled to a year's reduced service obligation, even though we served just three days. National Guardsmen enjoyed no such provision but Governor **Nelson Rockefeller** agreed to reduce their tours by a year as well.

31. **Victoria** and my parents made peace long before we separated in 1994, but it was an uneasy truce. When I told my mother that I was flying back to Maine one weekend to help sell some of our antiques with her at a show, there was silence and then she asked in an ominous tone, "You're not getting back together, are you?"

32. **John Cummings'** gruffness was as fake as his anecdotes. One Christmas Eve when Victoria was off singing, he invited me to bring Rebecca to his family celebration. She was nineteen months old, but thinks she remembers that night and told John and Lily Cummings so at my wedding to Leah in 2003. We spoke often before his death in 2016.

33. The most gnawing of my unanswered questions about **Attica** is whether a ricocheting bullet killed **Elliott Barkley** as authorities said or he was executed. In 2013, a former inmate told a documentarian filming *Criminal Injustice: Death and Politics at Attica* that he saw an officer shoot Barkley in the back.

34. Tony Marro left *Newsday* but returned to serve sixteen years as executive editor. In 1995, a new CEO closed the New York edition just as it seemed to turn a corner after losing $100 million in 10 years. Marro's successor, **Howard Schneider,** departed not long after and started a journalism program at Stony Brook University.

35. Maurice Nadjari lost his job but did not wind up in the dock, a fate that befell two disgraced contemporaries. Nassau County DA **Bill Cahn** served five months for double billing to feed a gambling habit. Brooklyn DA **Eugene Gold,** charged with molesting a ten-year-old girl, got off with probation and retired to Israel.

36. In 2016 a *Newsday* exposé led to the arrest of the Nassau County Executive on corruption charges, but like many dailies, it has struggled to meet the challenge of the Internet. By the time many of us old hands returned to Long Island for a 2010 reunion rounds of staffing cuts had rendered it a shadow of the paper we knew.

37. Perry B. Duryea, Jr. returned to private life on eastern Long Island after losing his race for governor in 1978, four years after our vote-siphoning exposé denied him the race he had been primed to run. He died at eighty-two in 2004 from injuries in an auto accident. A state building in Suffolk County bears his name.

38. Prosecutor **Stephen Scaring,** who suffered a rare setback in the **Jo Anne Brown** case, became a high-profile defense attorney. When I covered the murder of an Iranian-American mother of two in her Queens home in 1978, detectives said they suspected her ex-husband. Scaring advised him to say nothing. He was never charged.

PART FOUR: The Other Side

39. *Newsday* executives were not alone in underestimating **George Tedeschi**. The old guard gave him little chance when he ran for Graphic Communications International Union president in 2000. He won and in 2005 merged the GCIU into the Teamsters, solidifying its—and his—future in organized labor. He was still in charge in 2016.

40. Sentenced to twenty years, **John Hill** was freed in 1979 by Governor Hugh L. Carey who declared it time "to close the books" on Attica, saying it "lurks as a dark shadow over our system of justice." Decades later the state paid $12 million to inmates and a like amount to thirty-eight hostages and the families of the eleven who died.

41. A wire-service reporter took **Israel Karp** to the warehouse where he'd killed his boss a half-century before. It was a Chinese laundry. "I look at this," he said, "and it makes me think if I'll ever be free." He asked to return to the nursing home. "Time to head back. Take me back to the joint." He spent three years there before dying at 71.

42. Tim Dowd was promoted to deputy chief and retired a year later. When he died at the age of ninety-nine in 2014, his daughter recalled that when Dowd met the "**Son of Sam**" he said, "I told him we had never abused him or criticized him," and David Berkowitz agreed, adding, "Inspector, you finally got me. I guess this is the end of the trail."

43. Bus hijacker **Luis Robinson** initially pleaded not guilty by reason of insanity but changed his plea to guilty of murder a year later and served 34 years in New York State prisons. Stripped of his permanent U. S. residency status, he was paroled in 2011 and deported to Panama.

44. Released from Angola Prison after forty-four years, **Wilbert Rideau** wrote a memoir, *In the Place of Justice: A Story of Punishment and*

Deliverance. Thirty-one years after his award he spoke at the 2011 Polk Awards luncheon. "It's difficult to overstate what the award meant to me, a ninth-grade dropout and self-taught journalist who had once sat on death row," he said.

45. The Newspaper Guild transferred ownership of the ***Citizens Voice*** to the original strikers in 1989. They added a Sunday edition four years later and in 2000 sold the paper. The *Times-Leader* has been sold and reorganized a half-dozen times but survives, making Wilkes-Barre one of the few two-newspaper towns left in the U.S.

46. A quarter-century after organizing the Local 406 editorial unit, I was greeted like a returning hero at a ***Newsday*** retirement party. As upset as staffers were by the closure of *New York Newsday*, a union contract provision mandating generous buyouts before any layoff allowed employees to leave for other jobs with a significant nest egg.

47. After revelations of officer brutality on **Rikers Island** that earned two *New York Times* reporters a George Polk Award, in 2015 the city agreed to accept federal monitoring of its jails. Thirty years and three thousand miles away from my role as spokesman, I thought of the French proverb, *"Plus ça change, plus c'est la même chose."*

48. The strange story of the **"prison Dali"** became stranger still when it was discovered that it had been replaced by a fake. Three officers pleaded guilty stealing the original, which was valued at up to $500,000. It was never recovered. One defendant said he panicked and destroyed the painting before his arrest.

49. It was late, just about when **Chuck Ellington** usually called. This time it was his daughter Lee. He had died of a heart attack that day in Illinois. He had visited me in Ithaca that spring. Traveling to Conyers, Georgia for the funeral, I recalled how often my dear friend had invited me there. Now my first visit was to eulogize him.

50. Yeshiva University was still reeling from Bernie Madoff's theft of a chunk of its endowment when Mordechai Twersky, a student intern when I was there, revealed that **Norman Lamm**, its president from 1976 to 2003, protected one rabbi there who sexually abused Twersky and another who sodomized a friend. The boys were 16.

51. I was at **Colby** for six years and after a brief stay at Albright College in Reading, Pennsylvania, spent twelve more at Cornell. Why leave Albright? "To paraphrase Groucho Marx," I told Reed College interviewers in Portland, Oregon in 2005, "I should have known not to go to a college that would hire me as a vice president."

Acknowledgments

I owe much to two sets of individuals for "The Scorekeeper:" those (many gone now) who influenced the 35 years it spans and those who helped me bring the book to life, including a few who fit both categories.

Ralph Blumenfeld stands out among sportswriters who were generous to me when I was a teenager who dreamt of emulating them. The list also includes Morrey Rokeach, Dick Joyce, and Paul Zimmerman. The patient guidance of sports editors Larry Conroy and Ed Comerford meant a great deal when I knew less than I thought I did and, as I have written, Vic Ziegel and George Vecsey were outstanding role models. Bill McIllwain allowed me to cover the news and many *Newsday* colleagues—notably Ernie Volkmann, Jon Margolis, Pat Brasley, Pete Bowles, Bob Wyrick, Joe Treen, Manny Topol, and John Cummings—showed me how. Unionizing *Newsday*'s journalists remains one of my proudest moments and it would not have happened without George Tedeschi, Chuck Ellington, Bruce Lambert, Brad O'Hearn, Bettye Spinner and our attorney, Gerald Schilian.

As I recounted at his memorial service in 2008, Al Landa was a pivotal friend, mentor and unofficial employment counselor. Two other members of the George Polk Awards committee, Robert Spector and Len Karlin, were also dear friends and valued colleagues. I am grateful to Ben Ward for the chance to start a new phase in my career and for the advice and support I received from Sandy Smith at the New York City Correction Department, Roy Campbell at Yeshiva University, Peter Crescenti and David Grupper at L.I.U., and Earl Smith and Dick Whitmore at Colby. That's where this book concludes but insights drawn from the time it covers were abetted by subsequent wise counsel from Hank Dullea, Dorothy Pasternack, Sally Dutko, Scott Marsh, and Peggy Haine at Cornell; Mayor Allen Cohen and my

Ithaca Common Council colleagues; President Emeritus Paul Bragdon at Reed College; Michelle Brence Mortenson at the Oregonian; Jerry Cohen at AARP Oregon; Leslie Frane and Kathie Best at the Service Employees International Union; Ralph Engelman and my colleagues on the Polk Committee; and Rabbi Ariel Stone, whose insightful and non-judgmental guidance helped me revisit my religious heritage.

Families and friends matter and mine have inspired and empowered me. Because I wrote from a contemporaneous perspective, expressions of frustration are sometimes interspersed with the love, respect and gratitude I have for my parents. I treasure their memory. My daughter Rebecca has been a positive force in my life from the day she was born, as has my sister, the Hon. Nancy Hershey Lord. I am grateful, too, to my cousins Charles Simmons and Sandra Simmons Rudnick for advancing my career. Although we eventually parted, writing this book has reinforced how significant a role Victoria Mares played when we were together. I treasure my friendships with several people mentioned above as well as Jerry Glazer, Carole Stone, Pete and Marti Bowles, Steve Ende, and Fred Carlin.

This book bounced around in my head for years. The person most responsible for prodding it onto these pages is my wife, best friend, and Twenty-First Century life partner Leah Hershey, whose love, strength and counsel is reflected throughout. A number of friends encouraged me and commented on drafts of various chapters, among them Tom Drewes, Neal Hirschfeld and Ray Mathis in Portland and John Darnton, Aric Press, Steve Aiello, and Allen Weinberger on the East Coast. I am indebted to *Newsday* librarian Iris Quigley, now retired, for opening critical paths for my research; to Mary Ann Skinner for arranging permission to reprint two *Newsday* articles; and to Janet Marks at L.I.U. for digging information out of old *Seawanhakas*. Jenna Kern-Rugile provided a first edit that improved the manuscript and Kate King and Sheryl Kornman transformed the final draft into what you have read. Laura Duffy and Karen Minster designed the book outside and in, respectively, with great professionalism and my publisher Geri Hearne pulled it all together.